The Poetic Vision of
Robert Penn Warren

The Poetic Vision of

Robert Penn Warren

VICTOR STRANDBERG

The University Press of Kentucky

ISBN: 0-8131-1347-4

Library of Congress Catalog Card Number: 76-9503

Copyright © 1977 by The University Press of Kentucky

A statewide cooperative scholarly publishing agency
serving Berea College, Centre College of Kentucky,
Eastern Kentucky University, The Filson Club,
Georgetown College, Kentucky Historical Society,
Kentucky State University, Morehead State University,
Murray State University, Northern Kentucky University,
Transylvania University, University of Kentucky,
University of Louisville, and Western Kentucky University.

Editorial and Sales Offices: Lexington, Kentucky 40506

To Anne and Susan,
And with thanks to Penny
for her encouragement and support

Man lives by images. They
Lean at us from the world's wall, and Time's.
—"Reading Late at Night, Thermometer Falling"

Contents

Preface   ix

Introduction: The Critical Reckoning   1

1 The Themes of Robert Penn Warren   21
Passage   21
The Undiscovered Self   24
Mysticism   27
In Context: Warren's Criticism   33

2 Poems of Passage   46

3 The Undiscovered Self   121

4 Mysticism   190

5 Postscript: An Appreciation   255
Some Notes on Verse Texture   256
The Question of "Place"   267

Notes   277

Index of Warren's Works   285

General Index   289

Preface

TWELVE years have passed since publication of my earlier book on Warren's poetry, *A Colder Fire*, and in those years Warren has added some five volumes to his poetic canon. This fact and my own intense desire to rewrite much of my earlier criticism cause the appearance of the present volume. The only item that remains almost intact from the earlier book is the discussion of *Brother to Dragons;* otherwise, the salvageable fragments of *A Colder Fire* have been scattered and stitched into a largely reconceptualized analysis, featuring William James as the major guiding spirit.

I have written this book in pursuit of two purposes. First, I have tried to elucidate Warren's poetry through a close study of a great number of individual poems, because the fact is that, after over half a century of prolific creativity as a poet, Warren is not very well or very widely understood, though he is good enough that he ought to be. Second, I have organized this study around a thematic analysis that shows the development, from volume to volume, of three ground themes that span Warren's career as a poet: poems of passage, the undiscovered self, and mysticism. In passing these themes over his books like a magnet over iron filings, my study shows that the poems from all his volumes leap to the magnet in three large clusters that largely preempt everything there. If such a procedure looks dangerously reductive to some readers, I can only ask that they weigh my arguments and supporting evidence before resting in that judgment.

I wish to acknowledge here my debt—both practical and inspirational—to two students in my Faulkner-Warren seminar, John Stevenson and Marsha Kuhn, whose presence in my classroom I must hereafter count among the luckiest things to have happened to me in Academe. I also owe such scholarly debts as are indicated in my "Introduction: The Critical Reckoning"—above all to Mary Nance Huff for her magnificent bibliography, as well as to scholars and critics whose contribution might be only passing phrases (*e.g.,*

J. Hillis Miller's "poets of reality") but who show thereby how their thoughts have entered the climate we all inhabit together. I also want to thank my three typists for their good work and good cheer: Betty Goodbar, Anne Durden, and Susan Williford; and to acknowledge the four magazines in which I have published material partly reused here: *PMLA* (September, 1964), *Criticism* (Winter, 1968), *Shenandoah* (Summer, 1969), and *Four Quarters* (May, 1972). Lastly, I am most grateful, of course, to Robert Penn Warren, whose poetry from first to last is a treasury of riches that seems larger and more rewarding upon my every return to it.

In following an essentially thematic approach, I have found it necessary to dismember those volumes that treat disparate themes, so as to regather their several fragments under the appropriate thematic canopy. Other volumes, like *Eleven Poems on the Same Theme, Brother to Dragons*, and *Audubon: A Vision*, cohere around an inherent thematic unity that renders the dismemberment process needless and hence inadvisable. To clarify the development of Warren's poetic canon, the following list of his published volumes of poetry, with original publication dates, may be useful:

1. *Thirty-six Poems* (1935)
2. *Eleven Poems on the Same Theme* (1942)
3. *Selected Poems: 1923–1943* (1944)
4. *Brother to Dragons: A Tale in Verse and Voices* (1953)
5. *Promises: Poems 1954–1956* (1957)
6. *You, Emperors, and Others: Poems 1957–1960* (1960)
7. *Selected Poems, New and Old: 1923–1966* (1966)
   with *Tale of Time: New Poems 1960–1966.*
8. *Incarnations: Poems 1966–1968* (1968)
9. *Audubon: A Vision* (1969)
10. *Or Else: Poem/Poems 1968–1974* (1974)
11. *Selected Poems, 1923–1975* (1977)

In republication, a number of Warren's poems have undergone cuts and revisions. In general, I have used the later, revised versions of poems in this study, partly out of respect for the author's sense of self-improvement but also for the practical reason that the later, revised versions of these poems are what Warren's audience of the future will most likely be reading.

I am grateful to Mr. Robert Penn Warren and Random House, Inc., for permission to quote from his published books; to *Esquire* magazine for permission to cite passages from "Bicentennial" (December, 1976); to the *New Yorker* for permission to quote from "American Portrait: Old Style" (August 23, 1976); to the *New York Review of Books* and NYREV, Inc., for permission to reprint parts of "Youth Stares at Minoan Sunset" (September 30, 1976) and "Sister Water" (October 24, 1976); and to the *Atlantic Monthly* for permission to cite passages from "Waiting" (© 1976) and "Three Poems in Time" (to be published in 1977).

Introduction:
The Critical Reckoning

CRITICISM of the poetry of Robert Penn Warren falls into three chronological phases roughly corresponding to three periods of creativity in his career. Phase one covers the three volumes represented in *Selected Poems, 1923–1943*, which evoked a cacophony of critical voices that continued to echo into the late 1940s. Phase two embraces the three volumes written in the 1950s, after Warren had been publishing exclusively in prose for nearly ten years. The first two of these volumes, *Brother to Dragons* and *Promises*, engendered a sufficiently large and favorable response to represent the high-water mark of Warren's popularity as a poet, which culminated in a Pulitzer Prize for *Promises;* but the third volume, *You, Emperors, and Others*, raised more cacophonous critical voices, sharply divided between distaste and approval. Phase three, we may say, got under way at about this time and it continues to the present; in this period several large-scale studies of Warren's whole literary canon—fiction, criticism, and poetry—have gradually emerged to place their subject in the light of a well-informed and carefully considered judgment.

Criticism during the early years, though scanty, was generally highly laudatory, though Warren's satisfaction in this fact must have been tempered by his knowledge that the criticism originated mostly among close friends and literary acquaintances. John Crowe Ransom, for example, called Warren "one of the really superlative poets of our time" in a 1939 *Kenyon Review* article, and Allen Tate designated his fellow Fugitive "the most gifted person I have ever known" in a reminiscence published in 1942—by which time Tate had come to know some very gifted people indeed, including T. S. Eliot, Hart Crane, and William Faulkner.[1] At this time, moreover, judgment of Warren's poetry rested upon only one published volume, *Thirty-six Poems*, brought out in 1935.

It would be a mistake, however, to conclude that generous comments were confined to the friendly inner sanctum. Morton Zabel, in *Poetry*—a Modernist magazine but certainly not a Fugitive house organ—concluded that Warren is "a writer who more and more shows himself . . . one of the most serious and gifted intelligences of his generation."[2] With the publication of *Eleven Poems on the Same Theme* in 1942, Peter Monro Jack, writing in the *New York Times*, found reason to call Warren "very much a poet's poet" (an opinion substantiated by lavish praise from other poets in later years) who "is something of a Donne in the twentieth century."[3] Another reviewer, Peter Rushton, agreed, adding that, "It is from a mind such as Warren's that we may expect the best and most lasting poetry of our own times."[4]

Real critical controversy about Warren's poetry surfaced for the first time with the publication, in *Selected Poems, 1923–1943*, of "The Ballad of Billie Potts," which has generated sharply discordant opinions. Since I consider this poem both Warren's best and most important, it may be well to let critics ventilate their views at greater length than would otherwise be appropriate. Dudley Fitts, in a review entitled "Of Tragic Stature," treats *Selected Poems* as a whole in a judiciously balanced manner, accrediting Warren's use of influences like Ransom, Eliot, and Marvell, while complaining about the "metaphysical fog" that renders poems like "Toward Rationality" and "Aged Man Surveys Past Time" unintelligible, even "after the most painful rereading." The tempered judgment disappears, however, when Fitts compares "Billie Potts" to *At Heaven's Gate*, Warren's recent novel: "I find it hard to be temperate about *Billie Potts*, just as I find it hard to be measured in my praise of the unjustly neglected *At Heaven's Gate*, which it resembles. . . . The poem is . . . composed of two streams—the narrative itself, and a parenthesized commentary—which converge at the end. . . . (This technique resembles the double-thread method—narrative and Wyndham statement—of *At Heaven's Gate*.)" Contrary to many other critics, Fitts judges that "the concluding lines of the poem, narrative and commentary, meet in a perfect resolution."[5]

For John Crowe Ransom, however, "Billie Potts" represented a regrettable break with Warren's Fugitive past, the poem's "great skill" in the narrative section being outweighed in the philosophical stanzas by "a gloss far more implausible than that which Coleridge wrote upon his margins" in *The Ancient Mariner*. Like Ransom, F. W. Dupee found " 'Billie Potts' admirable as a folk narrative," but "weak and confused" in its philosophical interpolations.[6] But Horace Gregory came to the opposite conclusion, finding in the narrative ballad "such violent lapses in taste that I became confused as to whether or not it was Jesse Stuart or Mr. Warren himself who dictated the lines." It is Gregory's judgment that Warren's earlier metaphysical style remained his best, the "half-meditative, half-descriptive vein" in which "Bearded Oaks" was written being "definitely the vein in which Mr. Warren's verse promises its own rewards." [7]

In addition to this controversy about form, *Selected Poems* raised questions about Warren's choice of theme and subject. F. W. Dupee found in this book's proliferation of death images ("almost as many stones as bones") a quasi-Freudian wish for a "return to lifelessness," to "the inorganic that hides out within the organic." And Ruth Herschberger, while calling Warren "one of the best of living poets," fretted about the "*denial* of exuberance" in Warren's poetry, so extreme as to parallel John Webster's post-Elizabethan morbidity: "Contrast is the marrow of poetry. . . . But at some moments in Warren's poetry, one feels it is the blind agony that needs a contrast." [8] Willard Thorp defended this feature of Warren's verse (which James Dickey later defined as "The Outlook"— the poetic establishment's vision of "mutually understood helplessness"): "There are those who like to object that we have had enough of this mood. If this is so, then we have no further use for Webster or Melville or the Tennyson who hid himself." [9] But William Van O'Connor felt that Warren's "naturalism" constituted a permanent obstacle "against the likelihood of Warren's poetry ever cohering into the large imaginative fusion we call a vision of life." The "naturalistic view," O'Connor explained, "unfortunately has yet to offer any symbols around which a fully satisfying faith may cohere," leaving Warren to face a "limitation he shares with all contemporaries who cannot return with Eliot to the vision of

Christianity and who are yet unable to participate in any large, universally acceptable belief in which one's imaginative, esthetic, rational, moral and religious insights merge, mutually sustaining and explaining one another." [10] (This statement strikes me as an excellent formulation of the problem that Warren was to solve by means of his osmosis of being concept, which was already acting to merge Warren's "imaginative, esthetic, rational, moral, and religious insights" in "The Ballad of Billie Potts.")

To conclude this look at phase one, we turn now to the two most excellent essays (in my judgment) on Warren's poetry of the *Selected Poetry* era. W. P. Southard's "The Religious Poetry of Robert Penn Warren," a delightfully engaging piece for its tone and style, begins by noting a severe need for clear exegesis: "he has been so badly read, when read at all, the *Selected Poems, 1923–1943*, may really need . . . a little elementary unheroic plumbing." [11] Southard's own exegesis, though often very fine, is marred at times by excessive sarcasm, leading him to call Warren "the servant of the servants of the servants" and to compare Warren's irony to Hell, both having "the same inscription on the gates." But he does corroborate his judgment that the famous Ransom-Warren irony leads to dualities that "join action, and . . . blow hell out of each other," and he avoids conservative ill temper towards Warren's metrical experiments by calling the poet's "loose line . . . his favorite and his best. His tight metrics mostly don't come off, they're too tight, a strain." The new and important contribution of the Southard essay is its discussion of Warren's poetry in the light of religious psychology. "The first speculation of a religion is always on a loss of innocence," Southard observes—a crucial issue in all Warren's work—and thereafter the innocent, pre-logical self gets lost, like lost virginity, for keeps. The main reason for Southard's sarcasm, it turns out, is his revulsion against Warren's pessimism: "the Warren night goes on all day, the civilization itself having become an abyss." As a "religious" poet, then, Warren fails for lacking "the capacity for simple delight, and celebration of it—it is this that will make Dr. Williams 'indestructible'—and Warren seems to be suppressing evidence, conceiving his duty too strictly and humorlessly, which means dishonestly." (Again, I must interpolate that Warren was to resolve this issue in phases two and three via his

"Epiphany" poems, about "Delight" and "Time's irremediable joy.")

Finally, there is John L. Stewart's "The Achievement of Robert Penn Warren," which points to "the story of man's effort to flee from the problem of evil and of his ultimate return to that problem" as the "single narrative pattern" that permeates all of Warren's fiction and poetry.[12] According to this narrative pattern—common "to all myths of Original Sin," Stewart says—a child quarrels with his parents, flees, and returns to find his original innocence irrecoverable, as is the case in much of Warren's fiction and in poems like "The Return: An Elegy," "Revelation," "Letter of a Mother," and "Billie Potts," among others. "The flight and return of so many persons in so many places has one meaning," Stewart adduces: "Man cannot re-enter Paradise; he must learn to live adequately without hope of recovering his lost innocence." Failure to accept such loss of paradise accounts for the imagery of "destruction, malignant growth, and putrescent decay" that Stewart finds rampant in Warren's early *Fugitive* magazine poems, rendering them "often little more than lists of descriptive words suitable to these images: *withered, frosty, bloated, rotting, . . . leprous, clotted.*" And in the later poems (as well as in *All the King's Men*) this obsession appears in Warren's Freudian "use of water symbols—pools, the sea, and a variety of submarine landscapes—to represent the state of innocence for which man longs." The Ransom-Warren Agrarian flight from the modern world toward a simpler past likewise suits this theme, in Stewart's judgment, figuring into Warren's imagery of "a Golden Age of the past such as the Garden symbolized." Like O'Connor, Herschberger, and others, Stewart sees this obsession as seriously damaging, so that the poet's "preoccupation with the physical appearance of evil" and his lack of "any large moral scheme" have "spoiled" poems like "Eidolon," "Aubade for Hope," "Crime," and "Billie Potts"—which are further "spoiled" by "self-conscious violence and exaggeration of the language" and by (in the case of "Billie Potts") the "incongruity" of form that makes the poem a "failure" ("the passages of commentary are poetically inferior to the narrative passages").

Phase two of Warren's critical reception displays two salient and contradictory features: the high marks generally accorded

Brother to Dragons and *Promises,* followed by the foundering of Warren's popularity (especially regarding *You, Emperors, and Others*) upon the shoals of the Paleface-Redskin controversy described by Philip Rahv. This issue actually represented a massive shift in national cultural sensibility, away from the high-brow, densely intellectual, formally disciplined style of the high Modern period (best represented in the early Eliot) and toward the loosely structured, transparently readable, Whitmanesque style of the "New American Poetry," whose rising prophets in the 1950s were Beat and Confessional poets like Allen Ginsberg and the Black Mountain group. Back in 1939 Warren himself had touched upon Rahv's Paleface-Redskin dichotomy while sniffing a new Redskin uprising in the wind. "American poetry," he said then, "is reacting against the obscurities and complexities which characterized much of the post-war poetry." [13] But when that reaction came on in full force during the 1950s, Warren's own practice followed a middle course, much more personal in tone and subject matter and freer of formal restraint than had been the case ten years earlier, while yet stopping far short of extreme Redskin anarchy. The unhappy result was that Warren's verse was tested and found wanting by both warring camps.

Nonetheless, the decade of criticism got off to a generally benevolent start, with Warren's fellow poets leading the way in hailing *Brother to Dragons* as a masterpiece. Randall Jarrell pronounced it at once its author's best book, and more than that, "an event, a great one." [14] Robert Lowell, declaring that he had read it three times cover to cover without stopping, also proclaimed *Brother to Dragons* Warren's best book on the basis of both its "unfaltering, unstilted blank verse" and its rendering of character (Lucy and Laetitia Lewis in particular). Although slightly flawed by some fifty repetitions of the word "definition," this poem still ranked as "superior to any of the larger works of Browning" in Lowell's judgment.[15] Delmore Schwartz found "perfect proportion throughout" the poem, calling it "a work which is most remarkable as a sustained whole," while also admiring "Warren's mastery of a blank verse style of the utmost flexibility." [16] And Louise Bogan admired Warren's "perfect ear for folk speech," although she also touched on what other critics considered a disastrous weakness:

Warren's mistreatment of Thomas Jefferson, wherein sometimes "the tone slips from tragedy to melodrama." [17]

That Warren had performed hatchet work on the father of our American liberties proved the main burden of the poem's detractors. The poem was "not a masterpiece" in Parker Tyler's view precisely because "the air is full ... of ideological axes": "If ... Jefferson has wielded an axe on Lilburn as Lilburn has wielded one on George, Warren has wielded an axe on the author of the Declaration of American Independence." [18] The kind of damage that such a bias can wreak upon style is engagingly illustrated by another reviewer, John McCormick, who cites one of Jefferson's lines—"They should have thrown it [Lilburn's infant body] / Out where the hogs come to the holler"—and inquires: "Would Jefferson have said 'holler' for 'hollow'?" [19] While these critics found much to admire in the poem despite its flaws ("superb for lines, pages, and scenes at a time," said McCormick), Hugh Kenner was simply fed up with the poem's stylistic deficiencies. The poem's "prevailing texture proves strained and declamatory," its "characteristic voice . . . resembles that of a Kentucky preacher hypostatizing Sin," and its Jefferson is reduced to "a stoveside rhetorician," wrote Kenner, who concluded that "all Mr. Warren's talent and sincerity can't defeat those rhythms, that idiom, and that philosophy." [20]

As an early example of Redskin reaction—this time in Warren's favor—Leslie Fiedler's "Seneca in the Meat-House" constitutes an interesting defense of the poem precisely on the grounds of the high-pitched rhetoric that Kenner found intolerable. "We have somehow come to believe that bombast and melodrama are hopelessly corrupted," Fiedler says. "But we need them to complete our sense of ourselves, to do justice to the absurdity of terror, its failure to be well-behaved. That Warren has handled them with skill and poignancy in a time of careful and genteel [read: Paleface] poets, that he has made for perhaps the first time in a hundred years a successful long poem of them, . . . must be said first of all." [21] So Fiedler praises the "skill and courage with which Warren has pursued a difficult, improbable, heartbreaking rhetoric," though he admits that "the tone, the hysterical pitch" might well seem excessive to a reader unacquainted with Warren's earlier treatment of the "evil

Nightmare": "No one would scream like this who is trying to tell us something for the first time."

Like *Brother to Dragons, Promises*—winner of the Pulitzer Prize and National Book Award in 1958—evoked superlatives from some of Warren's fellow writers. James Dickey's review, though perhaps too intense of tone to be representative, nonetheless compellingly illustrates the effect of Warren's poetry on a distinguished man of letters. "Opening a book of poems by Robert Penn Warren is like putting out the light of the sun, or plunging into the labyrinth and feeling the thread break after the first corner is passed," Dickey writes. "When he is good, and often even when he is bad, you had as soon read Warren as live, a feeling you do not get from any of these others, expert as some of them are." (Dickey was reviewing some thirty or so contemporaries in anthologies.) Of all these poets Warren is "the only one to give you the sense of poetry as a thing of final importance to life." [22]

Thanks to the worsening Paleface-Redskin schism, however, some poets found Warren's verse not at all companionable. In a pro-Redskin satire called "Fresh Air," Kenneth Koch, bidding farewell to the "castrati of poetry" and their "stale pale skunky pentameters," singles out Warren as a target exemplar of the detested Paleface manner prevalent in Academe. The reference in the next to last line below is to Warren's Poem I of *Promises* (to Gabriel), "What Was the Promise That Smiled from the Maples at Evening":

> Where are the young poets in America, they are trembling in
>   publishing houses and universities,
> Above all they are trembling in universities, they are bathing
>   the library steps with their spit,
> They are gargling out innocuous (to whom?) poems about maple
>   trees and their children. . . .
> Oh what worms they are! they wish to perfect their form.

Adding to Koch's impatience with "all your talk about restraint and mature talent" is the gloom-and-doom mood (so ready to hand in Warren) that pervades the Modernist school at large as though sorrow were the only permissible emotion:

I am afraid you have never smiled at the hibernation
Of bear cubs except that you saw in it some deep relation
To human suffering and wishes, oh what a bunch of
    crackpots! [23]

Nor was such criticism limited to the "new" poets. Within Academe the New American Poetry—Confessional, Beat, Neo-Romantic—was gaining champions, among whom one of the most distinguished, M. L. Rosenthal, turned up as a reviewer of *Promises*. Rosenthal's review, "Out There in the Dark," focuses mainly upon Warren's unhealthy morbidity of mood. Although he detects "a painfully awkward bleat of optimism" amid the book's "world of grunts, growls, and bloody chompings," Rosenthal concludes that Warren's Southern regional heritage makes any true escape from his Faulknerian heart of darkness quite unlikely: "human possibility, as presented here, seems all but inaudible and invisible. Observed reality drowns it out." [24]

Fortunately for Warren, other academic critics were more temperate and—in my judgment—more knowledgeable and perceptive. Morgan Blum's "*Promises* as Fulfillment" finds in Warren a distinctive "ability to find emblems of grace and redemption in the most unlikely places," amid "conditions of filth and decay." So far as style is concerned, he sees the girl's song in "The Flower"—"And you sing as though the human need / Were not for perfection"—as signalling the end of Warren's "perfectionist" period in poetry, with the carefully polished and integrated earlier poems like "Watershed" and "Picnic Remembered" giving way now to something akin to Redskin poetics.[25] Leonard Casper, in probably the best review of *Promises*, approaches the book with the excellent insights of a mind long steeped in Warren's whole literary canon. (His book on Warren, the first such book-length study, was then in preparation.) Noting the new (what we might call Redskin) elements in this verse, Casper notes Warren's "abandonment of anonymity" in treating "affections personal and private" and he correlates the roughening of verse texture in *Promises* with Warren's comment about Melville's similar roughening of verse texture, "because truth is not easily trapped; it assumes contradictory shapes . . . ; it exudes . . . ambiguity." Moving to the level of myth criticism, Casper sees Warren's version of the "fortunate fall" in the "sacramental reunion" made possible by the speaker's sense of complicity and "sharing of human weaknesses." [26]

By the decade's end the Paleface-Redskin crossfire was catching Warren in its maximum degree of intensity. Reviving an older controversy, Floyd C. Watkins's essay "Billie Potts at the Fall of Time" presents some fine insights—tying Warren's water imagery to "the embryonic state before knowledge, the state of innocence," for example. But he too faults the poem on the (Paleface) grounds of defects in tone and form. Concerning tone, Warren has become much too personal for Watkins's taste (the "use of the second-person pronoun indicates once again that the poet is pointing his finger at the reader"); and the form, were it properly unified, would blend the philosophical meaning with the narrative stanzas rather than set it off in parentheses. Nonetheless, Watkins's conclusion calls "Billie Potts" "one of America's great narrative poems" that might point "toward even more significant achievements." [27]

The prime target of critical fury in phase two was *You, Emperors, and Others: Poems, 1957–1960*. Harshly denouncing the book from a Redskin perspective, Harriet Zinnes thinks it evidences not only Warren's failure but that of contemporary poetry at large, for its irrelevance—both in language and subject matter—to the contemporary world scene. Although singling out the "Mortmain" and "Garland for You" sequences as good, Zinnes otherwise finds *You, Emperors* indicative of "the desperateness of the situation of the poet in today's new world." The conquest of outer space and the emergence of Africa and Asia in the 1960s, she feels, "are more compelling today as sources of man's actions and anxieties than 'man's guilt.' What sense do little poems make which use as Warren's do such traditional and now incommunicative images as moonlight, night, sky, time, star, stone, heart, wind, and joy . . . ?" Somewhat regretfully, then, Zinnes concludes her review (titled "A New Word Needed") with the judgment that Warren has outlived his time as a poet: "Patently the skeptical twentieth-century man, Warren yet looks backward using a dead language and metaphors no longer rooted in contemporary experience." [28]

Over in the Paleface camp, meanwhile, outrage was brewing over Warren's transgressions against formal proprieties, notably evident in his metrical irregularity, his lack of high seriousness (or sincerity), and above all, his flagrant failure to maintain aesthetic distance between himself and his reader. John Edward Hardy's review ("You, Robert Penn Warren") typifies the Paleface reaction, especially concerning this last point, as he warns the poet that his "you" form (directly addressing the reader) is "certainly among the most difficult to employ without awakening a fatal antagonism in the reader who has any decent measure of personal vanity." Although he calls himself "a long-time enthusiast for Warren's work," Hardy's enthusiasm fades before the "unconvincing posturings" and "worn-out disguises" that reduce *You, Emperors* to "seventy-nine pages of poems largely about nothing in the world, except a desperate *striving* for significance. Or, striving for 'you.' " [29] John Thompson, too, finds much to resent in Warren's attempt—by way of sustaining his theme that men are "basically no good"—to "wound the feelings of us others, the readers, the 'you' of the title." Indeed, Thompson wonders at the mental sadism of it all, the poet making his poems "swirl and crack at us like painful whips" as though "determined to admit that there is pleasure in it . . . , even glee." As if that were not bad enough, there is also a catastrophic weakening of the versification as compared to Warren's triumphs in the "metaphysical" manner of yesteryear: "His first poems sounded, sometimes, like a fierce Marvell; these newest ones sound, sometimes, like a fierce Ogden Nash." [30] (In fairness to Thompson, one must admit that his task of reviewing twenty-two poets in a single clump—as his essay does—did not permit a leisurely contemplation of Warren's work.) Dudley Fitts was led by his impression of the book's overall frivolousness to title his review in the *New York Times* "An Exercise in Metrical High Jinks." Except for the six pieces called "Some Quiet, Plain Poems," where "the tone is perfectly true, the construction perfectly right," Fitts concluded that "Mr. Warren's new book is an exercise in metrical high jinks. Fairly high jinks"—an artistic phenomenon that he nonetheless finds perfectly defensible on the same grounds, perhaps, whereon we might defend T. S. Eliot's "Cat" poetry: "There's no law against a poet's taking an artistic vacation, and this binge was obviously fun." At the same time, however, Fitts cannot help but mourn the demise of the neo-metaphysical poet he used to read with pleasure: "one thinks back to the earlier work, to the tense demonic force of *Thirty-six Poems*, with longing. . . ."[31]

Taken collectively, these excerpts from phases one and two of Warren's critical reception yield many valuable insights. Yet they also suggest the need, in many cases, for a larger knowledge of Warren's whole literary corpus as a base from which to judge any part of it, as well as the need for a standard of taste broad enough to encompass both the traditional style of the high Modern period and the energizing anarchy of its successor, the "New American Poetry." The meeting of that need, through intensive and large-scale critical analysis and scholarly research (helped along by the lengthening time perspective of the passing years), has been a distinctive feature of phase three of our survey. Regrettably the very size of this multiplying commentary precludes my doing proper justice to it. In some instances, I shall have to barely summarize excellent commentaries, while mentioning others only in passing, and slighting some altogether. Inaccessibility of documents has been an occasional problem; in the case of one intriguing item, Louis Rubin's twenty-two page essay on "Religious Themes in Robert Penn Warren's Poetry," the author confessed to me that he had never seen the thing in print for lack of access to it.[32]

The new catholicity of taste which characterizes the best of our phase three criticism is admirably illustrated in Louis L. Martz's reaction to *You, Emperors, and Others*. Martz, who has written with great insight and affection about the "Paleface" poetry of the seventeenth century, finds Warren's recent "Redskin" (my designation, not Martz's) tendencies a welcome and rather astounding development. "Something remarkable has happened in Robert Penn Warren's career over the past seven years," he writes; and the three volumes of the fifties, as a consequence, are "of a finer quality than the work of the *Selected Poems*."[33] Pointing to the "utterly original" creations in *You, Emperors*, Martz concludes that "Warren's achievement in his last three volumes of poetry leads one to say what might have seemed impossible ten years ago: that Warren may come to be remembered as a poet who also wrote novels."

Hyatt Waggoner, in his *American Poets: From the Puritans to the Present*, also remarks that Warren's "steady progress toward the romantic, the direct, the personal, and the visionary" in the later volumes might well dumbfound anyone who knew of him only "as the third member of the Ransom-Tate-Warren trio, a Vanderbilt man, contributor to *I'll Take My Stand*, and co-author of the most influential New Critical textbook, *Understanding Poetry*." But he too finds great merit in this development, citing *Brother to Dragons* as "certainly a central *document* in American poetry" and "Billie Potts" as "the triumph of Warren's new voice and manner" and "one of the finest long poems in our literature." This judgment, which takes added strength from the panoramic scope of Waggoner's book, includes a defense of the "double focus" of "Billie Potts"—its lack of formal "unity"—on the grounds of long-rooted literary practice: "Traditional literary *genres* began to be meaningless with the English Romantic movement and have been increasingly meaningless ever since, even in British literature. In American literature, they have been almost totally irrelevant since Emerson."[34]

The final word, it seems to me, on the subject of Warren's Paleface-Redskin classification appears in Monroe K. Spears's excellent review of Warren's *Selected Poems* (1966) and *Incarnations* (1968). After noting that Warren's new verse is "far more open in texture and more explicitly personal in reference" than was his earlier poetry, Spears remarks "a certain large resemblance between Warren's later poetry and the open or naked or confessional poetry of which Robert Lowell is chief luminary and exemplar." Spears goes on, however, to specify "two important differences. . . . In the first place, Warren's poetry is never really confessional, . . . [having] no touch of the *poète maudit*, suffering exceptionally for us all. . . . Second, Warren never goes as far as Lowell, for example, . . . toward the abandonment of form." As a result, Spears says, "Warren's later poetry seems to me to embody most of the special virtues of 'open' poetry—accessibility, immediate emotional involvement, wide appeal—and to resist the temptations to formlessness and to moral exhibitionism, self-absorption, and sentimentality that are the chief liabilities of that school."[35]

Naturally enough, not everyone can take satisfaction in these arguments. M. L. Rosenthal, for one, continues to be unhappy about Warren's attempt to force complicity in guilt upon the reader by continued use of his "you" form. "But suppose," he asks, "the rest of us decline the pronominal gambit?" Instead of "still attempting the great transference implied in his earlier use of 'you' for 'I,' " Warren ought to be more overtly confessional about the guilt he is obsessed with, in Rosenthal's opinion; as it is, his later poems suffer because they never "close in on the precise character of what the returning 'you' is burdened with. . . ." Moreover, although Warren is most often at his best in the narrative poems "involving intransigent or sadistic cruelty," he has "waited too much upon this theme and depended too much on the excitement . . . of its realization in action."[36] Jean Garrigue, reviewing *Selected Poems* (1966), likewise sees Warren's "vision of the named and unnamed dark, the monsters (and no heroes to combat them)" as tending to make this poet "a melodramatist of terror and the irreconcilables. . . . The mire and woe of the human condition. That it dominates is the point. In the totality of the book, its shadow is the most weighty."[37] And Hayden Carruth, reacting to the same book, complains similarly about its thematic monotony— "the same melodrama repeated again and again" about "the horror of death," and "hence we yawn over many pages . . . ," even though at times "the old metaphysical gasp can still shake us" in "poems that come alive with a real shock, making all my psychosomatic symptoms twitch at once, like a school of minnows." These poems Carruth finds "quite simply unforgettable."[38]

The sizable body of "happy" poems in the later volumes has not sufficed to remove this stigma of pessimism. John L. Stewart thinks *Promises* is marred at times by the intrusion of such poems because Warren "was somewhat unskilled in the poetry of happiness, most difficult to write." Yet, in his concluding summation, Stewart finds Warren's obsessive morbidity equally unsatisfying, there being "too much terror, too much decay, too much sexuality, too much disgust" in the whole Warren corpus. "Self-knowledge is more than recognition of one's capacity for wrongdoing. Glory is more than bearing up under a nearly overwhelming load of self-loathing and fear of the grave."[39] At the same time, Allen Shepherd finds too much affirmation in Warren's later literature, locating in *Brother to Dragons* "a shift in Warren's moral vision" that gives *Band of*

Angels and *Wilderness* "uncharacteristically affirmative" conclusions which in each case "tasks our credulity" for their contrived or unearned quality.[40]

On the whole, the volumes of the later sixties worked to strengthen Warren's gradually developing Elder Statesman status, which received an extra boost from his capture of the Bollingen Prize for *Selected Poems* (1966). Writing in the *New York Times*, Louis Rubin, Jr. called this book "a notable event" which gives us "some of the best poetry of our day"; and Joseph Slater, reviewing it in the *Saturday Review*, was moved to claim that "it is clearly time now to say that one of the men who taught us to understand poetry is also one of our major poets." While still an admirer of the early poems like "Pondy Woods" and "Billie Potts"—"as shattering now as when they were new"—Slater judged the most recent poems to "possess the old virtues, enlarged and extended," particularly for being "more lyric and formally more inventive and flexible."[41] Bernard Bergonzi, too, thought it "a volume of great distinction" whose recent poems display "a remarkable ease and a striking intensity of language."[42] And John Wain was inclined to marvel at Warren's powers as a memory poet, capable of evoking perfectly his youth as a "Nashville boy" despite the "long academic years in New England, official posts in Washington, substantial trips to Europe—and marriage to Eleanor Clark," which "must in itself represent a thoroughgoing Europeanization, for she knows Europe as inwardly and passionately as any American since Henry James."[43]

Dissenting from this consensus opinion, George Core, for one, felt that Warren's poetry had "slipped noticeably" since *You, Emperors* in 1960, so that only one of the poems in *Incarnations* rated strong approval—that one, however ("Myth on Mediterranean Beach: Aphrodite as Logos") being "exceptionally good."[44] And William Dickey (also reviewing *Incarnations*) felt that Warren's fictional techniques had adversely affected the later poetry by giving it different voices—lyric, narrative, ballad, parodic—that speak like different characters in a novel. This tendency, Dickey said, threatens to "dissipate the singleness of his [Warren's] personal authority."[45] But Louis Martz—in the Winter, 1967 *Yale Review*—held that "This volume has a total integrity of great power," and G. S. Fraser found its metrics and imagery "exemplary for skill." (He cited an excerpt, "Wind / Lifts the brightening of hair," as constituting "a small one-line imagist poem in itself.")[46]

With the appearance of *Audubon* in 1969 a novel exercise of myth criticism comes into play—novel because the Audubon myth differs so greatly from that of Warren's Fall from innocence theme. Louis Martz, characteristically, was one of the first to see what Warren was up to—"like Aeschylus or Ovid, [he] is re-imagining a myth"—and he heralded this mythologizing of Audubon as "fully justified, since Audubon truly is an American legend and folk hero." Doing a bit of "reverent source-hunting" ("why not," he asked, "since the poem is bound to become a classic?"), Martz produced some fascinating specimens of the "alchemy of art" (as Henry James termed it) in comparing Warren's poem to its source material in Audubon's *Ornithological Biography*. In *Audubon* Martz saw "the accumulated power of a lifetime's skill and wisdom" producing "certainly the best poetic sequence written in English during the past decade."[47] Helen Vendler and Norman Martien also looked admiringly upon Warren's mythologizing of Audubon. As "a new hero for our time," Audubon "appeals irre-sistibly," in Vendler's judgment, because he "blended art and science, the natural and cerebral, the tender and the violent," with an ease "peculiarly acceptable to the American intellectual mind." Audubon's art is like Warren's own, she observes, in that "his birds and his rats alike inhabit a world of beak and claw and fang, of ripped-open bellies and planted talons," in the face of which "these striking vignettes of a man questionlessly happy in his environment map out for us a possible happiness."[48] Martien too sees both War-ren's and Audubon's art informed by a similar "doubleness," a "play of contradictory forces [that] makes him [Audubon] seem a type of the American artist" and "an example of how vision and fact can be brought together." This effect "works to make this Robert Penn Warren's finest poem," Martien maintains; "his eye and his voice teach us a new affection for the world."[49] Even Allen Shepherd, though begrudging Warren's mythologizing license somewhat (he found that the Audubon of the original *Ornitho-logical Biography* was "well-pleased" at seeing "the infernal hag" hanged for her turpitude), concludes that the poem "reinforces the not uncommon opinion that Warren is at least as good a poet as he is a novelist." [50]

Similarly, *Or Else—Poem / Poems 1968–1974* has evoked widespread admiration and some sensitive readings from reviewers. Robert F. Clayton speaks of the book's collective ensemble as comprising "a longer, stunningly beautiful poem of great depth and meaning. . . . Unquestionably, the most extraordinary and most significant work published by an American poet this year." [51] Among numerous other commentaries, J. D. McClatchy's deserves mention here because McClatchy cites a passage from *All the King's Men* that has immense relevance to all of Warren's poetry. Speaking of Warren's "obsessive" images in *Or Else*, McClatchy recalls Jack Burden's description of the kind of image a man lives by (the image Jack has in mind is that of Anne Stanton swimming as a gull passes over):

> What happened was this: I got an image in my head that never got out. We see a great many things and can remember a great many things, but that is different. We get very few of the true images in our heads of the kind I am talking about, the kind which become more and more vivid for us as if the passage of the years did not obscure their reality but, year by year, drew off another veil to expose a meaning which we had only dimly surmised at first. Very probably the last veil will not be removed, for there are not enough years, but the brightness of the image increases and our conviction increases that the brightness is meaning, or the legend of meaning, and without the image our lives would be nothing except an old piece of film rolled on a spool and thrown into a desk drawer among the unanswered letters. [52]

Critical reaction to *Or Else* and to Warren's most recent collection, *Selected Poems, 1923–1975*, indicates that, high as it has been, Warren's reputation as a poet is still rising. Speaking of *Or Else* as Warren's "Life Record," Charles Bohner remarks (in a paper for the Modern Language Association Robert Penn Warren symposium of December, 1976) that *"Or Else* is Warren at his best, that it demonstrates a mastery of the themes and forms he has been working toward for twenty years, and that its sustained level of excellence is unique among his published volumes of verse." Dabney

Stuart, in the *Library Journal* (October 1, 1976), feels likewise about the new *Selected Poems* (published too late for Bohner to consider them), saying: "This volume presents a marvelous career, revealing how much good work a man does getting ready for his best. . . . [The] book gives a splendid measure of that achievement, major in any century." And Harold Bloom, writing on "The Year's Books" in the *New Republic* (November 20, 1976), calls this latest collection "the great event in this year's poetry," remarking that its previously uncollected opening sequence "maps out an all-but-final-vision." While severely downgrading Robert Lowell, Archibald MacLeish, and Richard Eberhart—contemporaries of Warren who have published recent "collected poems" editions—Bloom finds assurance in "the wealth of Warren's half-century of poetry" that "our nation . . . again has a living poet comparable in power to Stevens or Frost." Surveying that half-century's work in *Selected Poems*, Bloom maintains that "Warren's greatness has been palpable," at least in his last four volumes. Like Bohner and Stuart, Bloom feels that "Warren's best poems are his most recent."

The final category of commentary is the most important in this survey. I refer to the professionally first-rate, book-length studies of Warren that, fortunately, are easily available in city and college libraries, so that I might get by here with just a brief mention of them. This scholarly endeavor originated during the late fifties with Louise Cowan's *The Fugitive Group: A Literary History* and John M. Bradbury's *The Fugitives: A Critical Account*, which naturally included Warren as one of the three major figures dealt with. These were followed in 1960 by Leonard Casper's *Robert Penn Warren: The Dark and Bloody Ground*, the first book-length study of Warren's work, whose superb bibliography has earned the gratitude of Warren scholars ever since. Casper's chapter on Warren's poetry, like Bradbury's, contains many fine insights, particularly with respect to *Eleven Poems on the Same Theme*. Concerning "Billie Potts," Casper sides with those who are unhappy with Warren's "ambiguous alliance" between ballad form and philosophical commentary; but he nonetheless declares the poem "one of Warren's most important and interesting works," and deftly intuits the profound religious meaning of its conclusion: "It is the natural creature—bee, goose, salmon—whose instinct beholds

great designs in the universe. Such imagery invokes religious corre-
spondences." [53] In 1964 Paul West's Minnesota Pamphlet (No. 44)
on Warren joined this groundswell, as did Charles H. Bohner's
Twayne Series study, both of these titled *Robert Penn Warren*.
Again, both works contain excellent insights, and I am inclined
to rate Bohner's gracefully written and knowledgeable book as the
best general study of Warren's work.

This groundswell crested in 1965 with three books dealing
largely with Warren's poetry: John L. Stewart's complex and
ambitious *The Burden of Time: The Fugitives and Agrarians*,
which devotes much of its last 115 pages to a close study of Warren's verse; John L. Longley, Jr.'s *Robert Penn Warren: A Collection of Critical Essays;* and my own study of Warren's verse, *A
Colder Fire*. Stewart's chapter on "The Long Apprenticeship" of
Warren is an excellent discussion of the poet's development prior
to *Thirty-six Poems* (which is essentially where my study begins).
Stewart also does some fine work with subsequent poems by trac-
ing developments in theme and technique and such influences as
Dante and Shakespeare. A judicious critic, Stewart freely exposes
his subject's failings: speaking of *Brother to Dragons*, he says that
"when Meriwether enters with his bullet-torn head and Jefferson
greets him with 'Well, Crack-head, who are you?' one is tempted
to lay the poem aside with disgust." Stewart is all the more con-
vincing, then, when he bestows encomiums: "In scope, tragic sense,
mastered substance, inventiveness, and plain power *Promises* sur-
passes all other volumes of verse published in this country since
the Second World War." This volume, like Warren's other best
work, is set in "that landscape lost in the heart's homely deep,"
Stewart says, citing the remembered world of boyhood about
which Stewart, like Warren himself, writes beautifully.[54]

Although John L. Longley, Jr.'s collection focuses mainly on
Warren's fiction, it does reprint some material relating to Warren's
poetry, such as Warren's own *Paris Review* interview and his
seminal essay "Knowledge and the Image of Man" and Frederick
P. W. McDowell's essay on *Brother to Dragons* that originally
appeared in the Winter, 1955 *PMLA*. "Now that Faulkner and
Hemingway are gone, Robert Penn Warren is clearly America's
most distinguished man of letters," Longley writes in his Introduc-

tion.[55] That opinion evidently belongs as well to George P. Garrett, whose essay "The Recent Poetry of Robert Penn Warren" was written expressly for the Longley collection. One of the "very small number of outstanding and genuinely productive poets of our time," Warren displayed in *Promises* "a new sense of freedom and expansion" that "can only be compared to that last astounding harvest of W. B. Yeats," Garrett writes. And with Warren's extension of "the full power and energy of his hard-earned liberation" into *You, Emperors, and Others,* Garrett feels "no hesitation in suggesting that Warren's later poems . . . are more important to us than the late poems of Yeats." For a proper analogue to this later poetry Garrett looks to the worlds of art and music, where Warren's "steady growth and blooming" as a poet evoke comparison to Picasso and Stravinsky.[56]

Other collections of criticism appear in the Autumn, 1963 *South Atlantic Quarterly* and the May, 1972 *Four Quarters,* which is a special Robert Penn Warren issue. Here Curtis Whittington, Jr., in "The Earned Vision: Robert Penn Warren's 'The Ballad of Billie Potts' and Albert Camus' *Le Malentendu,*" correlates Warren's poem not only with the French novel but also with the criticism Warren was writing during the "Billie Potts" period: "Pure and Impure Poetry," "Irony with a Center: Katherine Anne Porter," "Love and Separateness in Eudora Welty," and the long essay on *The Ancient Mariner.* By way of ending this survey of Warren scholarship, I extend my personal gratitude as well as professional esteem to Mary Nance Huff for her *Robert Penn Warren: A Bibliography,* whose coverage of writings by and about Warren through 1967 has made my task infinitely easier.

1

The Themes of Robert Penn Warren

PASSAGE

SINCE the Romantic period, few subjects have proved so obsessive to English-speaking writers as has the experience of a forced, one-way passage into a ruined world. The trauma of lost innocence has been a common denominator linking up the otherwise contrary personalities of a Wordsworth and a T. S. Eliot; the Jesuit priest Gerard Manley Hopkins and the freethinking lapsed Protestant, Mark Twain; Faulkner and Hemingway and their contemptuously sardonic detractor Vladimir Nabokov. Thomas Wolfe's *Look Homeward, Angel* and *You Can't Go Home Again* also spring, titles and all, from this sense of exile from Eden, as do Scott Fitzgerald's various surrogates lapsed from their Keatsian "golden moment." And then there is Robert Frost, wondering in rueful melancholy "what to make of a diminished thing" in poems like "The Oven Bird," "A Prayer in Spring," "Reluctance," and "Nothing Gold Can Stay," and the tragic intensity of Dylan Thomas in "Fern Hill" and "Poem in October." So too Theodore Roethke poetically yearns for the greenhouse his child-self once occupied; and John Updike causes his Rabbit Angstrom to call being mature the same as being dead, so far as he could see. And in that most popular book of its generation, *The Catcher in the Rye*, Salinger presents a protagonist who finds his initiation into the adult world unbearably traumatic. The list could go on and on, but suffice it to say that the theme of passage from innocence into what Warren calls "the world's stew" has been a tradition of such magnitude as to quite reasonably explain Robert Penn Warren's lifelong devotion to it. Roughly half of the poems Warren has written over a fifty-year career as a poet have dealt with this issue.

Philosophically, what has lain behind this astoundingly wide-spread obsession has been the collapse of the old religious certitudes that pointed to a paradise in the next world and their replacement by naturalistic suspicions that whatever of paradise may exist for us is not to be found up ahead in the time continuum, but rather is behind us, in our vanished childhood. Thus Mark Twain speaks of Hannibal (fictionalized as St. Petersburg, meaning "heavenly place") as his Paradise Lost: "the town of my boyhood— . . . we see now that we were in heaven then and there was no one able to make us know it. . . ." [1] And Faulkner constructs *The Sound and the Fury* around that day when the Compson children first tasted the forbidden knowledge of sex and death—Caddy's muddy drawers and Damuddy's death. Faulkner obligingly supplies a snake and a tree to buttress his point and causes the female to flout the Edenic injunction: "Your paw told you to stay out of that tree." For Hemingway, the Fall was somewhat delayed until his personal exposure to imminent death at the Italian front in 1918, causing a "loss of immortality" that Colonel Cantwell was to meditate upon some thirty years later in *Across the River and into the Trees:* "No one of his other wounds had ever done to him what the first big one did. I suppose it is just the loss of the immortality, he thought. Well, in a way, that is quite a lot to lose." [2] Nabokov, by contrast, suffered his fall into the world of time and loss precociously early, and all of his later literary conquests of time—via the "durable pigments and refuge of art" in *Lolita* and *Pale Fire,* and the deliberate anachronisms that favor his aged hero in *Ada*—are but delayed reactions to the fall of the child-self as recorded in *Speak, Memory.* "The cradle rocks above an abyss," this book begins, "and our existence is but a brief crack of light between two eternities of darkness." [3]

Behind these personal and literary episodes, moreover, we may say that passage into a ruined world has been realized on a civilization-wide scale through ideological catastrophes occasioned by events like World War I and by the rise of nineteenth and twentieth century natural sciences. Massive scientific proof of man's bestial descent, his warped mentality, his place in a universe doomed to entropic extinction—these discoveries of Darwin, Freud, Einstein and others have forced a loss of innocence upon the contemporary intelligentsia from which few serious artists if any have been exempt and have made a return to the child-self's paradise all the more longed after. John Updike, one of the best recent writers on the impact of science upon modern thought, writes in "Lifeguard": "Each of our bodies is a clock that loses time. Young as I am, I can hear in myself the protein acids ticking; I wake at odd hours and in the shuddering darkness and silence feel my death rushing toward me like an express train." And in *The Poorhouse Fair* Updike suggests how scientific knowledge has even displaced the human soul: "We've sifted the body in a dozen directions, looking for a soul. Instead, we've found what? A dog's bones, an ape's glands, a few quarts of sea water, and a mind that is actually a set of electrical circuits." [4] I do not mean to imply that Updike's own beliefs correspond exactly to these sentiments; but he obviously has grasped the issue of a ruined world very powerfully, and his fear that the religious answer has become defunctive is worth quoting, again from "Lifeguard": "I sway appalled on the ladder of minus signs by which theologians would surmount the void. . . . Newman's iridescent cobwebs crush in my hands. Pascal's blackboard mathematics are erased by a passing shoulder. The cave drawings, astoundingly vital by candlelight, of those aboriginal magicians, Paul and Augustine, in daylight fade into mere anthropology."

For the poetry of Robert Penn Warren, these speculations about passage into a reality hostile to the needs of the human soul add up to a central question—the same question whose rendering had made T. S. Eliot, in Warren's opinion, "the most important single influence on [contemporary] American poetry." The "question which is central in modern life," Warren says, is "can man live on the purely naturalistic level?" [5] In his poems of passage the answer to that question is sometimes no and most often, just barely. In a world broken into solipsistic fragments and dominated by the fear of extinction, Warren's personae naturally seek something better—that search leads to the other two grand themes that govern his development as a poet, the undiscovered self and mysticism.

THE UNDISCOVERED SELF

Passage into a world ruined by time and loss brings ramifications far deeper than the mere sense of an unsatisfactory environment. Typically, the experience of passage evokes the feeling that something has gone wrong in the basic structure of the self, so that one can no longer enjoy the perfect self-acceptance evident in animals and in prelapsarian children. Commonly a sense of alienation from one's deepest or truest self ensues, leading the Hindu or Buddhist sage to renounce both mind and body as obstacles to his quest for the atman; while the Judeo-Christian tradition espouses renunciation or cleansing of the worldly and carnal self as the condition for redeeming the eternal self. Even the Transcendentalist rebels against this very tradition have periodically stepped back from their ringing proclamations—that this world *is* the kingdom of God, that *every man* (not Christ only) is His incarnation—to acknowledge their own sense of a polluted selfhood. Thus, although Thoreau proclaims (at the end of *Walden*) "a tide . . . behind every man which can float the British Empire like a chip," he also admits in his "Higher Laws" chapter to being "conscious of an animal in us, which is . . . reptile and sensual, and perhaps cannot be wholly expelled"; and he ruefully concludes, "I fear that we are such gods or demigods only as fauns and satyrs, the divine allied to beasts, . . . and that, to some extent, our very life is our disgrace." And Emerson, although roundly censured for telling the Harvard Divinity School about the godhood in every man, was capable of a Calvinist sense of his own depravity, as seen in his early poem "Grace":

> Example, custom, fear, occasion slow,—
> These scorned bondsmen were my parapet.
> I dare not peep over this parapet
> To gauge with glance the roaring gulf below,
> The depths of sin to which I had descended,
> Had not these me against myself defended.

This sense of helplessness before the inner man has persisted in the mainstream of Western tradition since biblical times. The Book of Job (the source of Warren's title, *Brother to Dragons*) tells us,

"Behold, God putteth no trust in his saints; yea, the heavens are not clean in his sight. How much more abominable and filthy is man, which drinketh iniquity like water?" (15:15–16). And in the New Testament, Paul, though a man of truly transcendental willfulness who in effect actually conquered the Roman Empire for his Savior, was nonetheless impotent to conquer his own inner being, as the famous passage in Romans (7:19–24) laments loudly: "For the good that I would, I do not: but the evil which I would not, that I do. I find then a law, that, when I would do good, evil is present with me. For I delight in the law of God after the inward man: But I see another law in my members warring against the law of my mind, and bringing me into captivity to the law of sin which is in my members. O wretched man that I am! Who shall deliver me from the body of this death?" Passing over Augustine and Dante and medieval debates between body and soul, we find remarkably strong secular confirmation of this inner schism in the literature of the West since the Renaissance and the Enlightenment. So antimoralistic a non-Christian as Poe—looking only at American writers—shared Paul's sense of hopeless bifurcation of the self between "CONSCIENCE grim / That spectre in my path" (in "William Wilson") and the "Spirit of Perverseness" that forced Poe's hapless narrators to commit irrational crimes in stories like "The Black Cat," "The Tell-Tale Heart," "William Wilson," and "The Imp of the Perverse." Hence Poe's sardonic advice to aspiring young writers on "How to Write a Blackwood Article": "[Maintain] the tone transcendental. . . . Put in something about the Supernal Oneness. Don't say a syllable about the Infernal Twoness." And Hawthorne did not even need the spectacle of criminal behavior to proclaim, in "Fancy's Show Box," a universally innate depravity: "Man must not disclaim his brotherhood, even with the guiltiest, since, though his hand be clean, his heart has surely been polluted by the flitting phantoms of iniquity." Herman Melville, in "Hawthorne and His Mosses," cherished Hawthorne precisely because of "this great power of blackness in him" which "derives its force from its appeal to that Calvinistic sense of Innate Depravity and Original Sin, from whose visitations, in some shape or other, no deeply thinking mind is always and wholly free."

With the rise of both literary and philosophical naturalism later in the nineteenth and twentieth centuries, belief in man's inherent depravity gathered scientific—and pseudo-scientific—support, leading Mark Twain to condemn the "damned human race" as "of all creatures . . . the most detestable. Of the entire brood he is the only one—the solitary one—that possesses malice. . . . That puts him below the rats, the grubs, the trichinae. He is the only creature that inflicts pain for sport, knowing it to *be* pain." [6] And with psychologists' discovery of the unconscious mind—occurring in 1886 by William James's calculation—the Freudian id and Jungian shadow would add their secular weight to Paul's self-revelation and confirm by psychoanalysis what literature and religion had known for at least two millennia. "The primitive, savage, and evil impulses of mankind have not vanished in any individual," was Freud's sober conclusion in 1914, and he added that "they wait for opportunities to display their activity." [7] His onetime disciple Carl Gustav Jung was likewise moved to conclude, in *The Undiscovered Self*, that "The evil that dwells in man is of gigantic proportions. . . . We are always, thanks to our human nature, potential criminals." [8] And in the early years of this turbulent century, Sir James Frazer drew upon his decades of intensive anthropological study to utter a prophecy that applied his enormous learning to his contemporary scene: "The permanent existence of a solid layer of savagery beneath the surface of society . . . [is] a standing menace to civilization. We seem to move on a thin crust which may at any moment be rent by the subterranean forces slumbering below." [9] By the time Robert Penn Warren published his first volume, *Thirty-six Poems* (1935), Frazer's statement had become a present reality, so that Warren could exclaim in "Ransom": "What wars and lecheries! . . . / . . . ere dawn in rosy buskins laced / Delivers cool with dew the recent news-story." It was beginning to look like a new Dark Ages: "Defeat is possible, and the stars rise."

Both in the interior of the psyche and in the external world, then, impressions of depravity and ruin leaped to the lapsarian eye. And indeed, in the poetry of Warren's "middle" period in the 1940s and 1950s this recurrent obsession furnished the basic material for *Eleven Poems on the Same Theme* (1942), the three "New" poems in *Selected Poems, 1923–43* ("Variation: Ode to Fear," "Mexico Is a Foreign Country: Five Studies in Naturalism," and

"The Ballad of Billie Potts"), *Brother to Dragons* (1953), and much of *You, Emperors, and Others* (1960). Paradoxically, however, descent into the undiscovered self was to provide the long-sought escape from this waste land mentality, for although the deeper self arose in these poems brimming with pollution, it also brought important new possibilities for religious experience. William James had anticipated such a likelihood in his comment on the unconscious mind that "'seraph and snake' abide there side by side," and Jung went so far as to call the unconscious "the only accessible source of religious experience." [10]

Warren appears to have intuited similar insights in his religious psychology, particularly after the crucial turning point in "The Ballad of Billie Potts." Thereafter, in the running warfare between the conscious ego, usually designated "you," and the shadow self—a warfare between the Clean and the Dirty—Warren has largely taken sides with the Dirty. For it is the polluted animal self and not the surface ego that, in Warren's thought, holds the secret of ultimate identity. So "The bee knows, and the eel's cold ganglia burn" at the end of "Billie Potts," and man's unconscious mind similarly apprehends knowledge through dream and intuition in much of Warren's later poetry. Here then, we may gather Warren's three basic modes of religious experience—epiphany, "conversion," and "cosmic consciousness"—under the heading of mysticism, the final member of Warren's central thematic triad.

MYSTICISM

The most important thing that happens in *All the King's Men* is the "conversion" of Jack Burden: from the sardonic wise-cracking believer in the deterministic Great Twitch and escapist Great Sleep, to the humanistic believer in "history and the awful responsibility of Time." Here the "scholarly and benign figure of William James"—as Warren's Modern Library Preface to the book describes him—appears to have furnished the paradigm, for Jack Burden's conversion follows perfectly the model set forth in James's *The Varieties of Religious Experience.*

Conversion, as James defines it, is a psychological phenomenon whereby persons in a "morbid-minded" or "Sick Soul" condition may experience a profound change of identity: "To say that a man is 'converted' means . . . that religious ideas, previously peripheral in his consciousness, now take a central place. . . . All we know is that there are dead feelings, dead ideas, and cold beliefs, and there are hot and live ones; and when one grows hot and alive within us, everything has to re-crystallize about it." [11] Like one of James's "sick souls, who must be twice-born in order to be happy"—as James puts it in "The Divided Self, and the Process of Its Unification"—Jack Burden has his second birth after waking to his mother's scream over his father's suicide, so that the wise-guy pose gives way at last to a new and more genuine sense of self: "It was like the ice breaking up after a long winter. And the winter had been long." [12] Up to this point Jack's sardonic humor and his Great Twitch, Great Sleep, and Back-to-the-Foetus philosophy represent the second of the two ways William James identified as the only means of getting rid of "anger, worry, fear, despair, or other undesirable affections. One is that an opposite affection should overpoweringly break over us, and the other is by getting so exhausted with the struggle that we have to stop,—so we drop down, give up, and *don't care* any longer." [13]

The interesting thing behind this portrait of Jack Burden is the similar experience of "conversion" that evidently overtook its author, Robert Penn Warren himself, at about the time he was writing *All the King's Men* in the mid-1940s. Warren's previous novels, we might say, represent the Inferno stage of his vision. *At Heaven's Gate* (1943) is explicitly patterned after one of the circles in Dante's Hell; and contemporary poems like "Variation: Ode to Fear" and "Mexico Is a Foreign Country: Five Studies in Naturalism" reveal a similarly bleak outlook. What made the world particularly conducive to the "Sick Soul" condition in these works was a sense of solipsism much like that which caused T. S. Eliot to quote F. H. Bradley in his Notes to *The Waste Land:* "my experience falls within my own circle, a circle closed on the outside; and . . . every sphere is opaque to the others which surround it. . . . In brief . . . the whole world for each is peculiar and private to that soul." For Jack Burden before his "conversion," the world looked this way, "for to him the world then [during his Cass Mastern inquiry] was simply an accumulation of items, odds and ends of things like the broken and misused and dust-shrouded things gathered in a garret. Or it was a flux of things before his eyes (or behind his eyes) and one thing had nothing to do, in the end, with anything else." So he was unable to understand Cass Mastern's sense of guilt and complicity; but later, "I (who am what Jack Burden became) look back now," and know that "Cass Mastern lived for a few years and in that time he learned that the world is all of one piece. He learned that the world is like an enormous spider web and if you touch it, however lightly, at any point, the vibration ripples to the remotest perimeter. . . ." [14] Similarly, before *his* "conversion" in "The Ballad of Billie Potts" the chief burden of existence for Warren's persona seemed to be this sense of the isolated self cast adrift in a fragmented universe. In "Small Soldiers with Drum in Large Landscape" (from "Mexico Is a Foreign Country") Warren's persona suffers this sensation while watching the soldiers marching:

> The little drum goes rum-tum-tum,
> The little hearts go rat-tat-tat,
> And I am I, and they are they,
> And *this* is *this*, and *that* is *that*. . . .

As this poem ends the persona tries through an act of imagination to "march beside them in the sun." But in the following poem, "The Mango on the Mango Tree" (which concludes the "Mexico Is a Foreign Country" sequence), he renews his complaint at the highest level, bringing it to "the Great Schismatic's ear":

> For God well works the Roman plan,
> Divide and rule, mango and man,
> And on hate's axis the great globe grinds in its span.

What saved the poet—or his persona, and is there *really* that much difference between them?—from this oppressive sense of fragmentation was an irruption of what James called "cosmic consciousness" that melded the fragments into supernal unity. We may leave the poetic evidence of this cosmic consciousness for later discussion and proceed instead directly to the poet's description of this "monistic insight" (as James would call it) in his essay "Knowledge and the Image of Man," which declares that, "[Man is] in the world with continual and intimate interpenetration, an inevitable osmosis of being, which in the end . . . affirms his identity."[15] This osmosis of being, Warren went on to say, may produce a merger of "the ugly with the beautiful, the slayer with the slain," evoking—in whoever can see this—"such a sublimation that the world which once provoked . . . fear and disgust may now be totally loved." To love the world totally, despite all the filth, loss, and suffering revealed during the trauma of passage, is thus the ultimate achievement of Warren's figures of grace—Audubon in *Audubon: A Vision*, "who had loved the world"; Brother Potts in *Flood*, who prayed though dying of cancer, "Help me to know the life I lived was blessèd"; and Blanding Cotshill in the same novel, who restates Warren's above-quoted thesis: "Things are tied together. . . . There's some spooky interpenetration of things, a mystic osmosis of being, you might say."[16]

We are entitled to speak of Warren's mental experience as a form of mysticism if we may again rely on James's scholarly conclusions. (And perhaps we should interpolate here that even Freud, despite his implacable hostility towards all things "religious," grudgingly conceded the genuineness of "cosmic consciousness.") "This overcoming of all the usual barriers between the individual and the Absolute is the great mystic achievement," James says, adding: "This is the everlasting and triumphant mystical tradition, hardly altered by differences of clime or creed. In Hinduism, in Neoplatonism, in Sufism, in Christian mysticism, in Whitmanism, we find the same recurring note, so that there is about mystical utterances an eternal unanimity which ought to make a critic stop and think. . . ."[17]

It is reasonable to speculate upon two plausible causes of this mental transformation in Warren. One is simply to accept Jung's and James's finding that the unconscious is the only source of religious experience, and thereby to assume that the poet's unconscious came bearing gifts in response to an urgent need. As James puts it, "If there be higher powers able to impress us, they may get access to us only through the subliminal door." The phenomenon of conversion, then, may be "partly due to explicitly conscious processes of thought and will," but it is "due largely also to the subconscious incubation and maturing of motives deposited by the experiences of life. When ripe, the results hatch out, or burst into flower." [18] We shall see evidence of just such an incubation or "hatching out" process in *Eleven Poems on the Same Theme* (1942) and "The Ballad of Billie Potts," and the results may be seen in everything Warren has written since then in fiction and poetry. Even his criticism has reflected the new monistic insight, as when he defines Herman Melville's final outlook—in an essay called "Melville the Poet," dated 1945—in terms remarkably similar to those of his own "osmosis of being." While endorsing the words of another critic, William Ellery Sedgwick, Warren said: "Melville's act was toward humanity, not away from it. He renounced all the prerogatives of individuality in order to enter into the destiny which binds all human beings in one great spiritual and emotional organism. He abdicated his independence so as to be incorporated into the mystical body of humanity." [19]

Accelerating some such "incubation" process, a second major thrust towards the "conversion" experience may be plausibly surmised in Warren's mental life of the mid-1940s. This thrust derived from his reading of Romantic poets who themselves testified to experiencing cosmic consciousness, most notably Samuel Taylor Coleridge. In his preface to the Modern Library edition of *All the King's Men*, Warren mentions that his writing of the novel was "interrupted . . . by the study for and writing of a long essay on Coleridge." That essay, on *The Ancient Mariner*, turns out to be an explanation and vindication of Warren's own purpose and practice in poetry. Speaking against the opinion of Griggs and Lowes that "the poem is nothing more than a pleasant but meaningless dream," Warren endorses Coleridge's statements in the *Table Talk* that "Dreams have nothing in them which is absurd and nonsensical" and that "There is in genius itself an unconscious activity." [20] He further not only defends but endorses Coleridge's religious imagination, as against I. A. Richard's reduction of it to a mere psychological phenomenon: "Coleridge . . . was not content to leave the doctrine of the creativity of mind at the psychological level. There is a God, and the creativity of the human mind . . . is an analogue of Divine creation. . . . Furthermore, the world of Nature is to be read by the mind as a symbol of Divinity, a symbol characterized by the 'translucence of the eternal through and in the temporal.' . . . It might be said that reason shows us God, and imagination shows us how Nature participates in God." [21]

These ideas should be remembered particularly as we approach the crucial "Ballad of Billie Potts," but there are some further Warren / Coleridge affinities to consider. For example, the two central themes of *The Ancient Mariner* are—as Warren interprets them—precisely the two central obsessions of Warren's own writing of the time. Coleridge's primary theme, Warren says, is (exactly like his own osmosis of being) "the sense of the 'One Life' in which all creation participates"; and the other is (so like Warren's undiscovered self) the "story of crime and punishment and repentance and reconciliation." [22] Concerning this latter theme, Coleridge must stand apart from his fellow Romantics like Blake and Wordsworth and Shelley, for unlike them Coleridge expressed a firm belief in man's original sin or natural depravity. Warren's considerable satisfaction in this fact may be guessed from the passages that, garnered from vast fields of Coleridgean prose, he cites in his essay. "I believe most steadfastly in original sin; that from our mothers' wombs our understandings are darkened; and . . . that our organization is depraved," reads one such quote from a Coleridge letter. And from the *Table Talk*, Warren quotes: "A Fall of some sort or other . . . is the fundamental postulate of the moral history of Man. Without this hypothesis, Man is unintelligible; with it every phenomenon is explicable." [23] Warren adds on his own, "Original Sin is not hereditary sin; it is original with the sinner and is of his will." Both punishment for and release from sin in *The Ancient Mariner* represent, as Warren describes them, the spiritual stages that Warren himself denoted before and after his own "conversion" (as described above): "The Mariner shoots the bird; suffers various pains, the greatest of which is loneliness and spiritual anguish; upon recognizing the beauty of the foul sea snakes, experiences a gush of love for them and is able to pray. . . ." [24] The relevance of these beliefs to Warren's themes of the undiscovered self and the osmosis of being is obvious. But for our purpose in discussing mysticism the final paragraph of Warren's essay will serve for Warren himself, we may dare say, as well as for Coleridge: "If poetry does anything for us, it reconciles . . . (for by its very nature it is in itself a myth of the unity of being)."

Though conversion through an irruption of cosmic consciousness stands as the main event in Warren's career as a poet, there remains one other form of "religious" experience that is crucial to his poetry. That would be the experience of the epiphany. Whether of a secular character or "divine" (however such a word is defined), the epiphany in modern literature has commonly captured life's significance so intensively as largely to justify T. S. Eliot's cry in *Four Quartets:* "Ridiculous the waste sad time / Stretching before and after." Writers like Hemingway, Nabokov, and Wallace Stevens have obviously shared this feeling, basing their epiphanies on secular—and normally aesthetic— experience. For Nabokov and Stevens, the beauty of a Lolita or a Susanna suffices to evoke such transcendence, as when the "red- eyed elders" in "Peter Quince at the Clavier" feel "The basses of their beings throb" and "their thin blood / Pulse pizzicati of Hosanna" at the spectacle of Susanna bathing. James, in his chapter on mysticism, considers the aesthetic epiphany a valid form of mystical experience in its own right when carried to a sufficiently intensive level, so that "effects of light on land and sea, odors and musical sounds, all bring it when the mind is tuned right"; and again, "Certain aspects of nature seem to have a peculiar power of awakening such mystical moods."[25] When we later turn to the subject of Warren's epiphanies and especially when we consider that they convey in his words "The True Nature of Time," we may have further reason to reflect on James's judgment that such moments constitute a religious experience and even a kind of mysticism. But first let us examine Warren's themes in the context of his literary criticism.

IN CONTEXT: WARREN'S CRITICISM

A fundamental coherence unifies Warren's whole body of poetry, as though it constituted a single poem drawn out in a fugal pattern —somewhat like Pound's *Cantos* or Eliot's poetry, but more like Eliot's because its total design was not preplanned but simply "exfoliated" (a favorite Warren metaphor for discovering identity) according to some deep rhythm of development in the artist's temperament. Like many another artist—one thinks of Keats and his letters, Hawthorne and his notebooks, Eliot and his essays— Warren has maintained a running gloss on his creative literature through the incidental prose that he has turned out over the duration of his career in letters. By touching upon his reviews and criticism at different points in his poetic career, we may gain further insight into his ground themes and, in some cases, observe them in the process of modulating from one to another. Ultimately, in fugal fashion, his three master themes interlock, so that at any point in the poet's career we are likely to see simultaneous traces of all three themes—and in at least one instance, "The Ballad of Billie Potts," they fuse into perfect harmony. But for the most part each theme has in its turn a period of predominance over the other two. Warren's literary criticism helps to clarify this pattern.

Although admirably reasonable and elucidating in its own right, Warren's criticism—like that of his sometime mentor T. S. Eliot—serves the secondary purpose of illuminating and often vindicating his own practice in literature. Predictably, the young poet faulted his peers in the light of his own Eliotic, neo-Metaphysical practice of poetry. Thus, for example, he argued that the technique of borrowing is fine, but it must be done with original effect. As early as 1928 Warren complained of John Hall Wheelock, "not merely that he borrows, but that he fails to assimilate the borrowed material as his own"—a charge that he also laid to John Peale Bishop.[26] And Archibald MacLeish fails to measure up to the neo-Metaphysical creed that poetry requires tension and self-conflict to be interesting: his work is "carefully purged of all opposing stresses; it is singularly undramatic. It is poetry of the single impulse, which requires no resolution."[27] Lacking such tension, or "Impurity" as he would later call it, Masefield, De La Mare, and E. E. Cummings have become "perfectly predictable," each of their poems "certain to be indistinguishable from the one before it"—despite the gimmicks that Cummings, for example, was fond of exploiting. The poetry of Robinson Jeffers likewise suffers from its failure to develop in new directions: "when we pick up that recent book by the established poet, we expect . . . a continuity of some kind. . . . But we demand in the new book something new. . . . If not new concepts, at least new percepts . . . to feed the understanding." [28] These statements were to remain permanently valid descriptions of what Warren sought to avoid in his poetry, and did avoid. By virtue of their dialectical interaction, Warren's grand themes of passage, the undiscovered self, and mysticism imparted continuous tension and growth. This interaction meant that he could largely avoid the essential limitation which he saw circumscribing Cummings, whose poems (he said in 1944) have merely "celebrated a temperament . . . the tough-sensitive poet in a beautiful-ugly world." [29]

Innovations in style inevitably accompanied the poet's incursions into major new subject areas. In a review written in 1932 Warren discloses a purely technical reason why he wrote poetry for so long (nearly two decades) exclusively in the lyric manner: "Today the resources of prose are so enormous and generally superior for narrative and psychological analysis that poetry is on the defensive when brought into direct competition." [30] The point is well taken, but choice of theme also had much to do with Warren's sense of poetry's formal resources. Had he continued to write almost solely in the poetry of passage vein, as he did in the 1920s and 1930s, the lyric mode might have continued to be his primary vehicle of expression—the most natural outlet for the personal emotions inherent in the passage experience. As it is, the poetry of that period sometimes appears to be merely celebrating a temperament, the tough-sensitive poet in a fallen world. But with the development of the undiscovered self theme in *Eleven Poems*, dramatic conflict within the poet's psyche began to roughen the lyric texture. And with the mystical theme of "how Nature participates in God" added in "Billie Potts," the narrative form—under Coleridge's tutelage, it seems—was conjoined to Warren's lyric and dramatic resources to comprise a technique capable of sustaining such substantial thematic expansions.

Initially, there was no sign that Warren would ever adopt the sort of nature-mysticism that animates "Billie Potts." Quite the contrary, in 1933 he sharply objected to Sidney Lanier's concept of "a union 'of human nature with physical nature,' the embodiment of man's broadened love of the universe," which he dismissed as mere sentimentality; he favored Lanier's own earlier statement that "Nature is the tyrant of tyrants." [31] But as early as January

1935, in "John Crowe Ransom: A Study in Irony," Warren expressed a sense of deficiency in the theme of passage that was then predominant in his own poetry. "The world . . . has been stricken with an unheard of poverty of mind and unhappiness of life," he said, because modern men have no sustaining myths to live by; and "Where there is no vision the people perish." [32] Ransom's definition of the constructive mythmaker, which Warren quotes here, is interesting because it anticipates just what Warren himself would be doing some years later: "the myth-maker, Ransom says, sets up his God in response to two motives: an extensive and an intensive. God means, in response to the former, a universe of 'a magnitude exceeding its own natural history,' in response to the latter, of 'a richness of being that exceeds formulation.' " Those two quoted phrases, about a universe exceeding its natural history and about richness of being, might eventually be found at the center of Warren's "mystic osmosis of being" and his epiphanies of later years.

F. Cudworth Flint, reviewing *Thirty-six Poems* in 1936, evoked a sense of thematic deficiency by saying that these poems raised the crucial question of contemporary culture: " Who will show us our myths?" We need a mythology which is "credible," Flint said, and therefore, "Such a mythology will probably have to arise on a human rather than a supernatural plane." [33] Warren's osmosis of being, which as an overbelief for interpreting life's meaning is a myth, would eventually serve just so on a "human rather than a supernatural plane," as would his mythologized figures in American history (Jefferson, Audubon, Dreiser). But through the 1930s Warren simply continued to admit a deficiency. In a 1939 essay entitled "The Present State of Poetry in the United States" Warren, apparently feeling stung by Flint's earlier comments, quoted Flint and made a rejoinder: "But perhaps we do not need to have our myth pointed out to us. Perhaps we may know it, and know it too well, knowing that, as Stevenson said, 'it provides no habitable city for the soul of man.' " [34] Warren's own reigning myth at this time was that of the Fall, modulating by now into that of original sin and the undiscovered self motif; and as yet neither myth had made of Warren's verse a habitable city, nor would they until touched by the mystic consciousness of "Billie Potts." Each theme in turn thus seemed to summon the next grand theme into being.

Although in the 1940s Warren produced only a small amount of poetry (the decade being given instead to his most brilliant successes in fiction), it included his single most important poem; the period also generated the poet's most illustrious body of criticism. Gathered and slightly revised at times in *Selected Essays* (1958), these works of criticism, including his essay on *The Ancient Mariner*, greatly illuminated Warren's developing convictions about his craft at that crucial midpoint of his poetic career. Among those convictions, none is more basic or recurrent than the idea that theme is the *sine qua non* of serious literature. The essays mostly comprise thematic analyses—though supported by some excellent observations about technique, to be sure—of Hemingway, Conrad, Faulkner, Coleridge, Frost, Porter, and Welty. Even Warren's most theoretical essay, "Pure and Impure Poetry," was written mainly to defend the literature of ideas from its detractors. Two of Warren's chief mentors, Eliot and Marvell, are thus cited as "the exact opposite of poets who, presumably on the grounds of purity, exclude the movement of mind from the center of the poetic process; . . . Marvell and Eliot . . . are trying to emphasize the participation of ideas in the poetic process." [35] To buttress his point Warren calls in the philosopher Santayana to testify that "philosophy, when a poet is not mindless, enters inevitably into his poetry, since it has entered into his life" (p. 26). In his analytical essays the issue comes up again and again: the poet's "truth" as "an organizing and vitalizing principle in his poems" in "The Themes of Robert Frost"; the inevitable mediocrity of those "who work from no fundamental and central conviction" in "Irony with a Center: Katherine Anne Porter"; the "principle of presumptive coherence of development" in "A Poem of Pure Imagination"; the demand that "a piece of literature, new or old, . . . should intensify our awareness of the world (and of ourselves in relation to the world) in terms of an idea, a 'view,' " in "Love and Separateness in Eudora Welty" (pp. 119, 137, 273, 159). These excerpts imply the paramountcy of a thematic approach to Warren's own poetry.

Perhaps the next most important general conception in *Selected*

Essays is that of a dialectical design, or "tension," being inherent in literature. The one entry in *Selected Essays* of a disparaging nature, "A Note on the Hamlet of Thomas Wolfe" (written in 1935, it antedates the more generous tone of the 1940s), scorns Wolfe as one who, like Whitman, Sandburg, Masters, and Benét, "pants for the Word, the union that will clarify all the disparate and confused elements . . ." (p. 180). Every one of Warren's favorites in the book, by contrast, is cited as working with thematic contraries of some type: "the fact and the dream" in Robert Frost; "the humanism-naturalism opposition in Faulkner's work"; the "dilemma of idea as opposed to nature" in Conrad; "the fundamental ironical dualities of existence" in Melville; "a tissue of contradictions" in Katherine Anne Porter; and "the contrasts [which] provide terms of human effort" in Eudora Welty (pp. 124, 73, 54, 190, 142, 166). To these he might have added, had he cared to, his own tissue of contradictions: the rational consciousness and the unconscious, Time and "no-Time," solipsism and the osmosis of being, the "world's stew" and its "Delight."

Warren's design, too, makes for impure poetry—poems that "mar themselves with cacophonies, jagged rhythms, ugly words and ugly thoughts, colloquialism, clichés, sterile technical terms, headwork and argument, self-contradictions, clevernesses, irony, realism—all things which call us back to the world of prose and imperfection" (pp. 4-5). And finally, "nothing that is available in human experience is to be legislated out of poetry," because ultimately, "other things being equal, the greatness of a poet depends upon the extent of the area of experience which he can master poetically" (pp. 26-27). In the name of this mastery of experience, apparently, Warren would justify his own continuing thematic contradictions—between his poems of passage and his epiphanies, for example—for poetry "is a motion toward a point of rest, but if it is not a resisted motion, it is motion of no consequence" (p. 27). Or, as he said about Hemingway, "An artist's basic ideas do not operate in splendid isolation; to a greater or lesser degree, they prove themselves by their conquest of other ideas" (p. 117).

Except for the Wolfe essay—an anomaly from the 1930s—it is obvious that for Warren a powerfully attracting force in the works of other writers was affinity with his own work—the Melvillean "shock of recognition." Ideologically, the leading affinity was the osmosis of being theme as he conceived other writers to have rendered it: the "One Life" in Coleridge; the "human bond" in Faulkner (there are "no villains in his work, except those who deny the human bond"); Conrad's "human community, the solidarity in which Conrad finds his final values"; Melville's immersion in "the destiny which binds all human beings in one great spiritual and emotional organism. . . . the mystical body of humanity" (pp. 78, 40, 197). Among these Coleridge's impact must have been greatest. The ending of "Billie Potts" may well correlate with what Warren calls "a central fact" of *The Ancient Mariner*, "that the world is full of powers and presences not visible to the physical eye. . . ; that there is a spiritual order of universal love, the sacramental vision. . . ; that nature, if understood aright—that is, by the imagination—offers us vital meanings" (p. 266). Next in importance to the Coleridge essay is the tribute to Conrad, whose relevance to "Billie Potts" may be seen in Warren's statement that "the lowest and most vile creature must, in some way, idealize his existence in order to exist, and must find sanctions outside himself" (p. 43). This specific "vital meaning" in nature is evidenced in "Billie Potts" by the way the gathering creatures do find sanctions outside themselves and form their own osmosis of being in their intuitively purposeful odysseys. Other thematic affinities involve the concepts of the Fall and original sin, mythologically rendered in Coleridge and naturalistically rendered—as man's fall into "the black inward abyss of himself and the black outward abyss of nature" (p. 55)—in Conrad, Hemingway, and Faulkner. (Melville and Frost render these themes both naturalistically and mythologically, Frost dealing with the Fall and Melville with original sin as central concerns.) Warren's three grand themes, in short, find ample expression in these kindred artists, according to his analyses of them.

Although our main interest here is theme, it may be well in passing to note some technical modulations. In earlier essays through the middle 1940s, Warren's approbation extends—in proper New Critical fashion—to the honored devices of the high Modern period. In the Coleridge essay, for example, he upholds the Eliotic ideal of a unified sensibility that he finds in Coleridge,

"The opposition between thought and feeling he wished to abolish"; and he further admires Coleridge's use of symbol to express a unified sensibility: "The symbol serves to *combine* . . . the 'poet's heart and intellect' " (pp. 252, 218). Here Warren might have been writing for the Imagist Manifesto. In the same vein he adds an "objective correlative" type of stricture in writing about Miss Porter: "the thematic considerations must, as it were, be validated in terms of circumstance and experience, and never be resolved in the poverty of statement" (p. 155). By the end of the decade, however, in the Conrad essay, Warren's poetic theory was changing to something more compatible with his work then in progress, *Brother to Dragons*. Didacticism and open participation in his art, though still eschewed, might be more amenable to a writer who observes that "Conrad made no split between literature and life" and quotes Conrad as saying, "even the most artful writer will give himself (and his morality) away in about every third sentence" (p. 57). As "R.P.W.: The writer of this poem" in *Brother to Dragons*, Warren too would make no split between literature and life and he would not object to resolving issues in "the poverty of statement."

In the 1950s Warren wrote several pieces explaining certain of his own poems—"Pursuit," "Terror," "Revelation," and *Brother to Dragons*—as well as a very important essay on his general philosophy of life ("Knowledge and the Image of Man").[36] None of these pieces, however, reveals as much about his poetic compositions as do his recent critical essays on the poetry of Ransom, Melville, and Whittier. Concerning Ransom, Warren wrote two pieces in 1963 and 1968, the latter in honor of Ransom's eightieth birthday. In the earlier piece he credits Ransom with having taught him, in *Poems about God* (which Warren read at age seventeen) the significance of the local, rural Tennessee environment; Ransom "put the mystical shiver, as it were, into the back pasture." In addition, he found that "the great quality that shines through" all of Ransom's poems is charity, "a charity possible only to one who has understood and mastered the self so fully that he can turn outward upon the world his full power of sympathy." Such charity, in fact, as infuses Warren's osmosis of being concept: "This charity may not be Christian, but if not it shows us . . . a

world redeemed by, at least, natural love."[37] In the 1968 essay
further affinities loom large, such as (again) the paramountcy of
theme that makes Ransom comparable "to the philosopher-poet
Coleridge, the haunting force of whose poems cannot be understood except in the light of his philosophy—not as illustrations
of the philosophy but as life-thrusts toward the philosophy."
Moreover, Ransom's later poetry, like Warren's, appears strengthened by closer identification between the poet and his persona,
Ransom thereby "accepting the responsibility of a fuller use of
his own sensibility and his own history." Finally, although Ransom's subject has been (like Warren's) "the haunting dualism in
man's experience," the famous Ransom irony concerning that
dualism masks a deeper and surprising emotion: joy. "He had
written his poems out of joy, he said." In recalling that conversation with his old mentor, Warren comes near to mythologizing
him as he did Jefferson ("In joy, I would end") and Audubon:
"he must have meant more than the special joy of composition.
He must have meant that he saw poetry as a natural function
of . . . the process of living. . . . And so we come back to the notion . . . of living as the great art, and back, in a very special way,
to the ancient notion of a good man's life as a poem."[38]

In "Melville's Poems" (1967) extensive correlations and affinities make Warren seem something like a reincarnation of the
earlier poet-novelist. Although, unlike Warren, Melville turned
seriously to poetry only after the collapse of his career in fiction,
poetry functioned similarly for both men, as a record of their
search for beliefs to live by: "Melville had touched bottom, and
he was now seeking a belief by which life could be considered
and his own life rebuilt; and his poetry, in one dimension, may
be read as a record of that search."[39] Theme or "idea" is therefore paramount once again. In *Clarel*, for example, "the deep relation of personality and idea" leads to Melville's "trying to show
us ideas not as abstractions but as a function of the life process;
and here, as in so much, he is something of a pioneer" (p. 831).
As with Warren's own poetry, the specific idea that governs
Melville's work is the theme of passage into a fallen world, which
Melville renders in the metaphor of passage around Cape Horn
(Warren quotes *White Jacket* here): "Sailor, beware of it; pre-

pare for it in time" (p. 800). Whereas Melville's fiction grew out of his romantic adventures in the unspoiled South Seas Eden, his verse—and *Clarel* in particular—derived from his appalling vision of corruption and spiritual sterility in the Old World, which climaxed during his visit to the Holy Land. Thus, "Melville's poetry belongs to that second half of his life after he had rounded his Horn and was trying to beat north to a latitude where peace might, at last, be possible" (p. 800).

In his postlapsarian condition, Melville could attain such "peace" or "transcendence"—as Warren did—only by accepting the sovereignty of nature and by "redemptive recognition . . . of the human bond," a bond involving the "harsh fact" that "the human community is, in one perspective, a community of guilt" (pp. 854, 813). It is also a community of suffering. In citing Melville's vision of "Jew, Christian, Arab, and Turk on the Via Crucis . . . as 'cross-bearers all,'" Warren finds confirmation of his own view (expressed in *Or Else*, "Interjection #2") that "every man / is a sort of Jesus" (p. 854). By accepting these conditions Melville moved through the phase of "anger and irony" and found "the final joy in resignation to the cyclic pulse of the universe" (p. 835)—a fair description of the emotional curve in Warren's own poetic canon. "Melville's most perfect poem," Warren says, is "Billy in the Darbies," "in which he achieves complete mastery of style and, shall we say, of his life" (p. 840). This statement and Warren's further description of the poem evoke some striking resemblances to Warren's "The Ballad of Billie Potts." Not only does Warren find the "magic of reconciliation of our conflicting needs" in Melville's "Billy" but he also commends its hybrid form: "it is at once a broadside ballad and a high poetic elegy, . . . combining the resonance of both popular poetry and art poetry [in] . . . a complicated interplay, of fusion and contrast" (pp. 855, 849). It reminds him, Warren says, of *The Ancient Mariner*.

Melville's early poetry, on the other hand, strikes Warren as an "imitation of seventeenth-century metaphysical poetry" reminiscent of Marvell; but this style modifies in *Battle-Pieces* toward "a metaphysical style of his own, . . . a style rich and yet shot through with realism and prosaism, sometimes casual and open and sometimes dense and intellectually weighted . . ." (pp. 804, 807). A better description of Warren's own style, particularly during the *Eleven Poems* period, would be hard to find. To conclude this list of affinities, Warren calls *Moby-Dick* a prose work in which "the prose often strains toward verse." (Not any more so than some of Warren's prose, however: *Who Speaks for the Negro?* speaks of persons murdered for ideological reasons, who "do not bleed when blade or bullet bites.") [40] Melville's poems, however, are often "anecdotal or dramatic; they have, in other words, a 'prose' base" (p. 841). Again, Warren's self-description here is perfect. (It should be noted in passing that Warren refers to William James several times here, quoting "Pragmatism and Religion" in particular.)

We end this look at Warren's criticism with his two recent publications on John Greenleaf Whittier and Theodore Dreiser. Initially, two more disparate figures can hardly be imagined and neither seems significantly related to Warren's poetry. The essays function, however, as companion pieces that relate directly to Warren's most obsessive master theme, the Fall from Eden and subsequent passage into a ruined world. Between them Whittier and Dreiser comprehend Warren's two primary responses to that experience (as expressed in his poems): nostalgia for that "landscape lost in the heart's homely deep"; and the Waste Lander's outcry of anger, dread perplexity, guilt, and humiliation. "The subject that released Whittier's deepest energy," Warren says, "was the memory of the past, more specifically the childhood past, . . . the happy, protected time before he knew the dark inward struggle. . . . Almost everyone has an Eden time to look back on, even if it never existed . . . ; but for Whittier the need to dwell on this lost Eden was more marked than is ordinary." In *Snow-Bound*, Warren sees this motif symbolized by "the hearthside, that Edenic spot surrounded by the dark world"; and this poem "summarizes Whittier's life and work" because, in giving "definitive expression to the obsessive theme of childhood nostalgia," it treats (our final affinity) the "great question of how to find in the contemplation of the past a meaning for the future." [41]

The book-length essay called *Homage to Theodore Dreiser*

is too long to discuss meaningfully here. However, Warren's fascination with Dreiser generated not only this essay but its prefatory poem (later included in *Or Else*), on which I shall comment later. Of the essay, we may say that behind Dreiser's role as "a cosmic muckraker" lay two developments of special interest to Warren the poet. One was Dreiser's ability to imagine a beautiful lost childhood—he too had "an Eden time to look back on . . . even if it never existed." Warren quotes from Dreiser's poem, "On the Banks of the Wabash, Far Away," which his brother Paul helped write and set to music.

> Round my Indiana homestead waves the cornfield,
> In the distance loom the woodlands clear and cool.
> Oftentimes my thoughts revert to scenes of childhood,
> Where I first received my lessons, nature's school.
> . . . .
> I long to see my mother in the doorway,
> As she stood there years ago, her boy to greet!

The other fascination Dreiser has for Warren is the way Dreiser's character serves as an exemplum of Warren's "Original Sin"—original with and willed by the sinner after his exile from Eden. As evidenced above all in his depraved treatment of "the stream of different women" in his life, Dreiser was one who plunged headlong into "the black inward abyss of self" (as Warren's essay on Conrad calls it). "Outraged at old deprivations, haunted by a sense of insufficiency and inferiority, paranoidally suspicious, totally self-centered and brutally selfish," Dreiser makes a handsome addition to Warren's specimens of the Dirty in his gallery of the Clean and the Dirty discussed in my "The Undiscovered Self" chapter.[42] Ever since his 1929 study of his archetypal Clean man, John Brown, Warren has found his Dirty people—Lilburn Lewis, the Roman emperors, Dreiser—increasingly irresistible.

A final affinity: Melville, Whittier, and Dreiser disclose radical disaffection with a father-figure (one of Warren's lifelong motifs). "If a secret drama of Melville's work is the search for the father who died after failure, a secret drama of Dreiser's is the rejection of a father who, after failure, lived." Whittier's revulsion against Daniel Webster in "Ichabod" also figures as a symbolic father-rejection, in Warren's reading.

None of the previous commentary is meant to represent the primary significance of Warren's criticism, most of which renders serious, generous, and often brilliantly perceptive exposition. But in so far as his essays illuminate his own poetic themes and theories, they are fair game, I think, for such interpretation.

2
Poems of Passage

On looking over Warren's eleven volumes of poems written over the span of half a century, one must be surprised at how permanently and deeply embedded is the theme of innocence confronting—or trying to evade—the trauma of awakening into a fallen world. Like Jack Burden wanting to remain an unknowing foetus in *All the King's Men*, the persona in many of Warren's poems is either a child on the brink of this trauma or an adult who resists plunging into the pain, filth, and injustice of "the world's stew," as our poet calls it in *You, Emperors, and Others*. Over roughly half of Warren's poetic career, this resisting adult is the main figure; in the later decades, when Warren writes largely about his own children and his own childhood, the child-on-the-brink predominates. In either case, forbidden knowledge is the midwife of passage. Although "the end of man is to know," according to *All the King's Men*, the cost of knowledge is loss of paradise, as in the biblical archetype—the irremediable discovery of sex and death and time.[1]

SELECTED POEMS: 1923–1943

In Warren's first published volume, *Thirty-six Poems* (1935), this theme of passage from innocence into a fallen state is apparent in a number of poem titles—"Man Coming of Age," "Problems of Knowledge," "So Frost Astounds," "Aged Man Surveys the Past Time," "The Garden"—and it not only permeates all the poems in the collection but also spills over into the subsequent *Eleven Poems on the Same Theme* (1942) and the new poems in *Selected Poems: 1923-1943*. As a whole, this latter collection (representing some twenty years of poetry-writing) divides itself fairly evenly between the two emotional poles that are naturally implicit in the lapsarian material: nostalgia and regret concerning paradise remembered; guilt, dread, and despair prevailing after the Fall. Often the two emotional states occur in the same poem, locked in dialectical conflict; but sometimes a whole poem is given over to one perspective or the other.

Warren's career as a published poet evidently began in the postlapsarian mood, since his earliest poem—"To a Face in a Crowd"—is given over entirely to an after the Fall psychology. (Using reverse chronology, Warren put his earliest poems last in all his compilations of *Selected Poems;* "To a Face in a Crowd" terminates these volumes.) Here a Waste Land nihilism claims both the speaker and his "brother," the face in a crowd, as both are "weary nomads" in a "lost procession" hearing gulls "Rehearse to the cliffs the rhetoric of their woe." As conventional as this stance may now appear, some of the poem's effects display a very creditable technical virtuosity. The thud of the heart—"how black and turbulent the blood / Will beat through iron chambers of the brain"—is fairly well captured in "b" sounds, for example; and likewise the lines where the grass touches men's bones with sexual hunger—"among the rocks the faint lascivious grass / Fingers in lust the arrogant bones of men"—project their sibilance as if making a hiss of disapproval. We see here also a nice metaphorical melding of the two modes of forbidden knowledge, sex and death entwined with grass and bones.

If "To a Face in a Crowd" features despair as the chief postlapsarian emotion, other poems vent rage, fear, or black laughter. In "Pacific Gazer," the sea's fury objectifies the wrath of Eden's outcast. To the "gazer of saddest intent" who now "Stares where the light went," paradise remembered is the "land of no wrath" in the fifth stanza:

> Lands of no wrath
> Knew, perhaps, his story,
> Happier then ere his path
> To the billed promontory
> Led, and storm's scath.

Now, after the Fall, its victim takes the storm as a perfect mirror of his inner condition, somewhat like a modern Lear on the heath:

> What wrath he owes
> Abides in the water's might:
> Only the blind blast echoes
> His wrath to black night
> Could night oppose.

Two other very early poems contained in *Thirty-six Poems* display such a *personal* trauma concerning entry into a ruined world as to explain their deletion from *Selected Poems* (1944). "Genealogy"—addressed to the poet's grandfather, Gabriel, after whom Warren would later name his own son—sees the birth of Warren's father as a disaster, not only for the infant's mother (who died in childbirth) but also for the later issue of the event, Robert Penn Warren himself:

> Gabriel, Gabriel . . .
> . . . .
> Your grandson keeps a broken house.
> There's a stitch in his side no plasters heal,
> A crack in the firmament, maggots in the meal;
> There's a mole in the garden, fennel by the gate,
> In the heart a curse of hell-black hate
> For that other young guy who croaked too late.

And "To One Awake" sees respite from the fallen world only in sleep ("Get you to sleep"), though even in sleep nightmare visions of death like those in Poe's "The Conqueror Worm" may obtrude oppressively:

> If in the unclean flesh of sleep are caught
> The sightless creatures that uncoil in dream,
> Mortal, you ought
> Not dread fat larvae of the thought
> That in the ogival bone preform
> The fabulous worm.

Passage into a ruined world having been completed, the rage and despair of the young dwindle for the old into pure dread.

For the subject of "Aged Man Surveys the Past Time," nothing remains but one further passage, a "rocky and bituminous descent" whose imminence moves the aged man to tears of dread and sorrow. Dying (like Eliot's Gerontion) without faith—"a wry and blasphemous theme"—he can find no sustenance in our age's "well-adapted" secular philosophies, which, if anything, seem now like a catbird's mockery:

> By fruitful grove, unfruited now by winter,
> The well-adapted and secular catbird
> Whimpers its enmity and invitation.
> Light fails beyond the barn and blasted oak.

Given the futility of other responses, it was natural that the poet should turn at last to that contemporary refuge from mental pain, black humor. "Variation: Ode to Fear," the chief example of black laughter in these *Selected Poems*, takes dread of death as its central theme. "*Timor mortis conturbat me*" is repeated some eighteen times as the refrain following each stanza. Unlike "Aged Man Surveys the Past Time," however, this "Ode to Fear" conceives of death as a prospect just distant enough to render possible a comic rather than tearful mood—comic, that is, in a black humor mode, with the desperate gaiety that Emily Dickinson had in mind in saying, "Mirth is the Mail of Anguish," or Nathanael West in saying, "I must laugh at myself, and if the laugh is 'bitter,' I must laugh at the laugh." [2] Freud's theory that humor is the chief defense against psychic pain is borne out in this poem, or at least in the bulk of it, where the dentist's drill, the overdrawn bank account, and the leveling of heroes like Milton, Saint Joan, and Jesus lead to the *Timor mortis* condition. [3] Humor fails to deaden the pain, however, in some situations:

> When in the midnight's pause I mark
> The breath beside me in the dark,
> And know that breath's a clock, and know
> That breath's the clock that's never slow,
> *Timor mortis conturbat me.*

Throughout *Selected Poems* (1944), the motif of passage into a diminished world is underscored above all by Warren's use of an autumnal setting. Such a symbolic Fall is nearly all-pervasive in the early poems particularly: "Calendar" ("the days draw in"); "The Last Metaphor" ("The wind had blown the leaves away"); "Man Coming of Age" ("Walker in woods that bear no leaf"); "Late Subterfuge" ("The world dulls towards its eaves-dripping end"); "Croesus in Autumn"; and "The Garden." The Kentucky autumn in "Croesus in Autumn" suffices to convert the wealthy Lydian king into a minor version of a Stoic philosopher, for even his Midas touch cannot restore "the absolute gold of summer gone." "Though this grey guy be no Aurelius," the "dwindling sun" of fall in Kentucky might well "stir the bald and metaphysic skull" to thoughts of loss, now that "green is gone and every gold gone sallow."

As an indicator of Warren's future poetic development, the most important autumnal poem in *Selected Poems* (1944) is "The Garden." Subtitled *"On prospect of a fine day in early autumn,"* this poem initially typifies the poetry of passage in that the fine day in question follows the first frost of the season, which has transformed the garden into a "ruined state." By closely imitating the rhyme and metrical pattern of Andrew Marvell's "The Garden," Warren constructs a modern reply to Marvell (much as his fellow Fugitive and teacher John Crowe Ransom had done in "You, Andrew Marvell"). What withers Warren's garden, in contrast to the eternal lushness of Marvell's, is precisely the metaphysical difference between them. Whereas Marvell and his friend Milton could and perhaps did believe in the traditional prospect of paradise regained, Warren's problem in an age of defunctive faith was to find his paradise in a natural world that may no longer expect a supernatural cleansing of its pain, loss, and horror.

Unexpectedly, nevertheless, "The Garden" contains a preview of Warren's eventual answer to the trauma of passage, for its last three lines envision, if only momentarily, a "sacrament that can translate / All things that fed luxurious sense / From appetite to innocence." In looking for some higher innocence that might encompass and redeem the world's stew, these lines form an almost perfect parallel to the "infinitely gentle, infinitely suffering thing" that appeared similarly early in T. S. Eliot's career, a momentary vision that was quickly and sardonically wiped away in "Preludes." But just as for Eliot that gentle thing kept coming back, to metamorphose at last into the redeeming Christ in *Ash-Wednesday*, so for Warren this sacrament that changes appetite to innocence was to come back stronger and stronger until in the later volumes it would take over center stage as the osmosis of being process, a mystical synthesis that merges (to quote Warren's essay on the subject) "the ugly with the beautiful, the slayer with the slain," producing for the initiate "such a sublimation that the world which once provoked . . . fear and disgust may now be totally loved." [4] This vision, to be discussed more fully in our "Mysticism" chapter, would supplant the orthodox metaphysics of former times and obviate as well the wrath, dread, and black laughter of poems like "Pacific Gazer," "Aged Man Surveys the Past Time," and "Variation: Ode to Fear."

But it takes a long time to "come to Jesus," as Warren once described this capacity to accept and love the world absolutely, in all its pain, filth, and corruption.[5] Before moving to the stage where a Blakean higher innocence might redeem the fallen creation, the Warren initiate faces two formidable temptations, both of which reject the world's filth and misery. The first is the escape reflex—either ahead towards death or back towards paradise remembered—usually expressed in the wish to be either a corpse or a fetus: "Anywhere Out of This World," as Baudelaire put it. The other deadly temptation, even more dangerous and prevalent in Warren's people, is the proclivity to divide the world between the Clean, which one accepts, and the Dirty, which one rejects categorically. In these early poems the escape reflex predominates; in the later volumes, the schism between the Clean and the Dirty presents the greatest obstacle to Warren's osmosis.

A typical poem of the escape reflex is "Letter of a Mother," apparently dating from Warren's college days, wherein the son who receives the letter feels that his mother's gift of life to him is secondary to "the worthier gift of her mortality." Although the "mother flesh . . . cannot summon back / The tired child it would again possess," he hopes death may return him to the fetus stage, with "a womb more tender than her [mother's] own / That builds not tissue or the little bone, / But dissolves them to itself in weariness." Another poem that sees death as the boon is "Rebuke of the Rocks," the initial poem of the "Kentucky Mountain Farm" sequence, in which the rocks advise the organic world to beware the revivification of springtime, that "season of the obscene moon whose pull / Disturbs the sod, the rabbit, and lank fox. . . ." "Breed no tender thing among the rocks," they admonish, but rather, "quit yourself as stone and cease / To break the weary stubble-field for seed." In Part III of this sequence, "History Among the Rocks," a human body departs from the organic world and—like Quentin Compson in Faulkner's novel or Phlebas in *The Waste Land*—seems enviably serene as a result:

> Tumbling and turning, hushed in the end,
> With hair afloat in waters that gently bend
> To ocean where the blind tides flow.

This image of a body totally given over to the underwater realm recurs as the master metaphor in "Bearded Oaks," where a pair of lovers so intensely imagine the state of being dead as to achieve an hour's "practice for eternity." Although there is no hope in this undersea kingdom, neither is there fear or rage or contention:

> All our debate is voiceless here,
> As all our rage, the rage of stone;
> If hope is hopeless, then fearless fear,
> And history is thus undone.

For history to be undone is not at all a bad prospect for those to whom history represents merely a passage into a ruined world; Warren's best known student of history, Jack Burden, felt likewise during his Great Sleep period.

If the death wish seems a rather morbid escape from the trauma of passage, the paradise remembered motif is not. In their remembrance of lost childhood poets as divergent as Dylan Thomas and T. S. Eliot have mourned the loss of paradise, to say nothing of the Romantic / Transcendentalist laments voiced by Wordsworth, Emerson, and Mark Twain. In some of his poems and in his finest short story, "Blackberry Winter," Warren also associates the Edenic state with childhood, often so as to bring a child through the Fall. But frequently for Warren's people the trauma of passage is held off until young adulthood, probably because the fundamentalist religious faith of his native region could sustain a man's innocence until adult experience or higher education at last broke it down. In any event, our study of the paradise lost psychology might well begin with its most perfect specimen among these early poems, "Man Coming of Age." Another Fall poem, in both senses of the word, its opening lines complain of the frost ("rime," "tinsel pure and chill") that has covered the ground overnight. For all its beauty—"This brilliance in the night was wrought"—the frost signifies only a newly dead and ruined world for the speaker, who describes the arrival of frost in a grisly metaphor. "So settles on a dying face, / After the retch and spasm, grace." In thus losing paradise, the speaker has also lost a self that, for its innocence, was better than the present frost-watcher who mourns his lost identity:

> "Was it I who roamed to prove
> My heart beneath the unwhispering grove
> In season greener and of more love?"

Thus cut off from a better self as well as a better world, our initiate into the world's evil is left "Seeking under the snowy bough / That frail reproachful *alter ego*." The poem's narrator advises the Man Coming of Age to accept his Waste Land exile, lest he deprive his former self of paradise forever:

> Walker in woods that bear no leaf,
> Climber of rocks, assume your grief
>
> And go! lest he, before you tread
> That ground once sweetly tenanted,
> Like mist, down the glassy gloom be fled.

"Picnic Remembered," as the title implies, is entirely given over to the lapsarian experience. Paradise is remembered in the first four stanzas as a day in which love's communion reached such perfection as to seem eternal:

> our substances,
> Twin flies, were as in amber tamed

> With our perfections stilled and framed
> To mock Time's marvelling after-spies.

"Joy, strongest medium, then buoyed / Us when we moved, as swimmers," says the speaker who even then was in the child-on-the-brink position: "Thus wrapped, sustained, we did not know / How darkness darker staired below." By the fifth stanza Eden's day has ended—"But darkness on the landscape grew / As in our bosoms darkness, too"—and the effects appear permanent, with the heart compared to a hollow stone that has trapped "A corner of that brackish tide" of darkness. Here, as in "Man Coming of Age," the immediate result of the Fall is a divided self, the better half of which harkens directly back to paradise, leaving the postlapsarian self behind it as an empty shell that must carry on as best it can in the fallen world:

> Or are we dead, that we, unmanned,
> Are vacant, and our clearest souls
> Are sped where each with each patrols
> In still society, hand in hand,
> That scene where we, too, wandered once
> Who now inherit new province,
> Love's limbo, this lost under-land.

I have quoted this particular paradise lost (and remembered) passage at length because it echoes Milton so deliberately in its diction and grand style (the whole stanza being one complex sentence) and in its comparison of the Warren persona to a newly outcast Adam and Eve recalling their innocent "hand in hand" condition of yesterday. As the poem ends, the vanished self fleeing back towards paradise is compared to a hawk ascending into the sunset, leaving its "unmanned" earth-mate desolate in the lower darkness. Here Wordsworth, rather than Milton, suggests the appropriate analogue, for like Wordsworth's fallen persona in "Intimations Ode," Warren's fallen persona in "Picnic Remembered" can hope at best for only a chance glint of a distant "Uncharted Truth" coming from his anima in those now-inaccessible higher regions:

> Or is the soul a hawk that, fled
> On glimmering wings past vision's path,

> Reflects the last gleam to us here
> Though sun is sunk and darkness near
> —Uncharted Truth's high heliograph?

This sense of a better self that, on the occasion of passage, has vanished back to its prelapsarian home and carried with it the deepest secret of identity has persistently recurred throughout Warren's poetry. Its archetype, one might suppose, dates back not only to Edenic myth, wherein Adam exchanges his perfect self for a fallen self, but to pagan myth as well. The Cupid and Psyche story, for example, tells of the vanishing of Psyche's lover the moment she achieves the knowledge she has craved by having a look at him. In Robert Penn Warren's poetry we may trace this theme back almost to the beginning. In "Cold Colloquy," a very early poem, the mother senses this loss of self in her son who has been pouring out his grief to her. Although the son is angry that "of words so freighted with woe, so little she caught," she perceives a larger loss behind the son's immediate burdens and so she stands, in the last two lines, in a typical symbolic autumn scene, "pondering, as one who grieves / Or seeks a thing long lost among the fallen leaves." Another early poem, "The Return" (the final poem in the Kentucky Mountain Farm" sequence) renders the theme of a self divided and deprived of its better part through contrast between the human situation and nature. Here a leaf falling towards its image in a stream suggests a self-reunion that the human observer can only envy, as there will be no such "return" of the vanished self for him:

> Up from the whiter bough, the bluer sky,
> That glimmered in the water's depth below,
> A richer leaf rose to the other there.
> They touched; with the gentle clarity of dream,
> Bosom to bosom, burned on the quiet stream.
>
> So, backward heart, you have no voice to call
> Your image back, the vagrant image again. . . .

In "Eidolon" the world's stew that the vanished self flees from is portrayed in the metaphor of a hunt, its prospective prey being that same vanished self or eidolon, which disappears doe-like from the "fanged commotion":

Dogs quartered the black woods: blood black on
May-apple at dawn, old beech-husk. And trails are lost
By rock, in ferns lost, by pools unlit.
I heard the hunt. Who saw, in darkness, how fled
The white eidolon from fanged commotion rude?

And finally, in "The Ballad of Billie Potts" the experience of
passage leads to a dividing of the self. As a youth, Billie "like the
cicada had left, at cross-roads or square, / The old shell of self,
thin, ghostly, translucent, light as air." Some ten years later, when
Billie comes home in search of that missing part of his identity,
his last earthly act is to lean to the well, hungering like Narcissus
after his own image of a better self lost in some prelapsarian period:

But perhaps what you lost was lost in the pool long ago
When childlike you lost it and then in your innocence rose to go
After kneeling, as now, with your thirst beneath the leaves:
And years it lies here and dreams in the depth and grieves,
More faithful than mother or father in the light or dark of the
leaves.

"Letter from a Coward to a Hero" differs somewhat from the
typical poem of passage in that the pre- and postlapsarian identities
are invested in two separate individuals. The speaker (the Coward
mentioned in the title) shows the usual effect of adult awareness,
a sense of the world as full of cheat and compromise:

What did the day bring?

. . . .
The promise half-meant,
The impaired thing,
At dusk the hard word. . . .
All
In the trampled stall

He also reveals a keen feeling of dread concerning the future,
both the world's ("Empires collide with a bang / . . . And democracy shows signs of dry rot") and his own ("Though young, I
do not like loud noise / . . . Or clocks that tick all night and will

not stop"). From this perspective, the Wordsworthian child-self of time past seems closed off behind an impassable barrier:

> The scenes of childhood were splendid,
> And the light that there attended,
> But is rescinded:
> The cedar,
> The lichened rocks,
> The thicket where I saw the fox,
> And where I swam, the river.
> These things are hard
> To reconstruct. . . .

The hero, now dead, represents the prefallen identity. He owed his courage to that childlike condition: *"I cannot see what ways your feet in childhood walked. / In what purlieus was courage early caulked?"* For such a person "piety is simple / And should be ample," the speaker says, and he concludes the poem with an ambiguous tribute to the deceased, who won honor like a child's token—"Clutching between the forefinger and thumb / Honor, for death shy valentine."

"Love's Parable" is another parable of the Fall written in the high style of seventeenth century metaphysical poetry, complete with archaic diction ("unthewed," "felicity," etc.) and ingeniously extended metaphors. Here the paradise remembered is a love relationship in which, as though Donne were writing, "each was the other's sun," holding the other as a planet that "fed / On light and heat flung from the source. . . ." The center of the poem, stanzas three through six, recalls the one defect of paradise, namely the incapacity of its inhabitants to appreciate their stupendous felicity for lack of some knowledge of evil to measure it by. "No wonder then to us it was!— / For miracle was daily food," the poet tells us; "Then miracle was corner cheap." Innocence being (like beauty) in the eye of the beholder, the lovers found "that all the world proportionate / And joyful seemed" back then; the world "did but consent / That all unto our garden state of innocence was innocent." As this poem proceeds, the fact that "We did not know what worth we owned" seems to imply a fortunate Fall in the making, but the speaker finds nothing fortunate about

"A knowledge that, now bought too dear, / Is but ironic residue." The passage into tragic knowledge appears to be totally ruinous for the outcast Adam:

> But we have seen the fungus eyes
> Of misery spore in the night,
> And marked, of friends, the malices
> That stain, like smoke, the day's fond light,
> And marked how ripe injustice flows,
> How ulcerous, how acid, then
> How proud flesh on the sounder grows
> Till rot engross the estate of men. . . .

As for the love affair, nothing now remains but "the inward sore / Of self that cankers at the bone," producing "Contempt of the very love we bore / And hatred of the good once known." Togetherness now fosters disease rather than sustenance, as "we at length, / Itching and slumwise, each other infect." "Picnic Remembered" works out a similar pattern, with unsuspecting lovers stumbling out of paradise, though in a somewhat less bitter tone: "The bright deception of that day! . . . / But darkness on the landscape grew / As in our bosoms darkness, too."

Terminating our "pure" poems of passage material from *Selected Poems* (1944) is one of the "New" poems first published in this collection, called "The World Comes Galloping: A True Story," a part of the "Mexico Is a Foreign Country: Five Studies in Naturalism" sequence. "The World Comes Galloping" shows a ragged old man conveying knowledge of the fallen world to younger, less knowing initiates who "stuck out hand for alms." The old man's peach, devoured just before the horseman comes galloping, serves as the mythical fruit in this instance; and after the frenzied horse and its crazy rider have passed—"Wall-eyed and wheezing, the lurching hammer-head"—the old one drops the pit from his now-eaten peach and gives the younger observers the "alms" of truth they requested, telling them that this meaningless scene is really all that the world signifies: "Viene galopando . . . el mundo." Of the "Five Studies in Naturalism" this is the only study in pure naturalism—defining a world full of energy but without purpose, or having "many means but no ends," as Joseph Wood Krutch put it. On receiving insight from the old man, this poem's young people take their place in our poems of passage gallery.

The poems we have looked at depict passage from paradise into the ruined world as a wholly devastating experience, producing the emotions of dread, rage, and despair and the escape reflex towards death and paradise remembered. There remains, however, another cluster of poems from this early period that, by opening a different alternative, would point the direction for Warren's future verse writing. In these poems passage into the ruined world is accepted realistically; both the escape reflex and the bitterness are subdued under what Paul Tillich called the courage to be, the resolution to live in the only world we have. "Garden Waters" implies that paradise always was an illusory state, dependent upon our not seeing the delicate proofs of a wrecked world beneath the water's quiet surface:

> Though garden waters are not broad or black
> Within them still sometimes, I think, is hid
> The obscure image of the season's wreck,
> The dead leaf and the summer's chrysalid.

"Late Subterfuge" likewise, though hardly a cheerful poem ("The year dulls towards its eaves-dripping end"), insists upon accepting the fallen world without recourse to anodynes that might make the world's stew endurable. Hence the poet treats sardonically the philosophical rationalization of evil:

> Our grief can be endured,
> For we, at least, are men, being inured
> To wrath, to the unjust act, if need, to blood;
> And we have faith that from evil blooms good.

The poem similarly casts withering doubt on the love ethic in which writers like D. H. Lawrence and Hemingway sometimes took refuge:

> In pairs we walk, heads bowed to the long drizzle—
> With women some, and take their rain-cold kiss;
> We say to ourselves we learn some strength from this.

In place of these attempts to evade or rationalize the world's evil, Warren turns to the very instrument of man's Fall—knowledge itself, including knowledge of evil—as the only realistic recourse now available. If knowledge is in fact the "end of man," men's only choice after passage into reality is to consume the forbidden fruit to their utmost capacity, to gorge themselves upon it, no matter how dangerous they know it to be. After the Fall into knowledge of evil, innocence may never be recovered by striving backward after the original unknowingness, but only possibly by the opposite process of seeking total knowledge—a comprehensive vision of the whole such as the "sunset hawk" attains in "Watershed," an early poem that appears in the "Kentucky Mountain Farm" sequence. The bird's grand view implies some psychic cost or need for humility in its reduction of the human world to a small and fragile niche in the totality of time and nature:

> His gold eyes scan
> The crumpled shade on gorge and crest
> And streams that creep and disappear, appear,
> Past fingered ridges and their shrivelling span.
> Under the broken eaves men take their rest.

In representing his theme of total—or the largest possible—knowledge, this kind of bird's eye view was to become one of Warren's most recurrent motifs over the years, a way of objectifying his osmosis of being thesis.

To resacralize the world, then, one must first know it, no matter how vast or terrible or inhuman that knowledge might be. In "Watershed" the quest for knowledge, or "certitude," now supplants the yearning for love and happiness typical of the paradise remembered psychology, for only knowledge (or truth) is immutable:

> Not love, happiness past, constrains,
> But certitude. Enough, and it remains,
> Though they who thread the flood and neap
> Of earth itself have felt the earth creep. . . .

Knowledge of time is chiefly the form of knowledge that must be ingested by Warren's initiates of passage. Such knowledge, as we have already observed in the poems about frost and autumn, is seldom ingested gladly; but in several of the early poems the necessity to accept time is the explicit theme. The narrator's resolution in "Resolution," for example, is precisely to acknowledge time and its losses, although his lover denies time's reality:

> I spoke of Time. You said:
> *There is no Time.*
> Since then some friends are dead;
> Hates cold, once hot;
> Ambitions thewless grown;
> Old slights forgot:
> And the weeper is made stone.

Clinching the argument is separation between the lovers themselves: "We, too, have lain / Apart, with continents / And seas between." Rather than deny time's reality, or react against it, the narrator submits to its power fairly gracefully:

> *Old winnower!*
> *I praise your pacèd power:*
> *Not truth I fear.*
> How ripe is turned the hour.

In another poem, "Letter to a Friend," the fallacious posture is bravado defiance. Here the narrator and his friend have witnessed eternity, evidently through the medium of art: "Our eyes have viewed the burnished vineyards where / No leaf falls, and the grape, unripening, ripes." As a result of seeing this timeless, motionless, unchanging place, the friend presumes having removed himself from time's ruined kingdom and its pitiable needs of the spirit: "That voyage, then each to each we said, had rendered / Courage superfluous, hope a burden." The narrator, however, fails to share this affectation, for to live in the world's stew requires just those virtues of hope and courage, no matter how meager their proportions:

> But living still, we live by them, and only
> Thus, or thus, stuttering, eke them out,
> Our huddled alms to crammed Necessity.

The last stanza thus punctures the friend's bravado:

> In this, the time of toads' engendering,
> I write to you, to you unfrighted yet
> Before the blunt experiment of Time.
> Your triumph is not commensurate with stone.

Considered as a whole, then, Warren's early poems constitute a rendering of the lapsarian experience and a weeding out of false responses to it. Following this weeding out process, the rudimentary elements of Warren's own response begin to appear in fragmentary passages. This response centers upon the poet's decision to accept his passage into the fallen world and to search for a sacrament, preferably in greater knowledge, whereby that world might compensate for its loss of meaning. As even Satan proclaimed while prostrate in Hell, all is still not lost so long as the unconquerable will endures. While hardly ready to emulate Milton's heroic rebel, Warren's persona does insist upon that small measure of existential freedom that even a fallen world cannot extinguish, and in that freedom some few embers of hope and courage may yet be nourished. Just how limited those spiritual virtues are is indicated in "Aubade for Hope," where "Hope . . . like a blockhead grandma ever / Above the ash and spittle croaks and leans." But even this image may not be as disparaging as it seems; if we remember the old people in Warren's early novels, *Night Rider* and *At Heaven's Gate* and *All the King's Men*, we may recall that they too were unglamorous, malodorous imbeciles, like the Scholarly Attorney that Jack Burden took to be his father, for instance, with a snowstorm of dandruff descending on his seedy shoulders. Whatever it lacks for glamour, the hope connected with such figures bears the merit of realism; and we must not be put off by the croaking, spittle-drooling grandma. The secret of identity may repose after all behind this kind of authentic presence in preference to the world's more attractive appearances. In the later volumes, where Warren evolved his "One Flesh" ideology, and particularly in the mystic center of *Promises*, the sequence called "Ballad of a Sweet Dream of Peace," old granny would have much to do with the reality-seeker's initiation.

But such mystical possibilities were to develop much later. For

now in the early poetry there is much of the T. S. Eliot stance of
Ash-Wednesday: "Teach us to sit still / Even among these rocks."
And beyond this decision to live in the Waste Land with stoic
forbearance, a more active principle is beginning to assert itself:
the quest for larger knowledge. At the end of "Question and
Answer" this quest assumes religious overtones when the seeker
after reality uses his heart as a bow to "let the arrow fly / At God's
black, orbèd, target eye." A fuller definition of Warren's God
remains for our chapters on the undiscovered self and mysticism;
but here we may assume that Warren, like Spinoza, identifies God
with the whole of reality, connection with which may make one's
own definition complete. In any case, the quest proceeds with or
without a target God, and with or without any prospect of success, simply because it must: because men who have lapsed from
paradise into knowledge of evil can do nothing but seek out larger
knowledge that may redeem their condition. As Warren himself
put it in his "Knowledge and the Image of Man" essay, "Man eats
of the fruit of the tree of knowledge, and falls. But if he takes another bite, he may get at least a sort of redemption." [6]

Moreover, as we conclude our look at *Selected Poems* (1944)
and its theme of passage, we may note some doubts on the poet's
part concerning his present naturalistic knowledge: not whether
it is false, but whether it is complete in its grasp of reality. In "The
Last Metaphor," Warren seems to share T. S. Eliot's dictum that
"humility is the only wisdom," as he notes how the trees respond
to *their* "fallen" condition:

> Thinking that when the leaves no more abide
> The stiff trees rear not up in strength and pride
> But lift unto the gradual dark in prayer.

From similar doubts about his perspective on the Fall in "Love's
Parable," Warren finds some liberating possibilities in his own version of Emerson's dictum in *Nature* that "The ruin or blank that
we see when we look at nature, is in our own eye." [7] "Are we but
mirror to the world? / Or does the world our ruin reflect?" he
asks. The fact that this is an open question may be added to the
other glimmers that would eventually light a path out of Warren's
initial Waste Land. Meanwhile, after the various bouts of rage,

despair, fear, self-pity, and nostalgia for paradise remembered—
after, that is to say, the trauma of passage has vented its typical
range of emotions—the Warren persona of the early poems pulls
himself together much in the style of similarly traumatized Hemingway heroes and musters up the courage to be.

PROMISES

We have lingered over *Selected Poems* (1944) because, as with any
poet, Warren's early work is formative and shapes in large measure
the design of his later work. Having established the basic forms of
thought that lie behind these early poems, we may more profitably
look into the succeeding volumes. Since *Brother to Dragons*,
Warren's next venture in poetry, is a lengthy dramatic poem, we
will discuss it in a separate chapter and merely note for now that in
this quintessence of Warren's thought Thomas Jefferson is the reluctant initiate who suffers forced passage into the fallen world.
Promises, the 1957 Pulitzer Prize winner, evinces a built-in poems
of passage psychology through the centrality of Gabriel and
Rosanna Warren—the poet's infant son and baby daughter. The
title of the Rosanna sequence, "To a Little Girl, One Year Old, in
a Ruined Fortress," establishes the theme of a prelapsarian innocent
encompassed by a human project gone to ruin. Throughout the
five poems of the Rosanna sequence the passage psychology is
divided between the two main characters, with Rosanna not only
acting as a foil to the narrator's postlapsarian mentality but also
prevailing over it, almost as though she were the vanished self returned from paradise, with Wordsworthian efficacy—or, to use
Warren's own imagery, as though she were the sky hawk reflecting
sunset light into the lower darkness in "Picnic Remembered": a
human version of "Uncharted Truth's high heliograph."

In Poem I of *Promises*, "Sirocco," this conflict of perspectives
is represented by what the two characters observe in their sur-
roundings. The narrator, Rosanna's father, sees the "ruined stone"
of the aging fortress and imagines the escutcheon, now buried
under the moat's garbage, of the ruined fortress's more ruined
maker, Philip II of Spain, the pious unfortunate who sent forth
the Spanish Armada and "For whom nothing prospered, though

he loved God." Into these melancholy meditations, Rosanna's laughter intrudes like the sirocco that providentially delights the two of them, bringing "Sun blaze and cloud tatter, . . . air like gold gauze whirled"; for she sees nothing but the beauty among the ruins—"rosemary with blue, thistle with gold bloom," and a mountain, "Giannutri in blue air."

The same pattern holds in Poem II, "Gull's Cry," where the narrator's initial gloom is substantially deeper than in "Sirocco," since here he is fixing his postlapsarian eye upon the wretchedness of the immediate present rather than on King Philip's bygone miseries. Goat droppings (soon to provide food for beetles), the defective child of the hunchback next door, and the hunchback's suffering wife arrest in turn the narrator's attention and produce a mood too deep for anything in nature to remedy. Thus the scenic beauty of Stanza 2, with the gull hanging white "under blue shadow of mountain, over blue-braiding seashadow," only adds to his sense of nature's soullessness, a feeling objectified in the harsh noise of the gull's cry. Adding to the black mood is the presence of a pair of adult innocents, lovers sitting "in the privacy of bemusement, heads bent: the classic pose," oblivious to the ruinous prospect around them. Into this mood Rosanna's laughter again penetrates, opening "a moment of possibility" that evokes Warren's osmosis of being mysticism:

> But at your laughter let the molecular dance of the stone-dark
>   glimmer like joy in the stone's dream,
> And in the moment of possibility, let *gobbo, gobbo's* wife, and
>   us, and all, take hands and sing: redeem, redeem!

In Poem III, "The Child Next Door," the narrator is set off against a different prelapsarian character, the twelve-year-old sister of the child next door, who "Is beautiful like a saint. / Sits with the monster all day, with pure love, calm eyes," and "smiles her smile without taint." Here, at the midpoint of the five-poem sequence, the dialectical configuration ceases to operate. No scenic beauty or mystic "moment of possibility" moves in to lift the narrator from his awareness, in seeing the defective child next door (a victim of attempted abortion), of the "malfeasance of nature or the filth of the fate." Prelapsarian innocence in this instance only stirs "hate / —Is it hate?—in my heart," and the child's laughter of Poems I and II is supplanted by the initiate's stoic grimace:

> I think of your goldness, of joy, how empires grind,
>   stars are hurled.
> I smile stiff, saying *ciao*, saying *ciao*, and think: this
>   is the world.

Since the capacity to revere the world just as it is forms the crucial test of the Warren character's ideology, these lines define a central slough of despond in the sequence, which is followed by a reversal of the passage psychology in Poems IV and V, allowing the fallen initiate to acquire some of the higher innocence of Blakean / Wordsworthian precedent.

Poem IV, "The Flower," again divides its theme between pre- and postlapsarian perspectives, but with the child's view predominant. Hence the lyric note prevails for the first time, expressing itself in the poem's short trimeter cadences—with many rhyming triplets—and its richly harmonious sound effects, as opposed to the rougher texture and philosophical bent of the preceding three sonnets. This is the poetry of epiphanies, its rhythm slowing from time to time "in the season's pulse and flow" to let the senses linger, "Bemused with sea, and slow / With June heat and perfume" in a place "Bee-drowsy and blowsy with white bloom." Now again the girl's epiphanies, springing out of what Emerson would call an original relationship with nature, overcome the narrator's gloom, though the approaching fall forces the problem, as Robert Frost put it, of what to make of a diminished thing:

> But the season has thinned out.
>
> . . . .
> By the vineyard we have found
> No bloom worthily white. . . .
> We give the best one to you.
> It is ruined, but will have to do.

To the girl's prelapsarian eye the flower is not ruined—"And you sing as though human need / Were not for perfection"—and something of this mood affects the narrator, who now "accepts the incipient night" as does the rest of nature: the mountain, sea, and gull being absorbed in the gathering darkness.

In the other section of *Promises*, the sequence of poems to Warren's infant son Gabriel, a substantial number of the poems recall
the poet's own boyhood passage into a perception of the world's
stew of injustice, violence, and evil. Poem I tells of that great
trauma of passage in anyone's life, the death and burial of a parent:

> And the house shrunk to silence, the odor of flowers near gone. . . .
> Recollection of childhood was natural: cold gust at the back.
> What door on the dark flings open, then suddenly bangs?
> Yes, something was lost in between, but it's long, the way back.
> You sleep, but in sleep hear a door that creaks where it hangs.

In Poem II, "Court-Martial," the initiation experience affects a
boy who hears, for the first time, a horror story from his kindly
old grandfather, a former Confederate soldier (like both Warren's
grandfathers) who reveals his part in a multiple hanging of dubious
legality. Despite the old man's fervent self-vindication (" 'By God,
they deserved it,' he said. / 'Don't look at me that way,' he said. /
'By God—' and the old eyes glared red"), the boy is possessed by
an awful vision of the hanging scene: "Each face outraged, agape, /
Not yet believing it true . . . / Tongue out, out-staring eye. . . ."
From out of that grisly scene, a horseman rides hither as the poem
ends. It is grandfather, the young cavalry officer of time past,
"Riding toward me there, / Through the darkening air," and carrying the inescapable message of initiation: "The world is real. It is
there."

Poems III and IV, "Gold Glade" and "Dark Woods," are companion poems on the theme of passage, but with an inversion of the
usual seasonal setting: the fall being the setting for a prelapsarian
epiphany and the spring (as in *The Waste Land*) being the season
of the "Dark Woods" experience. In the fashion of Wordsworth,
"Gold Glade" recalls the poet's boyhood encounter with nature in
its "golden age" of autumnal splendor: "Beyond any heart-hurt,
or eye's grief-fall, / Goldmassy the beech stood in that gold light-
fall." In this instance, almost supernaturally, there is also the
Wordsworthian hush that accompanies the soul's absorption into
nature:

> There was no stir of air, no leaf now gold-falling,
> No tooth-stitch of squirrel, or any far fox bark,

No woodpecker coding, or late jay calling.
Silence: . . . the great shagbark
Gave forth gold light. . . .

As always—even in Wordsworth—the Fall comes to darken the golden moment, though to the boy entranced by immersion in nature that had seemed impossible: "There could be no dark. / But of course dark came. . . ."

"Dark Woods" is subdivided into three lyrics in which, contrary to "Gold Glade," death prevails over beauty. The first lyric, "Tonight the Woods Are Darkened," shows the speaker arising alone in the night, summoned by some indefinable hunger to go forth to a ghostly encounter:

Trapped in that *déjà-vu*,
Déjà-fait, déjà-fait, you hear whispers,
In the dark, say, "Ah." Say: "You, too?"

Was there a field full of folk there,
Behind you? Threading like mist?
All who, dark-hungry, once had flung forth
From the house, and now persist. . . .

In Lyric 2, "The Dogwood," the hunger that moves him, as it did these now dead people in years past, is a "werewolf thirst" for such beauty as we see in the later "Man in Moonlight" poems; but the path to beauty is here strewn by *mementos mori:* "In green grass the skull waits, has waited: A cathedral for ants. . . ." Heart "made tight now as a nut in the hull," the nocturnal seeker finds more pain than joy in the dogwood's heartless beauty: "then you felt a strange wrath burn / To strike it, and strike, had a stick been handy there." In "The Hazel Leaf," the falling leaf and a little green snake by the path provide premonitions of the Fall as boys still in the prelapsarian state "shout and kick up the gold leaves there." Years pass, the psychology of passage has done its work, and the little green snake "waits, head crushed, to be observed by the next to pass."

In "Country Burying (1919)" the narrator recalls his indifference to a funeral to which his mother had taken him when he was a lad ("Who was she? Who knows? I'd not thought to ask it? / . . . old face yellow as a gourd"); but after the burial a passage "from what is, to what will be" elapsed, "And I passed toward voices and the foreign faces" of the adult's world-view. Now although the funeral is only a memory, the narrator can so intently identify with the deceased as to rival one of Emily Dickinson's famous exercises in morbidity: *"Why doesn't that fly stop buzzing—stop buzzing up there!"* [8] Poem VI, "School Lesson Based on Word of Tragic Death of Entire Gillum Family," must stand out as a shocker even in a poems of passage series, for it tells how a cluster of hillbilly school children learned of the ice pick murder of five classmates— the type who "sat right mannerly while teacher spoke"—by their father. So for this afternoon the school lesson largely assumes the configuration of the passage psychology, with the class spending the afternoon

> Studying the arithmetic of losses,
>> To be prepared when the next one,
> By fire, flood, foe, cancer, thrombosis,
>> Or Time's slow malediction, came to be undone.

As class ends that day one last stage in the passage experience remains unrealized, but that stage—the full consciousness of their own mortality—can wait: *"We studied all afternoon, till getting on to sun. / There was another lesson, but we were too young to take up that one."*

Poem VII, "Summer Storm (Circa 1916), and God's Grace," provides a fine example of Warren's statement that he stopped writing short stories because he found them turning into poems.[9] In this case he wrote the short story before the itch to make it a poem overcame him and so we have both poem and story stemming from the same recollections of childhood. The story, "Blackberry Winter," is reckoned Warren's finest and one of the classic initiation tales in American literature. The poem focuses only upon one feature of the tale, namely the storm itself, whose aftermath introduces the story's nine-year-old into the adult world of poverty, alienation, and loss. An admirable exercise in imagery and sound texture, it ushers in the storm's wrath with cacophonous fury:

> And darkness rode in on the wind.
>> The pitchfork lightning tossed the trees,
> And God got down on his hands and knees

> To peer and cackle and commend
> His own sadistic idiocies.

Apart from the possible question of theodicy in this passage, the main link between the poem and the initiation motif of the story lies in the social disaster facing the ruined farmers in the storm's aftermath:

> Next morning you stood where the bridge had washed out.
> A drowned cow bobbled down the creek.
> Raw-eyed, men watched. They did not speak.
> Till one shrugged, said he thought he'd make out. . . .

In *Selected Poems* (1966) Warren dropped his final stanza from the original, which was a prayer that God send them "one summer just right." The effect of the revision is to accentuate more sharply the initiation motif.

"Dark Night of the Soul" (the original version in *Promises* omits the last two words from this title) nicely rounds out Warren's reuse of his "Blackberry Winter" material. This poem focuses on the tragically rootless wandering bum who warned the boy not to follow him in the short story's ending: " 'You don't stop following me and I cut yore throat, you little son-of-a-bitch.' . . . But I did follow him, all the years." The poem operates almost like a parody of Wordsworth's man-in-nature motif, for here the boy who encounters the man-in-nature—a homeless derelict, like Wordsworth's people—loses his Wordsworthian communion with nature as a result and assumes instead a postlapsarian knowledge of fear and pity: "Cold prickles ran in my hair. / Beneath elder bloom, the eyes glare." New and bitter experience follows quickly:

> He says: "Caint you let a man lay!"
>
> I stared down the dank depth and heard
> That croak from cold slime. . . .

From this moment the Wordsworthian age of innocence is past forever, as the boy follows the cows home,

> There to enter and understand
> My plate laid by a loving hand,

And to sleep, but not understand
That somewhere on the dark land,

. . . .

By age, rage, rejection unmanned,

. . . .

[His head] gleams with the absolute and glacial purity of despair.

Poem XIII, the "Man in Moonlight" sequence, comprises an interesting rebuttal of the Romantic conviction (mentioned in Warren's *Ancient Mariner* essay) that the moon is the presiding symbol of the transfiguring imagination. In Lyric 1, "Moonlight Observed from Ruined Fortress," it at first appears that the Romantic poets Wordsworth and Coleridge were right, in that the moon *does* transfigure the speaker's world magically and evoke memories of how it "smoothed the sweet Gulf asleep, like a babe at the breast" or "spangled spume-tangle on black rock, and seal barked at sea-roar." Even a "Tennessee stock-pond is not beneath your contempt," nor "a puddle . . . too small for respect," the moonlight-observer concedes; but "Be it a sea or a sewer" the moon lights, the lapse into the world's stew cannot be thus amended, despite men's "werewolf thirst for plenilune":

> We stand on the crumbling stone and ruins of rage,
> To watch your Tyrrhenian silver prank the sea.
>
> . . . .
>
> We stare, we stare, but will not stare for long.
> You will not tell us what we need to know.
>   Our feet soon go the way that they must go,
>   In diurnal dust and heat, and right and wrong.

In Lyric 2, "Walk by Moonlight in Small Town," the setting shifts from Italy to America, and from present time to a time when the speaker had attended school in this place. It is unsettling to picture ghostly classmates from that age of innocence and to think how awareness grew upon them:

> Their eyes were fixed on me, and I
> Now tried, face by pale face, to find
> The names that haunted in my mind.

> But something grew in their pale stare:
> Not reprobation or surprise,
> Nor even forgiveness in their eyes,
> But a humble question dawning there,
> From face to face. . . .

Since—after the Fall—knowledge is the end of man, lack of knowledge becomes the essential problem, not alleviated in the slightest by the moonbeams: "Might a man but know his Truth, . . . / Then never . . . / Need he stand and shake in that cold blaze of Platonic light."

As we round out our look at *Promises* in the light of the lapsarian experience, "Dragon Country: To Jacob Boehme" brings us to Warren's basic premise that man's spiritual destiny, though unknown, requires that knowledge of the world's evil must be accepted and ingested entirely: "the human heart / Demands language for reality that has no slightest dependence / On desire, or need." Thus it is an error for the beast-ravaged community first to rationalize its losses ("What . . . they agreed couldn't be true") and then to pray "only that evil depart." To the contrary, the lapsarian experience means precisely that the Beast—Warren's image for the irrational horrors that circumscribe the ruined world with pain and death and dread—claims the whole fallen world as dragon country, just as sacred writ has long insisted. This Kierkegaardian (or Jacob Boehmean) dread alone gives the world its tragic possibility of a larger meaning—the hope that the monster's corpse-littered spoor might prove the path to whatever of paradise might be recoverable in actual reality:

> But if the Beast were withdrawn now, life might dwindle again
> To the ennui, the pleasure, and night sweat, known in the time before
> Necessity of truth had trodden the land, and heart, to pain,
> And left, in darkness, the fearful glimmer of joy, like a spoor.

Poem XVII, "Boy's Will, Joyful Labor Without Pay, and Harvest Home (1918)," indicates in the middle part of its title the innocent state of its main character, a boy bursting with eagerness to achieve passage into the man's world of productive labor. Part 1, "Morning," shows the boy, after a hasty breakfast, poised on the brink of transition:

> . . . you must feast the eye
> An instant on possibility,
> Before finite constriction is made
> To our pathos of rapacity.

Part II, "Work," shows the eager aspirant, with "hand that aches for the pitchfork heft," duly earning his credentials as a working man (" 'Boy, save yore strength, 'fore you got none left' "). And Part III, "The Snake," provides the mythical emblem of transition. Here the callous killing of the snake—"Snagged high on a pitchfork tine, he will make / Slow arabesque till the bullbats wake"— provides the disturbing element of the initiation, similar to the "little green snake" with "jeweled head" that is crushed in "The Hazel Leaf." Rearing "big in his ruined room," the snake "Defiant . . . swaps his stare. / . . . Yes, they are men, and a stone is there." Enmity between man and serpent, the symbol of an evil to be exorcised and destroyed, is as much a consequence of the Fall as is the imperative of work that these harvesters are following: "By the sweat of thy brow shalt thou earn thy bread." But though he accepts the work imperative gladly enough, the boy—or the man he has become—is haunted in the final lyric, "Hands Are Paid," by the ritual killing. He thinks how "The little blood that smeared the stone / Dropped in the stubble, has long since dried," and how "In the star-pale field, the propped pitchfork lifts / Its burden, hung black, to the white star." For the boy, an important part of the day's harvest has been this grisly image of death and "our pathos of rapacity."

YOU, EMPERORS, AND OTHERS

Of all the volumes of poetry Warren has published to date, *You, Emperors, and Others* remains the least satisfactorily understood and appreciated. Called "seventy-nine pages of poems largely about nothing in the world" by one critic, and "an exercise in metrical high jinks, . . . an artistic vacation" by another, the volume is best understood, I think, in the light of Warren's earlier poetry, particularly with reference to our three grand themes.[10] If we leave the "Garland for You" and "Emperors" sequences for our undiscovered self discussion, the poems of passage in *You, Emperors, and Others* properly begin with "Mortmain," the sequence on the death of the poet's father, an experience harrowing enough to set Time's reel moving backwards to both the poet's and his father's prelapsarian boyhood. In Poem 1, "AFTER NIGHT FLIGHT SON REACHES BEDSIDE OF ALREADY / UNCONSCIOUS FATHER, WHOSE RIGHT HAND LIFTS / IN A SPASMODIC GESTURE, AS THOUGH TRYING / TO MAKE CONTACT: 1955," the father's dying gesture spins the speaker backward past various landmarks of his growing up and to his "Naked" state of infantile dependency:

> . . . Like an eyelid the hand sank, strove
> Downward, and in that darkening roar,
> All things—all joy and the hope that strove,
> The failed exam, the admired endeavor,
> Prizes and prinkings, and the truth that strove,
> And back of the Capitol, boyhood's first whore—
> Were snatched from me, and I could not move,
> Naked in that black blast of his love.

Poem 2, "A Dead Language: Circa 1885," takes us back to the father's own rites of passage in adolescence: his work ("Cutting crossties for the first railroad in the region, / Sixteen and strong as a man—was a man, by God!") and his study of Greek. Later, as a grown man and father, he tells his son (our poet, the boy watching him shave) the Greek words from St. John which have acquired a bitter ambiguity—as "A Dead Language" implies—in the light of the preceding poem about the father's death: ". . . in the beginning / Was the word, but in the end was / What?"

Poem 3, "Fox-fire: 1956," projects the pattern into the future, gathering the three generations of poet, poet's father, and poet's son under his question of beginnings and ends. While the speaker broods over the father's old grammar with its dead language and its ghostly memories, he hears his small son's laughter from another room, and it evokes a prelapsarian world that is still invulnerable:

I know he sits there and laughs among his toys,
Teddy bear, letter blocks, yellow dumptruck, derrick, choo-choo—
Bright images, all, of Life's significance.

Surrounded, by contrast, with morbid imagery of extinction ("Beyond my window, athwart that red west, / The spruce bough, though snow-burdened, looks black"), the narrator puts the grammar with its riddle of beginnings and ends back on the shelf, where, "in the dark / Amid History's vice and velleity," it "burns / Like fox-fire in the black swamp of the world's error." Thus deprived of even its fox-fire, the poet's mind surrenders to "the thickening / Darkness" of inner and outer landscapes in which time's velocity is so appalling that it has become audible—"that sound / Like wind, that fills the enormous dark of my head." (Such imagery of time's velocity becomes obsessively recurrent in the later volumes.)

Poem 4 also identifies time as the chief agent of the world's ruin, both in its splendid title phrase "In the Turpitude of Time" and in its imagery of passage: the prelapsarian scene of the father's shaving in stanza one (" Hope dances on the razor edge. . . . / I see the song-wet lip and tossing hair") giving way to the fall and its losses in stanza two, where the autumn hunting season is a paradigm of the world's stew ("the hunter, weeping, kneels" to his prey, and "the dappled fawn weeps" for its manifest destiny). A prospective answer to the problem of time's turpitude opens in the final stanzas, which postulate a mystic knowledge of the whole that might lift all creation—even the inorganic—into a disclosure of inherent meaning:

> Can we—oh, could we only—believe
> What annelid and osprey know,
> And the stone, night-long, groans to divulge?
> If we could only, then that star
> That downward slants might sing to our human ear. . . .

Within the poem's scope, however, such knowledge is only the object of wishful thinking; and resistance to time's turpitude relies solely upon the time-transcending powers of the human imagination.

Those powers do produce a memorable effect in the final poem of the "Mortmain" sequence, "A Vision: Circa 1880," where the poet reverses time's reel to afford a glimpse of his father in the prelapsarian state:

> . . . look,
> Out of the woods, barefoot, the boy comes. He stands,
> Hieratic, complete, in patched britches and that idleness of boyhood
> Which asks nothing and is its own fulfillment.

Staring down "the tube and darkening corridor of Time," the speaker finds the boy's innocence intolerable, and he wants to cry out a warning: *"Listen! I know—oh, I know—let me tell you!"* But he cannot prevent the boy's lapse from paradise:

> . . . I strive to cry across the dry pasture,
> But cannot, nor move, for my feet, like dry corn-roots,
>   cleave
> Into the hard earth, and my tongue makes only the dry,
> Slight sound of wind on the autumn corn-blade. The boy,
> With imperial calm, crosses a space, rejoins
> The shadow of woods, but pauses, turns, grins once,
> And is gone. . . .

Far removed from this family setting, the next victim of passage into the world's stew in *You, Emperors, and Others* is Achilles in "Fatal Interview: Penthesilea and Achilles," where Warren continues his longstanding practice of reinterpreting myth and history to suit his private system. Written in the Homeric grand style, with admirably graphic details and vivid metaphors, the poem in its first half describes the Amazon queen's lust to kill her mighty adversary in battle. When the encounter with Achilles finally arrives, it at first augurs a farcical conclusion: "She leaps from horse, hurls spear; hears laughter, then, from the Greek." Boylike, Achilles grins; now it is his turn at spear-chucking, and a Homerically grisly spectacle ensues:

> Where lungs divide to hang belly, the spear-flight first pricks her;
> Under breastplate slides weightily in; in blood-darkness shears
>   backbone;
> Emerges in sunlight, though briefly; finds the mount waiting,
>   faithful,
> And with the same force unallayed it had used to transfix her,
> Transfixes the brute, knocks it down; and thus on that pincushion
>   sticks her.

Too late, Achilles finds that "this sweet blood I spill now / . . . is my True Love." "His life . . . like dust on his tongue," he withdraws his spear, as "flesh-suction sighs sad," and a carrion crow approaches to feast on the blue eyes of the bereaved hero's victim.

In "Some Quiet, Plain Poems" Warren returns to his familiar world of childhood memories, looking back at paradise remembered and counting losses. In these six poems, whose lyric texture is nicely reinforced by delicate imagery and elaborate rhyming patterns, memories of paradise may be cruelly evoked by any chance agency: a bird call or owl swoop at evening, bright moonlight or night rain at the bedroom window, snatches of distant music. The governing metaphor seems to be the scene in the ruined well house in Poem 3, where the narrator leans like Billie Potts with unslakable thirst for an earlier, prefallen identity:

> Though guessing the water foul now, and not thirsting to
> take it,
> With thirst from those years before
> You might lean over the coping to stare at the water's dark-
> glinting floor.

In Poem 1, "Ornithology in a World of Flux," a bird call in the evening stillness suffices to evoke the sense of loss between now and then: "Years pass, all places and faces fade, some people have died, / And I stand in a far land . . . ." In Poem 2, "Holly and Hickory," the land is not far, but the time is, as the narrator pictures himself lying awake in the house of his youth, "meditating some old folly / Or trying to live some old pleasure again" while listening to rain. But someone else lives there now:

> And if any car comes now up that lane,
> It carries nobody I could know,
> And who wakes in that house now to hear the rain
> May fall back to sleep—as I, long ago. . . .

Following a pattern like a miniature *Four Quartets*—"to arrive where we started/And know the place for the first time"—the narrator leans above his reflection in Poem 3, "The Well House," and finds that, as Eliot had warned, human kind cannot bear too much reality:

> What happened there, it was not not much,
> But was enough. If you come back
> *Not much* may be *too much*, even if you have your old knack
> Of stillness, and do not touch
> A thing, a broken toy or rusted tool or any such. . . .

Poem 4, "In Moonlight, Somewhere, They Are Singing," captures an exceptionally powerful epiphany from a prelapsarian memory of the speaker, as a boy, waking at night to hear his young aunt and her husband singing outdoors in the moonlight. "Too young to know what they meant, I was happy," the speaker recalls, but now that he's older he must think of the singers' other auditor:

> But what of the old man awake there,
> As the voices, like vine, climbed up moonlight?
> What thought did he think of past time as they twined bright in
>   moon-air,
> And veined, with their silver, the moon-flesh of night?

Beauty, like time, hurts for its losses; but in this instance it may be sufficient to sustain "Some life-faith yet, by my years, unrepealed," if ever the speaker awakes again to hear singing in the "white moon-fire."

As meager as this sustenance is, it gives way in Poem 5, "In Italian They Call the Bird Civetta," to an unqualified sense of loss thanks to "Time's adept trickery" (as Poem 2 had called it). Irremediably placed "in this far land"—literally Italy, but mainly the " World of Flux" described in Poem 1—the speaker finds the evening hush around him, with its "thin moon" and "owl-call," reminiscent of a similar evening in his lost paradise: "Ah, I see that Kentucky scene / Now only behind my shut eyelids." The central tactic in this moving little poem is the juxtaposing of two owl-calls, one occurring in the present scene in Italy and the other remembered from the lost time in boyhood, so as to "frame between owl-call and owl-call / Life's bright parenthesis." In this fashion, "Time is crumpled like paper," so that the owl of boyhood audibly answers its Italian mate "Across all the years and miles that / Are the only Truth I have learned." The evocation of time past is, as always in Warren, rendered in heartwrenching detail; few poets have achieved, in the aggregate of their work, so Proustian a recovery of lost time. Here, "back from the present owl-call,"

> . . . the passage of years, like a tire's scream,
> Fades now while the reply
> Of a dew-damp and downy lost throat spills
> To quaver from that home-dark,
> And frame between owl-call and owl-call
> Life's bright parenthesis.

Poem 6, "Debate: Question, Quarry, Dream," concludes our paradise remembered sequence with a self-portrait that dates from the poet's prelapsarian period but conveys an emotion recollected not altogether in tranquillity. Unlike his adult successor, a dread-ridden night-walker in cities, the boy enjoys perfect immersion in nature, conversing with a muskrat in stanza one, spotting a deer in stanza two, lying on a hillside in stanza three, "While far away, before moonrise, come the town lights, one by one." Looking back towards that vanished alter ego, he cannot reconstitute the whole mentality of the dweller in paradise—"*asking what? / . . . seeking what? / . . . dreaming what?*" But he can remember how time, no dread adversary then, "leans down to kiss the heart's ambition." Passage into the world's stew has changed all that, and so, none the wiser:

> Long since that time I have walked night streets, heel-iron
> Clicking the stone, and in dark in windows have stared.
> Question, quarry, dream—I have vented my ire on
> My own heart that, ignorant and untoward,
> Yearns for an absolute that Time would, I thought, have prepared,
>
> But has not yet. . . .

Rounding out the irony of the passage psychology, the poet thinks of his small son asleep with a toy, while he will go forth "where the cold constellations deploy" to "consider more strictly," in the light of these epiphanies and their heartwrenching evanescence, "the appalling logic of joy."

"Ballad: Between the Boxcars (1923)" is yet another sequence about forced passage into the world's stew. Reluctance is here occasioned by the bloody death of a fifteen-year-old who foolishly went for the rear rather than the front ladder of a passing freight car. "I Can't Even Remember the Name," says the speaker in Lyric 1, but he does remember one thing very clearly—"whether or not he managed to get off his yell, / I remember its shape on his mouth, between the boxcars." Lyric 2, " He Was Formidable," documents the speaker's exceptional sense of this death's wasteful-ness, for the lad had shown great promise as an athlete and lover:

> Oh, his hair was brown-bright as a chestnut, sun-glinting and
> curly,
> And that lip that smiled boy-sweet could go, of a sudden, man-
> surly,
> And the way he was built
> Made the girls in his grade in dark stare, and finger the quilt. . . .

But now death has substituted its climax for theirs, making a rude joke of that old Renaissance pun about sexual orgasm being a kind of dying: "He spilled, as boys may, too soon, between the boxcars." In Lyric 3, "He Has Fled," the narrator first describes the boy's dissolution into nature and then terminates the sequence with a vain wish to reject his postlapsarian knowledge:

> For we are in the world and nothing is good enough, which is
>   to say that the world is here and we are not
>   good enough,
> And we live in the world, and in so far as we live, the world
>   continues to live in us,
> Despite all we can do to reject it utterly, including
>   this particular recollection, which now I
>   would eject, reject,
>   but cannot.

"Ballad: Between the Boxcars" thus shows a narrator rueing his passage into knowledge of an untimely death. "Nocturne: Traveling Salesman in Hotel Bedroom" discloses a still more ruinous specta-cle: a dead soul, who must continue his meaningless life and work simply because he has no alternative. Attesting what John Updike called "the irremediable anguish of simply having to go on," the naturalistic artifacts in the salesman's routine—toothbrush, soap, toilet, sales sheet—bespeak the totally initiated man whose passage into a fallen world is complete.[11] Feebly attempting to offset this condition, the last stanza asserts that "vision is possible, and / Man's meed of glory not / Impossible . . . in life's upshot," but nothing in the poem justifies this conclusion. We would have to look outside the poem to Warren's mysticism to substantiate any such vision.

In the final three sections of *You, Emperors, and Others* we find Warren's psychology of passage somewhat departmentalized according to life's major phases. "Autumnal Equinox on Mediterranean Beach" is an older man's mood poem, wherein gusty blasts of autumn wind are welcomed as a correlative of the speaker's disillusion with summer's phony paradise:

> For I am sick of summer and the insane glitter
> Of sea sun-bit, and the wavelets that bicker and titter,
>
> And the fat girls that hang out brown breasts like fruit over-
> ripe,
> And the thin ones flung pale in rock-shadow, goose-pimpled as
> tripe,
>
> And the young men who pose on the headlands like ads for
> Jantzen,
> And the old who would do so much better to keep proper
> pants on,
>
> And all Latin faeces one finds, like jewels, in the sand. . . .

With cleansing force, the wind is urged to "Come howl like a prophet the season's righteous anger, / And knock down our idols with crash, bang, or clangor." Chief among these idols is the setting's inherent hedonism, which fails to mitigate the fact that "our pleasures, like peaches, get rotten, not riper." The mood turns sourer yet at the poem's conclusion, which observes that in this fallen world neither nature nor its God cares who suffers or who benefits in the turn of its seasons. The poem's cacophonous noises seem to objectify the speaker's black mood:

> For pain and pleasure balance in God's year—
> Though *whose* is *which* is not your problem here.

> And perhaps not even God's. So bang, wind, batter,
> While human hearts do the bookkeeping in this matter.

In form, content, theme, and setting, this poem sufficiently resembles Shelley's famous "Ode to the West Wind" to suggest possible parody: oh, wind, if autumn comes, can winter be far behind?

The penultimate sequence in *You, Emperors, and Others* is a set of four "Nursery Rhymes," where the contrast between form (suggesting childhood innocence and security) and content (death, copulation, and drunkenness) underscores the theme of passage. Poem 1, "Knockety-Knockety-Knock," makes the Fall literal for the child-victim in the first stanza, with the clock—symbol of time's turpitude—as the poem's master metaphor:

> The clock struck one,
> And I fell down,
> Hickory-dickory-dock.
> God let me fall down. . . .

Stanzas two and three look back to the lost world of infantile paradise—"My father took me / For a ride on his knee"; "When I'd wake in the night / Mother held me tight"—but a ticking clock has marked off losses of familial and religious certitudes:

> Hickory-dickory-dock,
> And Ma's deader than mackerel,
> And Pa pickled as pickerel,
> And oh! knockety-knockety-knock,
> God's red eyes glare
> From sockets of dark air—
> Knockety-knockety-knock.

Poem 2, "News of Unexpected Demise of Little Boy Blue," begins with the traditional scolding of Boy Blue for his dereliction of duty; but by stanza three the narrator's adult perspective of the world's stew has blotted out the child's-eye view of the original:

> I should have known you'd be derelict.
> From a family like yours what can we expect?
> Born of woman, and she grunted like a pig,

Got by man just for the frig,
Dropped in the world like a package of offal,
Demanding love with wail and snuffle. . . .

Knowledge of sex, the first fruit of the Fall from Eden, is quickly followed by knowledge of death, the Fall's other main consequence, as that nap under the haystack promises to be a long one.

Poems 3 and 4, "Mother Makes the Biscuits" and "The Bramble Bush," take the sequence beyond the poems of passage psychology and into a Blakean higher innocence. But even here a child's passage into lapsarian knowledge occurs through a juxtaposition of prelapsarian order and security—"Mother makes the biscuits, / Father makes the laws"—with some nonparadisical observations: "Grandma wets the bed sometimes, / Kitty-cats have claws." The final sequence in *You, Emperors, and Others*, "Short Thoughts for Long Nights," is a series of nine poems, most of them consisting of a single rhyming quatrain, wherein various character types respond unhappily to passage into the gross world. Poem 1, "Nightmare of Mouse," presents a character who rejects passage by simply not believing in the reality of evil, somewhat in the manner of the community in "Dragon Country: To Jacob Boehme": "It was there, but I said it couldn't be true. . . ." As the poem ends, the world proves itself real when "Teeth crunched on my skull." Poem 2, "Nightmare of Man," presents the logical positivist, a scientific type who "assembled, marshaled, my data" with perfect induction, but crumbled at last to the nightmare of losses, "For I'd thought of the death of my mother, and wept; and weep still." In Poem 3, "Colloquy with Cockroach," the cockroach's auditor is an innocent neophyte who tries but fails to establish his cleanliness as against the insect's assertion, "I know I smell. But everyone does. . . ." Poem 4, "Little Boy on Voyage," shows the lad's first chilling intimations of eternity while "standing on ship-shudder, wide eyes staring / At unease of ocean, at sunset, and the distance long." Though he is called in "for supper and sleep" at the poem's end, presumably that "gray distance past hoping or despairing" has changed his simpler mind of yesterday. Poem 5, "Obsession," begins with heavy assonance and a spondaic slowing of the rhythm to approximate an insomniac's tired brain-pulse: "Dawn draws on slow when dawn brings only dawn. . . ."

This insomniac—whose weary intelligence seems to lie behind the title of the whole sequence, "Short Thoughts for Long Nights"— resembles Eliot's and Hemingway's sleepless night-people in that his obsession is evidently naturalistic dread of nada, which he has unsuccessfully sought to escape in sleep:

> ... slow milk-wash on window, star paling, first bird-stir,
> Sweat cold now on pillow, before the alarm's *burr*,
> And the old thought for the new day as day draws on.

Poem 6, "Joy," provides a dialectical contrast to the trend of the sequence as a whole; but Poem 7, "Cricket, on Kitchen Floor, Enters History," returns us wholemindedly to the world's *angst*. Here history is seen as naturalistic oblivion that swallows up the individual much as the hen in the poem devours a cricket; the whole thing reminds us of the "tomb of Roman citizen of no historical importance" in the book's first poem, "Clearly about You." Poem 8, "Little Boy and General Principle," presents a last vignette of the psychology of passage:

> Don't cry, little boy, you see it is only natural
> That little red trucks will break, whether plastic or tin,
> And some other things, too. It's a general principle
> That you'll have to learn soon, so you might, I guess, begin.

Taken together, these "Short Thoughts for Long Nights" do not represent a high achievement in either form or thought, but they do illustrate yet again just how deeply the problems of passage, or psychology of the Fall, are ingrained in Warren's poetry. Better than half the poems in *You, Emperors, and Others* relate directly to this continuing obsession. Perhaps the poem "Obsession" was uncommonly well titled in referring to this lapsarian mentality as "the old thought for the new day."

TALE OF TIME

During the six years between *You, Emperors, and Others* and the publication of *Tale of Time: New Poems, 1960-1966*, several changes in the materials of the poet's art occur: a shift in geography with Vermont replacing Italy as a favored setting; an interest in biblical characters supplanting Achilles and the Roman emperors of classical antiquity; and the development of his children's minds providing a foil to his own melancholy meditations. In other respects, however, *Tale of Time* fastens upon the recurrently familiar, most importantly in the poems of passage situation. Of the six major poem sequences that comprise the collection, five treat the Fall from a more innocent view of life as the predominant issue; the two poems that lie outside the sequence format also treat the theme of bitter knowledge. (One of these, "Shoes in the Rain Jungle," is an early protest poem that sees the Vietnam war as evidence of an ominous national innocence; and the other, "Fall Comes in Back-Country Vermont," exploits symbolically the poet's favorite seasonal setting.)

Opening the collection is a sequence of ten poems called "Notes on a Life to be Lived"—the life in question evidently being whatever remains of the speaker's. Operating in his usual dialectical fashion, Warren's persona sporadically relieves his gloom with intimations of joy and vision, doing his best to garner from his children's unfallen perspective some approach to a Blakean or Yeatsian higher innocence; but as a whole the ten poems accentuate the adult's negative. Poem I, "Stargazing," establishes the contrary perspectives of postlapsarian narrator and prelapsarian child by means of setting. Stars, black spruces, the fall coming on, and a premonition of wind gathering "Far off in arctic starlight" provoke in the narrator unwanted memories of his own passage into dread of the world (much as in Wallace Stevens's "Domination of Black"), while the child sees only the scene's beauty:

> And the girl is saying, "You do not look
> At the stars," for I did not look at
> The stars, for I know they are there, know
> That if I look at the stars, I
>
> Will have to live over again all I have lived
> In the years I looked at stars and
> Cried out, "O reality!"

Poem II, "Small White House," recalls a child's cry overheard in the infernal heat of a long ago summer; and Poem III, "Blow, West Wind," darkens the mood still further with a morbid mem-

ory of "how cold / Was the sweat on my father's mouth, dead."
These sweatbeads in turn evoke a scene from paradise remembered,
when "I, a boy, crouching at creekside, / Watched in sunlight, a
handful of water / Drip, drip, from my hand. The drops—they
were bright!" Poem IV, "Composition in Gold and Red-Gold,"
brings the time setting to the present, a fall day alive with golden
colors as in an impressionistic painting: sunlight, leaves, apples,
chipmunk, little girl's hair, cat fur, cat eyes. But gold, as Robert
Frost observed, is nature's hardest hue to hold: the girl's scream
marks passage out of her golden day, while the narrator, observing
the "faint smear of flame-gold" at the base of the chipmunk's skull,
notes: "This effect / Completes the composition." Poem V, "Little
Boy and Lost Shoe," is yet another exercise in juxtaposed perspectives, with the boy showing that carelessness about time which
typifies the resident in paradise ("Home he hobbled, not caring,
with a stick whipping goldenrod"), while the speaker's vain warn-
ings bespeak his postlapsarian time-consciousness: "Oh, hurry, boy,
for the grass will be tall as a tree . . . : / Hurry, for time is money
and the sun is low."

   In the next three poems of the sequence, VI through VIII, the
dialectic between innocence and knowledge develops toward a
Blakean higher innocence. Nevertheless the sequence remains
heavily freighted toward the "Songs of Experience" side. In "Patriotic Tour and Postulate of Joy," for example, the postulate of joy
must survive screening through a weltschmerz like that of the
senator who, wakened by the mockingbird,

> Rose with a taste in the throat like bile,
> To the bathroom fled
> And spat, and faced the mirror there, and while
> The bicarb fizzed, stared, feet cold on tile.

"Dragon-Tree" likewise looks for gilt leaves from a tree whose
roots plunge deep into the naturalistic fear of the fallen soul and
his sense of life as a diminished thing: "Do you feel, in your heart,
that life has turned out as you expected?" Our narrator's characteristic insomnia generates images of dread in relentless profusion: a
faucet dripping all night, cats in coition squalling "like Hell's
honeymoon," icy black water pounding the boulders in the neigh-

boring gorge, geese passing overhead in dawn-light, the eating of human flesh in the Congo, the eating of one's own heart. "The world drives at you like a locomotive / In an archaic movie," and you are its rails.

"Vision Under the October Mountain: A Love Poem" blissfully escapes this world scene, but only by returning the speaker to his prelapsarian state *in utero*, when "we in the / pulse and warm slosh of / that unbreathing bouillon" had "blind eyes with / no lashes yet, unbrined by grief yet. . . ." Since this is a love poem, the usual scenario of loss and regret does not obtain; yet even here the speaker's request for the whole story of his lover's life, with "particular emphasis on the development of / the human scheme of values," denotes the scepticism of a man after passage. Poem IX, "Chain Saw at Dawn in Vermont in Time of Drouth," displays our speaker, as "New light gilds the spruce-tops," possessed upon waking by two images of "the outraged heart": a crow-call in the silence (a recurrent image in Warren's later poetry), and the sound of a chain saw singing *"Now, now, now*, in the / Blood-lust and lash of an eternal present. . . ." What makes these images outrageous is disclosed in section 2 of the poem, wherein our fitful waker, wondering "Have I learned how to live?" has a secret sharer, a dying man who, hearing the same chain saw and picturing likewise "the first light spangling the spruces," thinks *"I have not learned how to die."* Knowing neither how to die, on his sharer's behalf, nor how to live, on his own, the speaker finds in the drouth-ridden landscape a correlative of his soul's condition:

> . . . soon I must rise and go out in the world where
> The heel of the sun's foot smites horridly the hill,
> And the stalk of the beech leaf goes limp,
> And the bright brook goes gray among boulders,
> And the saw sings. . . .

The sequence ends in Poem X, "Ways of Day," as it had begun, with the narrator's postlapsarian gloom juxtaposed against his child's prelapsarian joy of life. From his symbolic shade watching his son play in symbolic sunlight, the speaker recapitulates his Fall from paradise and his subsequent insomnia in imagery of memorable power and delicacy:

> Night heaved, and burning, the star
> Fell. Oh, what do I remember?
> I heard the swamp-owl, night-long, call.
> The far car's headlight swept the room wall.

Now in his fallen state, the narrator has learned from his life in the world merely devious tactics of survival: "I am the dark and tricky one. / I am watching from my shade." And so our brooder in the night ends his "Notes on a Life to Be Lived" sequence with a barely tenable plea for a return to innocence: "I watch you at your sun-lit play. / Teach me, my son, the ways of day."

"Tale of Time," the sequence that gives this whole collection of poems its title, touches upon all three of the major themes of our discourse: poems of passage, the undiscovered self, and the osmosis of being. The poems of passage motif is obviously inherent in the traumatic subject matter, which involves the near-simultaneous deaths of two mother figures: the narrator's biological mother and her helper, the family's old black Mammy. Betokening this "time of endings" (Poem IV, 1) is the ominous imagery of the passage experience: an autumn setting, water rushing down the gorge at night, a night freight passing ("It will move all night into distance" —Poem IV, 5), death observed rather too closely (Poem IV, 3):

> . . . life
> Spinning out, spilling out, from
> The holes of the eyes: and the eyes are
> Burning mud beneath a sky of nothing.
> The eyes bubble like hot mud with the expulsion of vision.

"Between the clod"—on mother's coffin at burial—"and the midnight" (of insomniac unrest) is ample time for full assimilation of the day's dread knowledge, reflected in images like "Water deeper than daylight" or "The sun-dappled dark of deep woods and / Blood on green fern frond" (Poem I, "What Happened"). Passage into unwanted knowledge is marked off also by the night visitation of faces long dead, who "lean at my bed-foot, and grin fit to kill, / For we now share a knowledge I did not have in my youth" (Poem II, "The Mad Druggist"). Thus the insomniac's nightly burden (Poem IV, 7):

> Planes pass in the night. I turn
> To the right side if the beating
> Of my own heart disturbs me.

As with the sequence on his father's death in *You, Emperors, and Others*, Warren musters his most affecting powers when reversing time's reel to glimpse his mother's prepassage identity. Poem V ("What Were You Thinking, Dear Mother?") restores the deceased to her prelapsarian childhood, before "you found it necessary to live on . . . / Into our present maniacal century, / In which you gave me birth." Like similar portraits of his own lost self and his father's in *You, Emperors, and Others*, Warren here strives to capture the mind frame of Eden's inhabitant, which after the Fall becomes nearly unimaginable:

> What were you thinking, a child, when you lay,
> At the whippoorwill hour, lost in the long grass. . . .
>
> In lamplight, your father's head bent at his book.
>
> What did you think when the last saffron
> Of sunset faded beyond the dark cedars,
> And on noble blue how the evening star hung?

Now much older than his mother was at the time of her death, the speaker in Poem VI (appropriately titled "Insomnia"), section 3, longs to "Reach out that I might offer / What protection I could" to that child in the grass of yesteryear, telling her "I am older than you will ever be," and trying to forestall her coming exile from Eden:

> "Your hand—
> Give it here, for it's dark and, my dear,
> You should never have come in the woods when it's dark,
> But I'll take you back home, they're waiting."
> And to woods-edge we come, there stand.

One of Warren's fine poetic vignettes follows, with the narrator watching hapless from his time frame as his mother moves blindly back to hers:

I watch you move across the open space.
You move under the paleness of new stars.
You move toward the house, and one instant,

A door opening, I see
Your small form black against the light, and the door
Is closed. . . .

Warren's quarrel with Ralph Waldo Emerson, which structures the seven poem sequence called "Homage to Emerson, On
Night Flight to New York," has been long-standing. As a Waste
Lander who began his poetic career under the shadow of Eliot's
ascendency in the 1920s and launched his prose career with *John
Brown: The Making of a Martyr* (1929), which spotlights the
folly, depravity, and self-deception of a man Emerson predicted
would "make the gallows glorious as the cross"; as a writer who
further demolished Transcendental high-mindedness via fictional
creations like Adam Stanton in *All the King's Men* and Tobias
Sears in *Band of Angels;* and as an analyst of America's heritage of
perverted ideologies in *The Legacy of the Civil War: Meditations
on the Centennial,* Warren is predictably in Hawthorne's corner,
another sceptic who might sometimes have admired Emerson as a
poet but "sought nothing from him as a philosopher." [12] Warren's
basic quarrel with Emerson is precisely over the question of the
Fall. For Emerson, who never took a Night Flight—symbolic or
otherwise—and who, if he had, would assuredly never have
alighted in so grubby a cesspool of corruption as New York City
(a symbol of modern society's soulless depravity since Warren's
Fugitive-Agrarian days), there never was a Fall. There was merely
a failure of men's faith in themselves owing to misconceptions
perpetrated by the Puritan tradition, a regrettable circumstance
needing only the corrective of the "new eyes" of Transcendentalist
promulgation. For Warren Emerson's path to redemption seems
much too short and easy. It is all very well for Emerson, in Poem I
("His Smile"), to have "forgiven God everything"—in fact, that is
precisely what Warren's personae must do by "loving the world" in
all its filth and suffering—but there is little to forgive if a man has
never accepted the trauma of passage. And so Warren's purpose in
these "Homage to Emerson" poems is to subject the chief Emer-

sonian doctrines to a reality test drawn up by the Warren persona.

Those chief doctrines are twofold: at the heart of his mission, Emerson rose to proclaim that this world is in fact the kingdom of God, there being no other; and that, as the "Divinity School Address" announces, not Christ only but every man is the incarnation of God. A third doctrine or corollary useful for Warren's sceptical purposes is the sovereignty of this deified man over nature, which "receives the dominion of man as meekly as the ass on which the Saviour rode," according to Section V of "Nature." For the postlapsarian soul, ridden by naturalistic dread to the point of insomnia, such an ideology may be all too easily lacerated. To the airborne speaker in Poem I, Emerson's benignly assuring smile seems inadequate to offset the sense of night's dark immensity as perceived from 38,000 feet, which even the lights of our greatest city cannot dispel in Poem V, "Multiplication Table":

> If the Christmas tree at Rockefeller Center were
> A billion times bigger, and you laid it
> Flat down in the dark, and
> With a steam roller waist-high to God and heavy as
> The Rocky Mountains, flattened it out thin as paper, but
> Never broke a single damned colored light bulb, and they were all
> Blazing in the dark, that would be the way it is, but
>
> Beyond the lights it is dark. . . .

Nor does Emerson's sweet smile ease the distress of the speaker's seatmate who "begins, quite audibly, to recite / The multiplication table" as the plane sinks towards landing. Afterwards, though the landing proved safe enough, the night-flight delivers the speaker to a grubby wasteland:

> The wind comes off the Sound, smelling
> Of ice. It smells
> Of fish and burned gasoline. A sheet
> Of newspaper drives in the wind. . . .

This wasteland is surrounded by an even chillier inhuman earthscape: "Eastward, the great waters stretch in darkness" (Poems VI and VII). So much for Transcendental immersion in nature. Nor does the doctrine of the deity of man escape a bit of postpassage meditation. In Poem II, "The Wart," the speaker recalls being told as a boy to cure his wart by not masturbating; and in Poem IV, "One Drunk Allegory," an inebriate practices some Emersonian advice ("Let a man look at the stars") in a prostrate position: *"This is as good a position as any / From which to watch the stars . . . . / Until, of course, the cops come."*

In the light of Emerson's genuinely epochal achievement such statements may seem slanted and unfair; so it is good that Warren ends the sequence with something of a real "homage to Emerson." First, although he had ridiculed Emerson's assertion that "significance shines through everything" in Poem IV, "One Drunk Allegory," his final poem in the sequence, "Does the Wild Rose?," strives to grasp some such significance with respect to two enigmatic images: the wild rose itself—*"Does the wild rose know your secret / As the summer silence breathes?"*—and a human face breaking into expression. The face, "half in shadow," with "muted glitter" of tears in the eyes but perhaps about to smile, follows the question, "What constitutes the human bond?" Second, Warren enlists himself in the search for "A way by which the process of living can become Truth," thereby endorsing Emerson's splendid statement in "The American Scholar" and the "Divinity School Address" that the poet-scholar-preacher aims "to convert life into truth."

Sandwiched between the longer sequences are two short poems about passage into tragic knowledge. "Shoes in Rain Jungle," a 1966 protest against the Vietnamese war, sees the whole Republic about to lapse from political innocence into the terrible knowledge of history as an unsolvable mess:

> All wars are righteous. Except when
> You lose them. This
> Is the lesson of history. . . .

But in the fallen world "History is what you can't / Resign from," and so men will continue to march into history "On rotting shoe leather," and when they get there will look around, "lost / In the . . . beaded / Rain," and say, " '*Mot de Cambronne* [i.e. *merde*], this / Is history.' " Such protest poetry is fortunately rare in Warren. The other short poem, "Fall Comes in Back-Country Vermont," is much more in his true vein of elegiac meditation. It exploits once again Warren's favorite symbolic season for a setting, and it represents the speed and thrust of Time by enclosing its four sections and 116 lines all within a single sentence concerning a death in the village.

"The Day Dr. Knox Did It" is a vintage lapsarian poem, whose "Place and Time" (title of section I) is the precarious high point of both the narrator's and the world's age of innocence: nine years old for the boy and August of 1914 for the world. In the terrific heat a setter "pants in his cave / of cool back under the rotting floor boards," and another beastie with traditional mythic properties appears briefly: "the head of the moccasin parts the green / algae and it slides up out of the slough. . . ." Part II, "The Event," tells us what happened—a suicide in a neighboring barn loft. In section III the boy asks from his prepassage state, " 'But why did he do it, Grandpa?' " The old man answers, from his postpassage knowledge (" 'Yes, by God, and I've seen 'em die. / I've seen 'em die and I've seen 'em dead' "), that some people simply cannot accept their passage into the world's reality: " 'Son—' the tongue said. / 'For some folks the world gets too much.' " In Poem IV the narrator is visiting the loft with the son of the deceased and " wondering who had cleaned up the mess." But in Poem V, "And All That Came Thereafter," he retreats towards the unknowing fetal state *à la* Jack Burden, as symbolized by the underwater, eyes-shut posture, and lets the world wash away:

> But ran from such wondering . . .
> toward that stream that was silent and silver
>
> in willow and water, and I would lie
> with my eyes shut tight, and let water flow
> over me as I lay, and like water, the world
> would flow, flow away, on forever. . . .

But of course the Fall ensues, "for there is / no water to wash the world away." In fact, "We are the world, and it is too late / to pretend we are children at dusk watching fireflies." So the rest of this poem—one of Warren's finest in this book—depicts the speaker's own experience of loss. This loss has two dimensions, the first being the evanescence of epiphanies so intense that "my own heart, in a rage like joy, / burst." Now, decades later, he cannot even remember the face of the girl whose body he entered on a night,

> when sea-salt on the laurel leaf
> in moonlight, like frost, gleamed, and salt
>
> were the tears to my lips on the girl's face, for
> she wept, and I did not know why. . . .

Still another intense memory is mocked by the subsequent decay of the poem's setting, with Telegraph Hill in San Francisco being presently occupied by "wearers of pin-stripe and of furs by I. Magnin . . . in their hives of glass." The other primary loss—which relates to our undiscovered self discussion—is replacement of the "clean" prelapsarian self by a "dirty" successor, the "I" who,

> have lied, in velleity loved, in weakness
> forgiven, who have stolen small objects, committed
> adultery, and for a passing pleasure,
> as well as for reasons of sanitation,
>
> inflicted death on flies. . . .

The poem—and the whole sequence—ends like several others we have noted, with the lapsarian experience impinging cruelly upon a new generation: "My small daughter's dog has been killed on the road. / It is night. In the next room she weeps."

The final poem of passage in *Tale of Time*, "Saul at Gilboa," the second of the two "Holy Writ" poems, is perhaps the grimmest Warren has ever written. Gilboa alludes to the mountain where Israel's first hero-king, after the rout of his army, fell on his sword to escape being tortured by the Philistines, who thereupon desecrated his body and took his severed head to be fastened in their temple of Dagon (I Chronicles, 10). With that grisly spectacle already evoked by the title, the central action of the poem—the prophet Samuel's anointing of young Saul—becomes bitterly ironic, especially since Samuel, the poem's speaker, foreknows this wretched destiny even as he applies the oil to Saul's innocent head. Thus Samuel is the postlapsarian man whose knowledge of the world's stew has reached unbearable dimensions (especially since he speaks from his posthumous state, the ghost summoned by the witch of Endor) and who, much in the manner of a chorus in Greek tragedy, is powerless to enlighten the tragedy's victim. In Part I Saul comes out from the desert as a prelapsarian innocent seeking his father's lost asses, but instead he finds Samuel—"for what / We seek we never / Find, find only fate." "How beautiful are the young," Samuel laments in Part 2; "He walks / In his youth, which is the sweet affront / Of ignorance, toward me. . . . / In beauty toward / My knowledge, walks." Part 3 describes the actual anointing as a cruel juxtaposition of knowledge and innocence: "Before the knowledge in me, he, beautiful, down in the dirt, kneels./. . . He / Is ignorant, and I pour / Oil on those locks. . . ." In Part 4 as the oil glistens on the head destined for Dagon's temple, Samuel describes his anguish as "the membrane between the past and the future" as "I, / In my knowledge, close my eyes." Though full of prophecy, Samuel cannot bring himself to precipitate Saul's fall from innocence— "oh! / Beautiful is ignorance kneeling"—and so he withholds his dark visions: "Say he will dance, but I do not say / That that dance is a dance into self-hood /. . . He himself will become a friend to darkness, be counseled by wolves." In Part 5, the witch of Endor episode, Saul has indeed fallen into ruinous knowledge and so he seeks from Samuel's ghost that larger knowledge which is the fallen soul's only hope for amelioration, or so Warren and his Samuel believe:

> . . . for, in the end,
> To know is, always, all. To know
> Is, whatever the knowledge, the secret hope within
> Hope. So to the cave.

Unfortunately, what Samuel knows (in Part 6) is only that vision of coming disaster that is Saul's fate, destined to reduce Saul from "A king" to being merely "Himself." Saul's reaction, after waking from his fit, is to revert to the prefallen self of childhood— "She feeds him, morsel / By morsel, he like a child." And Part 7 is an extended paradise remembered evocation, taking us back once again to the anointing—"How beautiful are the young, walking! / I closed my eyes. I shuddered in a rage of joy." Immediately following this reenacting of the anointment comes the grisly spectacle at Mount Gilboa. The anointed head lies severed ("The ant has entered / The eye-arch") while its trunk, "The great torso, a stake / Thrust upward to twist the gut-tangle," hangs above the city wall of the Philistines. Part 9, which concludes the "Saul" sequence, ends with the prophet Samuel totally traumatized, even after his death ("a death / In which I cannot lie down"), by his tragic knowledge; so that he cannot derive any meaning from either religion or history:

> I have forgotten, literally, God, and through
> The enormous hollow of my head, History
> Whistles like a wind.

The final two lines of the poem sum up the lapsarian experience in an innocence/knowledge juxtaposition that Wordsworth might have called a thought too deep for tears:

> How beautiful are the young, walking!
> If I could weep.

INCARNATIONS

Incarnations: Poems 1966–1968 consists of three sections: an *Island of Summer* series with a Mediterranean setting, an *Internal Injuries* collection about a doomed convict and an accident victim, and a brief section called *Enclaves*. The *Island of Summer* sequence introduces in Poem 1 ("What Day Is") the lapsarian theme of ruinous knowledge. Knowledge of time hits the speaker in double-barreled fashion as he measures the island's long sweep of history, featuring domination by Phoenicians, Celts, Romans, Moors, and English, against this day in his own life. This day, as he watches, is producing a bit of sawdust as "All day, cicadas, / At the foot of infinity, like / A tree, saw." Similar days, he reflects, have left random human artifacts strewn carelessly rather like the cicada filings: "A handful of coins, a late emperor. / Hewn stone. . . ." The poem ends with a look at the sea, that ancient symbol of eternity that surrounds the island of summer, accompanied by a belated warning against such long views of reality:

> Do not
> Look too long at the sea, for
> That brightness will rinse out your eyeballs.
>
> They will go gray as dead moons.

Poem 3, "Natural History," roots up yet more morbid knowledge in contemplating the many who have died here, nameless bodies "eaten by dogs, gulls, rodents, ants, / And fish" until by now even "the root / Of the laurel has profited," and the leaf of the live-oak "achieves a new luster." Natural history, then, is a study of incalculable losses in nature and history, for which "Neither has tears." From the next island a rocket rising at dusk from its scientific laboratory affords unexpected beauty and a healing metaphor for our natural historian—"Beauty / Is the fume-track of necessity." But on further reflection this "therapeutic" thought that aesthetics might heal the sick soul requires the further recourse to "consult your family physician."

Further doubts about the therapy of beauty arise in Poem 7, "Moonrise," which seems a companion poem to "What Day Is." Warren himself in his essay on "The Ancient Mariner" had drawn the contrast between Daylight/Reason and Moonlight/Imagination, with the moon symbolizing the Romantic preference for the transfiguring power of imagination over the mere daylight glare of reason that shows reality harshly. Warren's moonrise, however, discloses the experience of beauty to be almost as painful as the knowledge of evil. The speaker himself is the first to be smitten as,

> From the widening throat of the valley,
> Light, like a bugle-blast,
> Silver, pours at us. We are,
> In that silence, stunned.

Casting his eye downward at diners on the café *terrasse*, he notes that they too, with eyes that yearn from their sockets, look moonward in insatiable werewolf hunger, their faces "Washed white as bone." The air, too, "is heavy with blossom," adding olfactory to visual hunger; and the scene as a whole makes the moonrise almost as unbearable as the brightness of sea in "What Day Is." Consequently, some diners, who "have shown more judgment," have retreated into the shadow of laurel, while the narrator himself reflects ruefully on the Romantic solipsism of such epiphanies: "We wait. We do not even / Know the names of one another."

The naturalistic cul-de-sac of burdensome knowledge in *Island of Summer* is Poem 13, "A Place Where Nothing Is." Portraying death with the intensity of Eliot's hollow men or Hemingway's nada-obsessed insomniacs, this poem also resembles one of Emily Dickinson's best poems on the subject, "It Was Not Death, For I Stood Up." Warren's persona, like Dickinson's, foresees personal extinction in a series of negative definitions: "it is not / silence, for there are voices," "nor / echo, for the dark has / no walls." Needlessly, the poem concludes by explicating the sea-metaphor of "What Day Is," a sea "like the inestimable sea of / Nothingness Plotinus dreamed."

Three poems in *Island of Summer* advance the theme of lapsarian knowledge through a mythological framework. Poem 4, "Riddle in the Garden," resounds with Edenic overtones complete with a proscribed fruit: "I warn you, do not / touch that plum, it will burn you. . . ." The "Riddle" itself evinces the osmosis of being theme, which for Warren is not symbol or myth but literal reality. The "One Life" in which all things live means that eating a plum is an obverse correlative to the laurel and live-oak "profiting" from the human dead in "Natural History." The Fall in "Riddle in the Garden" thus implies awareness of one's irremediable participation in the one life of the world, both as guilty benefitter and powerless victim. And any plum will do as literally a fruit of knowledge, capable at a touch of raising a blister that you must not bite open, since,

> exposing that inwardness will
> increase your pain, for you
> are part of the world. You think
> I am speaking in riddles. But I am not, for
>
> The world means only itself.

Poem 8 conjoins in its title, "Myth on Mediterranean Beach: Aphrodite as Logos," the Christian and Classical elements, with the ironies of a fallen world undermining both. The Logos of Saint John's Gospel has given way to its naturalistic successor, the "Polyphiloprogenitive" impulse to copulate spoken of in T. S. Eliot's "Mr. Eliot's Sunday Morning Service," which is the only primordial creative force visible in living nature. Hence the "Aphrodite as Logos" in Warren's title. But Greek myth has also been undercut by the naturalistic awareness of our era, in particular the knowledge of time that renders the goddess of love a "Botticellian parody." An "old hunchback in bikini," whose "breasts hang down like saddle-bags, / To balance the hump the belly sags," she chills the ardors of the young among whom she passes: "Her pince-nez glitter like contempt / For all delusion." One of the chief "Incarnations" after which this volume of poems is titled, this paradigm in flesh at last subdues erotic love to the burden of knowledge:

> She passes the lovers, one by one,
>
> And passing, draws their dreams away,
> And leaves them naked to the day.

The final poem in the *Island of Summer* sequence—Poem 15, "The Leaf"—focuses once more on the Garden of Eden mythology. Implicitly the whole sequence, with its "Island of Summer" and Mediterranean ("Middle of the World") setting, has measured the ruins of paradise. Here at the end of the sequence the specific reference is to the fig leaves wherewith, after the Fall, Adam and Eve covered their genitals. In Part A of "The Leaf" Warren has a little fun with this sexual motif, as the five-fingered fig leaf "drops, / Shamefast, down" like an "innocent" hand to cover him, as though he were the genitalia to be hidden "from the blaze of the wide world": "I am / What is to be concealed." As the poem ends, however, it is not sexual shame but grief that has prompted this concealment: "To this spot I bring my grief. / Human grief is the obscenity to be hidden by the leaf." Part B identifies one cause of grief as knowledge of self—"We have undergone ourselves, therefore / What more is to be done for Truth's sake?"—which

correlates nicely with Emerson's concept of self-consciousness in
"Experience": "It is very unhappy, but too late to be helped, the
discovery we have made that we exist. That discovery is called the
Fall of Man."[13]

The major cause of grief, however, is the naturalistic evidence
of death scattered through Parts B and C. This is the design of
incarnations—a running sacrifice of the world's flesh that the one
life may continue. Ascending to the nesting place of the hawk,
high on a cliff like nature's great stone altar, our speaker has seen
"The clutter of annual bones, of hare, vole, bird, white / As chalk
from sun and season. . . ." In a symbolic gesture of empathy he
stretches himself out like the next victim on that "High place of
stone," and "the small exacerbation / Of dry bones was what my
back, shirtless and bare, knew." Looking up, he can see "The
hawk shudder in the high sky," its eye fixed on "the flicker of
hare-scut, the movement of vole." For such knowledge "there is
no solution"; the speaker ruefully compares his original innocence
in seeking worldly knowledge to his present soul-sickness:

> I
> Have opened my mouth to the wind of the world like wine,
>   I wanted
> To taste what the world is, wind dried up
> The live saliva of my tongue, my tongue
> Was like a dry leaf in my mouth.

At the end Part B reverts to the fig leaf image, with the knowledge of evil being the shame that drives its human observer from
the world's "flame" in search of shadow.

Part C of "The Leaf" begins with the garden momentarily
like Eden again, its lushness reinforced by a rich sound texture:

> The world is fruitful. In this heat
> The plum, black yet bough-bound, bursts, and the gold ooze is,
> Of bees, joy, the gold ooze has striven
> Outward, it wants again to be of
> The goldness of air and—oh—innocent. . . .

But the ripeness of grapes obtrudes the theme of harvest into the
picture and evokes in turn the thought—yes, "The world / Is

fruitful"—of a human harvest, going back through "my father's father's father." Such knowledge, like a bitter grape, has "set the teeth on edge"—"I have cried out in the night." So Eden fades under the recollection that, "From a further garden, from the shade of another tree, / My father's voice, in the moment when the cicada ceases, has called to me."

Part D closes out the poem (and the sequence) by extending the setting of the incarnation theme from the minimal and the personal—the animal bones and the death of fathers—to the cosmic. Here the *"teeth set on edge"* attitude previously ascribed to his father describes his own dread of eternity, glimpsed in an instant of silence:

> In the momentary silence of the cicada,
> I can hear the appalling speed,
> In space beyond stars, of
> Light. It is
> A sound like wind.

Here and in Warren's later poetry a recurring sound like wind signifies too much reality: the speed of light or the immensity of time overpowers the minds of men in their earth- and time-bound feebleness of flesh. That sound completes the passage of our narrator into the world's reality, and *Island of Summer* terminates.

Part II of *Incarnations* is *Internal Injuries*, a collection that consists of two sequences of poems ("Penological Study: Southern Exposure" and "Internal Injuries") and three main characters: a convict waiting for his electrocution next morning, an elderly woman dying from an auto accident, and a narrator-observer whose own "internal injuries" are a result of his passage into this dreadful knowledge of a reality he would prefer not to think about. The convict in Poem 1 of "Penological Study" at least has recourse to morphine to help him through the night—" 'Jest keep that morphine moving, Cap, / And me, I'll tough it through.' " But the speaker, lacking any such buffer between his imagination and the coming event, vicariously lives out the moment of death in the execution chamber (Poem 2, "Tomorrow Morning"): "Truth will embrace you with tentacles like an octopus. It / Will suck your blood through a thousand suction-cups." Poem 3, "Wet

Hair: If Now His Mother Should Come," juxtaposes the present moment, with the convict's hair drenched with sweat, against the convict's boy-self of yesteryear, when his wet hair had earned him punishment for playing in the creek. Poems 4, 5, and 6 are all "Night" poems. They move the sequence through the narrator's insomnia-wracked night towards the concluding Poem 7, "Dawn," which on this execution morning will come "Like a blast of buckshot through / A stained-glass window." The sense of guilt implicit in this image spills over into a prayer—"Forgive us, this day, our joy"—which is then modified to reflect the *need* for joy caused by the burden of terrible knowledge: "Forgive us—oh, give us!—our joy."

The other sequence, titled "Internal Injuries," begins in Poem 1, "The Event," with one of the world's victims—old, black, poor, female, alone, and just fired from her job—who is further victimized, mortally, in a car accident. A reluctant but intimate witness to the event, the narrator watches from a taxi that is stuck in the traffic jam caused by the accident. From this proximity the woman's scream in Poem 2, "The Scream," is loud enough to make the pneumatic hammers working nearby seem, "In the period / Of non-scream, . . . merely a part of the silence." Surrealistically, the scream grows in Poem 4, "The Only Trouble," to resemble a "Soap bubble, it is enormous, it glitters / Above the city," until it "Explodes, and over the city a bright mist / Descends of—microscopically—spit." But unlike the scream of Jack Burden's mother that gave Jack a new birth into reality at the end of *All the King's Men*, this death-scream produces resistance to passage. The police ignore it, "doing their duty"; "The three construction workers are looking at you like a technical / Problem"; and the narrator also draws back: "How long since last I heard birdsong in the flowery hedgerows of France?" The woman herself undergoes a reverse passage in the narrator's mind, which associates the zinnia-colored helmets of the construction workers with her girl-self long past: "When you were a child in Georgia, a lard-can of zinnias bloomed by the little cabin door. / Your mother had planted them in the lard-can." Symbolizing this retreat from too much knowledge is the jet plane that, passing over at the moment of the accident, is now "so far off that there is no sound"; it carries people safely distant from and ignorant of the microscopic drama down below in the city streets.

But one thing thwarts this withdrawal of attention. Singling him out from the onlookers, the woman stares the narrator straight in the eye and thus impales his identity like "a piece of white paper filed for eternity on the sharp point of a filing spindle." Now there is no escaping the world's stew, and the familiar cry of passage—"Oh, reality!" (a cry that appears in "Stargazing" in *Tale of Time* and elsewhere)—begins our narrator's final frantic spasms of resistance. His first panicked act is to beg the woman to "Be Something Else," as the title of Poem 6 pleads, so that he can go on practicing a total acceptance of reality and even harboring love for it—which is becoming very difficult in the presence of her screaming:

> oh!
> We love you, we truly
> Do, and we love the
>
> World, but . . .
> For God's sake stop that yelling!

Since, however, the woman cannot "Be something else, . . . something / That is not what it is," the narrator scrabbles to the next best escape from the reality before him: a change in *his* condition, or identity, to something or someone free of this knowledge that has been forced upon him. Poem 7, "The World Is A Parable," thus shows the narrator recoiling from passage into reality with every scrap of sail hoisted for his getaway:

> I must hurry, I must go somewhere
> Where you are not, where you
> Will never be, I
> Must go somewhere where
> Nothing is real. . . .

The poem's title metaphor—"The world / Is a parable and we are / The meaning"—may be seen as part of this flight reflex, for though the statement may be true, the larger truth of the moment is that the dying woman is not a parable at all, but rather palpable flesh. Luckily for the speaker, the traffic jam untangles—a movement he hoarsely encourages: "Oh, driver! / For God's sake catch that light. . . ." The poem ends with the speaker rationalizing his flight reflex: "There comes a time for us all when we want to begin a new life./ All mythologies recognize that fact."

Poem 8, "Driver, Driver," concludes the "Internal Injuries" sequence with the speaker still seeking escape by ordering the driver to "change the address, I want to go to / A place where nothing is the same." But it is already too late. There is no disgorging of the poisonous fruit of knowledge; once it is eaten, the Fall is irreversible. So now the speaker's "guts are full of chyme and chyle, of Time and bile, my head / Of visions." These visions, drawing upon what he has just seen, add a new if unwanted focus to his title theme of incarnations by fixing upon

> All those fat slick slimy things that
> Are so like a tub full of those things you
> Would find in a vat in the back room of a butcher shop, but
> > wouldn't eat, but
>
> Are not that, for they are you.

This is about as far as the speaker's passage into knowledge of reality can go. The poem and the sequence ends with the speaker not knowing "what flesh is" or if it is, "as some people say, really sacred"; but there is a good chance that the answers may (regrettably) be soon forthcoming. The poem's last line notes "an awful glitter in the air" and asks for the weather forecast. Snow—an archetypal image of death—is pending.

OR ELSE

In the same vein, whiteness has served as an image of the final stage of passage into annihilation, timelessness, and solipsism in Warren's recent poetry. *Incarnations* itself ends with "Fog," whose "Blank mufflement of white" presses through the nostrils and into the guts until "an eye / Screams in the belly." The eye screams because it "Sees the substance of body dissolving," and so "The body's brags are put / To sleep—all, all." In *Audubon:*

A Vision, "snow thatches . . . with white, like wisdom," the heads of the three hanging victims who stiffen on their ropes "As wind lifts its burden." And in his more recent volume, *Or Else,* the image recurs with memorable effect. The speaker in "Reading Late at Night, Thermometer Falling" recalls the death of his father, suddenly deceased ("So disappeared. / Simply not there"), and feels time's movement creep down the "green valley at a gla- cier's / Massive pace" until the great ice-mass is now at hand, containing his own death like a frozen Frankenstein monster about to be loosened:

> And there it is.
> It looms.
>
> The bulk of the unnamable and de-timed beast is now visible,
> Erect, in the thinly glimmering shadow of ice.

From this chilling prevision the poem shrinks back into the relative comfort of reading late at night, thermometer falling, but the comfort seems foreshortened now: "The mercury falls. Tonight snow is predicted. This, / However, is another country."

Snow provides the setting for a similar trauma of passage in "Time As Hypnosis," Poem III of *Or Else.* Here Warren's twelve- year-old persona, wandering in the first snow to have fallen in several years, finds some tracks of a field mouse that abruptly vanish:

> I saw the tracks. But suddenly, none. Nothing
> But the wing-flurried snow. Then, small as a pin-head, the single
> Bright-frozen, red bead of a blood-drop. Have you ever
> Stared into the owl's eyes? They blink slow, then burn. . . .

Looking back, the boy sees his own tracks advancing like those of the mouse, while "Ahead, / Was the blankness of white," the snow a "glittering metaphor / For which I could find no referent." The point at which the tracks end, or where absorption into the blankness of white occurs, must therefore stand for the last stage of passage in this and Warren's other eschatological poems. And this is, again, about as far as the poetry of passage can go.

The symbolism of winter, however, is not the only motif of

passage threading through Warren's tenth volume. In *Or Else*, as in all the earlier volumes, the fall season weighs in once again with its archetypal cargo of losses. The book's first poem, "The Nature of a Mirror" ("Time / Is the mirror into which you stare"), gives us a narrator who looks at the sky with "murder in the heart" because of the "murder in the eye" that the sky bears towards him. The sky's eye is the sun of autumn ("The solstice of summer has sagged") which sinks, "redder than / A mother's rage," and in setting makes the whole landscape look monstrously carnivorous, silhouetting a "western ridge of black-burnt pine stubs like / A snaggery of rotten shark teeth." Similar images of fall, or the Fall, permeate the seven poems from "Notes on a Life to Be Lived" that Warren republished in *Or Else* from the *Tale of Time* collection: "cold . . . sweat on my father's mouth, dead" in "Blow, West Wind"; a dying landscape where "the heel of the sun's foot smites horridly" in "Chain Saw at Dawn in Vermont in Time of Drouth"; a child's cry coming from the house in "Small White House"; a reversion to the fetal state ("our blind eyes with / no lashes yet, unbrined by grief") in "Vision Under the October Mountain: A Love Poem"; fear of the universe ("and the fall comes on") in "Stargazing"; precarious prelapsarian innocence ("The mountains lean. They watch. They know.") in "Little Boy and Lost Shoe"; and a little girl weeping over her cat's killing of a chipmunk in "Composition in Gold and Red-Gold."

Or Else concludes with the final prospect of passage, death, presented in a fine bit of understatement as "A Problem in Spatial Composition." Part 1 of the poem gathers some archetypal metaphors in a sort of verbal painting. Framed by the window, the "Composition" features a beautiful sunset over the darkening forest: "Sun now down, flame, above blue, dies upward forever in / Saffron." Giving upon such a sky, "pure, pure, and forever . . . / Upward," the window frame bespeaks man's limited vision of the whole, while below the window a brook (its running water a recurrent image of time) "utters a deeper-toned meditation" as darkness gathers. Part 2 completes the landscape painting with "the stub / Of a great tree, gaunt-blasted and black" that "Stabs, black, at the infinite saffron of sky." Now that "All is ready," a hawk enters the "composition," glides past the "upper left frame /

Of the window," and perches on the black bough. Part 3, the poem's conclusion, consists of seven words: "The hawk, in an eyeblink, is gone."

Since this is the concluding line of Warren's recent book, a word about his bird metaphors may be in order. As far back as "Picnic Remembered" (in *Eleven Poems on the Same Theme*) Warren had compared the soul to a hawk riding the sunset; and even before that, in *Kentucky Mountain Farm*, he had used a "sunset hawk" to represent a longed-for synthesizing vision. In all his volumes of verse bird-against-the-sunset imagery has served as Warren's "Man Against the Sky" motif, with much the same import as in Edwin Arlington Robinson's masterpiece. Speaking of Coleridge's imagery in *The Ancient Mariner*, Warren defended such cumulative power of the recurrent image: "My reasoning is this: Once the import of an image is established for our minds, that image cannot in its workings upon us elsewhere in the poem be disencumbered, whether or not we are consciously defining it." [14] It would seem reasonable, then, to see "A Problem in Spatial Composition" as another eschatological poem, ending in an implicit question concerning the soul or hawk that, "in an eyeblink, is gone": gone where? "What we know, we know," the speaker says; but as always in the psychology of passage, the initiate's knowledge is both too much and too little. Looking into the depths of evening, the speaker sees more than he wishes to see of spatial infinity, unframed and unframable by any act of imagination, thus confirming "what the heart knows: *beyond* is *forever*." This book that began with the menace of time represented in an autumnal sunset thus concludes with a similar impression of space as the burden of postlapsarian knowledge, its "problem in Spatial Composition" being rationally unsolvable.

Besides Warren's own persona, several other characters undergo the trauma of passage in *Or Else*. "Rattlesnake Country" projects several of these in the persons of the Indian youth Laughing Boy, who began by burning rattlesnakes alive and ended up in the pen for murder, and of some of the speaker's fellow guests at the resort: two of the girls, then young, who "after their pain and delusions, worthy endeavors and lies," are now dead; a third girl who "Committed her first adultery the next year"; and this woman's husband, who "Would, by this time, be totally cynical" if still alive. There is, in addition, the pathetic subject of "News Photo," a man acquitted (dubiously) of the charge of murdering an Episcopal minister active in the local civil rights movement. After heroically blasting this "Communist" to death, "he / is not happy. Nothing / is like he had expected"; and his wife has attained that absolute stage of passage wherein "she hates the world." At the end of the poem, black humor—that condition "beyond tragedy"—takes over as the statue of Robert E. Lee "shakes all over with laughing. . . . But / there are tears in his eyes." Something similar to this death of innocence, but on a nation-wide scale, makes up the subject of "Interjection # 4: Bad Year, Bad War: A New Year's Card, 1969," a poem that takes as its headnote John Brown's favorite verse of scripture: "and without shedding of blood there is no remission [of sin]." One of the better antiwar poems to come out of that agonizing period, this piece looks at America's lost innocence with a scathing sarcasm that culminates in the poem's closing mockery of its headnote: "Dear God, we pray / To be restored to that purity of heart / That sanctifies the shedding of blood."

The most important figures of passage in *Or Else* besides Warren's persona would be the two novelists in the realist-naturalistic mode, Flaubert and Dreiser. "Flaubert in Egypt" shows the great French stylist steeped in the grubby sexuality of the Middle East. But despite bouts with venereal disease, he could still elicit some beauty from his sojourn in that ancient center of civilizations. Not so Dreiser, who in "Homage to Dreiser" describes beauty only in the song about the Wabash for which he helped to write the lyrics and his brother Paul composed the musical score. On the whole, because of his upbringing in grinding poverty, his lumpish bad looks, and his pathological discontent, this American writer is a fine representative of the trauma of passage inherent in the naturalistic view of life: "Full of screaming his soul is. . . ." Despite his compulsive masturbation and fornication whenever opportunity offered, he "knows that no kiss heals his soul, it is always the same." An offshoot of Warren's lengthy study of Dreiser published a few years ago, this poem shows Dreiser vainly seeking relief from his "self-contemplative distress" in gluttonous recourse to food and sex. But the knowledge of pain is finally all that is real, as William

James affirmed was true of "every merely positivistic, agnostic, or naturalistic scheme of philosophy." In his chapter of *The Varieties of Religious Experience* called "The Sick Soul," James commented that "the purely naturalistic look at life . . . is sure to end in sadness. . . . Let sanguine healthy-mindedness do its best with its strange power of living in the moment and ignoring and forgetting, still . . . the skull will grin in at the banquet." [15]

Dreiser, then, in this book of poems that appeared in 1974 represents the stage of passage into a ruined, naturalistic world that Warren himself had depicted back in his earliest volume, *Thirty-six Poems* (1935). Consequently, this repulsive man elicits the poet's serious empathy, despite his "filth of self"—his "lies, masturbation, vainglory, and shame." Even the internal schism typical of passage befalls Dreiser, whose "only gift is to enact," in his life of moral turpitude, "All that his deepest self abhors." This sense of his own unworthiness paralleling the outer world's ruins was finally irremediable: "Sometimes he wept for the general human condition," but "Nothing could help nothing, not reading Veblen or even Freud. . . ." And at last for Dreiser the only hope reposed in the paradox of finding "The secret worth / Of all our human worthlessness."

CAN I SEE ARCTURUS FROM WHERE I STAND? POEMS 1975

In his *Selected Poems, 1923–1975*, Warren included a previously uncollected cluster of poems, "Can I See Arcturus from Where I Stand?" Here we find the themes of his earlier volumes extended, modified, or otherwise "made new" through strikingly novel achievements in imagery, tone, and form. Concerning the theme of passage, the main event of these poems is a return to his motif of the bifurcated self—the unified prelapsarian psyche having been split, after the trauma of passage, between the fallen self in a ruined world and an alter ego or anima disappearing toward a higher realm of being. It was some forty years ago, in *Thirty-six Poems* (1935) and the first few of the *Eleven Poems on the Same Theme*, when Warren last addressed this subject so intensively. In these recent poems he extends the motif to what one must suppose is an ultimate level of intensity. There is also increasing use of the pronoun "you" to refer to the fallen self. (This "you" is sharply distinguished from the "you" of Warren's middle period, the 1940s and 1950s, when it referred to an idealized self-image.)

Recurrently in the "Arcturus" sequence the fallen self is defined by typically lapsarian responses: dread of the world, a solipsistic sense of isolation, insomnia. Dread of the world emanates particularly from Warren's images of death—death that applies to man, beast, and even inanimate earth. Death's kingdom in "A Way to Love God" thus embraces your father (whose "death rattle / Provides all biographical data required for the *Who's Who* of the dead"), Mary, Queen of Scots (whose lips, of her severed head, "kept on moving, / But without sound"), the herd of sheep in the white night-mist (whose eyes "Stared into nothingness. . . . Their jaws did not move"), and even the mountains, which in daylight serenely accept their gradual erosion ("not going anywhere except in slow disintegration") but which at night "moan in their sleep." Perhaps the focal image for this theme is that of "Season Opens on Wild Boar in Chianti," where—in the familiar autumnal setting ("Gold light of October")—the newly slaughtered creature hangs on its pole like a death's head in the dark: "the great head swings weighty and thoughtful / While eyes blank in wisdom stare hard." As the poem ends the speaker shuts his door to too much knowledge: "And we bolt up our doors, thus redeeming / From darkness, our ignorant dreaming."

Solipsistic isolation likewise afflicts our victim of passage. In "Midnight Outcry" the husband who hears his wife cry out in her sleep finds that nothing in her daytime life—her "sunlit smile," her "Endearment and protest," her tenderness toward "the infant to whom she gives suck"—can assuage his separation from that part of her being which cried out, something "Much deeper and darker than anything love can redeem." A similar attenuation or loss of relationships is indicated in the speaker's references to various vanished girl friends: one who had slept with him after praying that he be happy, one he had chased down the beach without catching her, one who had shared with him an unforgettable evening of dancing.

Separation from nature is also a burden, implicit in "A Way to Love God" and explicit in "Brotherhood in Pain." In the former poem a resemblance to Wordsworth's sonnet "The World Is Too Much With Us" is evident in the juxtaposition of nature's quiet splendor with the frenzy of human affairs (the sound texture, and notably the shift from *v* to *b / p* labials, nicely reinforces this contrast):

> [I urge you to think on] stars, silver, silver, while the silence
> Blows like wind by, and on the sea's virgin bosom unveiled
> To give suck to the wavering serpent of the moon; and,
> In the distance, in *plaza, piazza, place, platz,* and square,
> Boot heels, like history being born, on cobbles bang.

In "Brotherhood in Pain" the natural object—dead leaf, hunk of chewing gum, discarded sock, or brookside stone—has the advantage over its human spectator of belonging to a larger matrix of being from which the human feels separated. So the object, though removed from its original environment, "pityingly knows that you are more lonely than it is." The human's irremediable separation from *his* environment is occasioned by his lapse into self-consciousness, an event that correlates closely with his acquisition of language. The child-self's "original relationship with nature" (as Emerson put it) thus dwindles until "You exist only in the delirious illusion of language."

Even at his luckiest, in "Answer to Prayer," the fallen persona finds only "the savvy insanity and wit / of history" in the wealth and success that have apparently resulted from his girl friend's prayer "just for you to be happy." As against his subsequent period of "Lights flashing, fruit spinning, the machine spurting dollars like dirt— / . . . all just a metaphor for the luck I now had," he now yearns back toward that time when, by being with her, he was already as happy as he would ever be. In the perversity of destiny, which "Has the shape of a joke—if you find the heart to laugh at it," their tender love relationship has long since faded into a heart-wrenching memory of certain details: of the girl, "cocking her head to one side" with "an impudent eye-sparkling grin"; of the two of them moving "with hands again nakedly clasped, through the soft veil and swish / Of flakes falling, . . . / To the unlit room." Hence, the poem's regretful subtitle, "A Short Story That Could Be Longer," and hence also the rueful and belated insight: "In such a world, then, one must be pretty careful how one prays."

Perhaps the vintage lapsarian poem of the "Arcturus" sequence is "Loss, of Perhaps Love, in Our World of Contingency." Here the lost object in the first stanza—"Think! Think hard. Try to remember / When you last had it"—is the former child-self's love of the world (thus the "Loss, of Perhaps Love" in the poem's title). The pre- and postlapsarian phases of identity are figured, respectively, in "The earliest thing you remember, the dapple / Of sunlight on the bathroom floor while your mother bathed you," and in the adult image of yourself ("under no circumstances look / In the mirror") as an old bum:

> . . . the night wind
> Shuffles a torn newspaper down the street with a sound
> Like an old bum's old shoe-soles that he makes
> Slide on the pavement to keep them from flopping off.

Whether one traces one's life backward from this bum-like present condition or forward from that child-self's paradise, one cannot retrieve that lost love of the world, vanished like "Violets, / Buried now under dead leaves (later snowdrifts)." The best the postlapsarian man can do is to accommodate himself to his new knowledge, the "new electric tang of joy—or pain—like ammonia" after the thunder. In closing, the poem states starkly the paramount problem facing the victim of passage: "We must learn to live in the world."

As against these motifs of a fallen self trapped in a ruined world, Warren's recent verse establishes in contrapuntal fashion a vision of the lost anima hearkening toward a better, or in any case ultimate, realm of being. In the "Arcturus" sequence, the anima figure is primarily the bird in "Evening Hawk" and secondarily the vanished girl in "Paradox," while the realm of higher—or deeper—being is imaged primarily in the stars (including Arcturus) and secondarily in references to Plato.

The Platonic element of Warren's vision is announced in the first line of the first poem of the "Arcturus" sequence: "Here is the shadow of truth, for only the shadow is true." The idea that this world is a mere shadow of some more perfect realm is enlarged upon in the second poem, "Evening Hawk," where the bird ascending into sunset resembles the similar anima figure of "Picnic Remembered." In that earlier poem (in *Eleven Poems on the Same Theme*), the soul was explicitly compared to "a hawk . . . [that] fled on glimmering wings" from the darkening world below; in "Evening Hawk" the comparison is implicit between the vanished prelapsarian self and the bird that, "climbing the last light," simply leaves, "unforgiving, the world [that], unforgiven, swings / Into shadow." Like the unfallen anima self, the bird "knows neither Time nor error" as it flees the ruined world below for some higher sphere that is represented here by the conjunction of star and Plato: "The star / Is steady, like Plato, over the mountain." For the fallen persona the inaccessibility of that Platonic realm of being is underscored in the poem's closing lines, where the speaker can almost hear "The earth grind on its axis, or history / Drip in darkness like a leaking pipe in the cellar."

"Paradox," which refers to Zeno's paradox of Achilles chasing but never catching the hare, appears to cast the anima figure in its more familiar Jungian embodiment of a woman. Though the poem may read perfectly well as a love story, it is also quite plausible that this beauteous but unattainable lady refers—as in Jung's formulation—to a lost, idealized image of self such as existed before the trauma of passage caused the psyche's bifurcation. Seen in this light, the girl whose "smile . . . mocks / Pursuit down . . . / Our flickering passage through the years" might be a correlative to T. S. Eliot's similar females, from (quite possibly) Prufrock's unattainable lady to the Hyacinth Girl and the intercessory Lady of the *Four Quartets*.

As we approach the final "Arcturus" poem, "Old Nigger on One-Mule Cart Encountered Late at Night When Driving Home from Party in the Back Country," the predominant impression left by the previous poems is of an unbridgeable schism separating the fallen self from its vanished anima and this ruined world from an unreachable Platonic sphere of being. The only existing connection seems to be mainly through pain, as in "Loss, of Perhaps Love, in Our World of Contingency," where "your heart bleeds far / Beyond the outermost pulsar." Similarly, in "Brotherhood in Pain" the object torn from its matrix "Bleeds profusely. . . . Its experience / Is too terrible to recount." Perhaps the best image of the schism is the juxtaposition of boar's head and stars in "Season Opens on Wild Boar in Chianti," the "great head swinging down, tusks star-gleaming. / The constellations are steady."

In "Old Nigger on One-Mule Cart" Warren attempts to reconcile his contraries. He does so through the figure of the "Nigger," an impolite term but one which Warren justifies by making this old fellow a secret sharer and a man who has learned how to live in the world. Like Warren's other old people—and unlike the persona who enjoyed wealth and success in "Answer to Prayer," the Old Nigger has attained perfect acceptance of both his own lapsarian self and his place in a ruined world. The poem's speaker, whose rejection of his lapsarian life is indicated by his insomnia and his hearkening after the lost child-self ("Recollection of childhood brings tears / To the dark-wide eyes"), now sees the Old Nigger as a figure of wisdom, much as Wordsworth saw his beggars, hermits, and leech-gatherers. The Nigger with his cargo of junk is not torn from his matrix, nor is he out of sorts with a fallen world: "his face / Is lifted into starlight, calm as prayer." Through sharing identity with this "Brother, . . . Philosopher past all / Casuistry," the speaker attains a perspective that will enable him to "arrive and leave my own cart of junk" peacefully enough, in "the world's monstrous blessedness," when his time comes to enter the Nigger's shack and lie down in darkness.

"Entering into that darkness to fumble / My way to a place to lie down," he may now regard the record of the life he had lived (corresponding to the Nigger's cart of junk) as something worthwhile: "a name— / Like a shell, a dry flower, a worn stone, a toy— merely / A hard-won something" that is his "trophy of truth" from having lived. For a victim of passage, this transmutation of one's life into truth, on however modest a scale, is about the best that can be hoped for. Its implicit acceptance of things at least opens the possibility of a larger reconciliation in the closing line of this poem sequence: "Can I see Arcturus from where I stand?" "Old Nigger on One-Mule Cart" thus terminates the "Arcturus" poems with a twofold consolation for the speaker's lapsarian losses: though he may never recover the vanished anima of yesteryear, it is possible to find some worth in the life that remains in the fallen world; and though he may never attain the Platonic realm of being, he may at least be able to see Arcturus from where he stands.

RECENT POEMS (1976–1977)

Now settling into his seventies, Robert Penn Warren shows not the slightest sign of any flagging in his creative energy. What he calls "spasms" of poems have been coming on to such an extent that a new collection is shaping up for late 1977 or early 1978, even while the ink has barely had time to dry in his *Selected Poems, 1923–1975*. Out of his seemingly bottomless well of creativity, the poet fetches forth in recent poems a continuing flow of images, characters, incidents, and verbal craftsmanship having a power and significance equal to any period in his career. Without sharing the bias or neglect that has caused some readers to underrate Warren's earlier verse, we may yet understand why a number of reviewers have referred to his recent poetry as his best.

These latest poems, like his "Arcturus" series, contain a great deal of lapsarian material. Whether by coincidence or by design, their chronological order of appearance, generally speaking, also enhances the theme of passage. "Youth Stares at Minoan Sunset," the first of our recent selections (in the *New York Review of Books* for September 30, 1976), renders its theme of passage through the juxtaposition of a prelapsarian youth watching the sunset, with a postlapsarian speaker watching the youth. The appalling speed of Time, implicit in the title's reference to a lost civilization, is made explicit in the image of the youth silhouetted against the setting sun like a figure on a coin or vase of Minoan antiquity:

> . . . one instant, one only,
> The great coin, flame-massy and with
> The frail human figure minted black thereon,
> Balances: Suddenly is gone. A gull
> Impairs at last the emptiness of air.

To the youth's parents (evidently the speaker is one), the child immersed in the sunset appears to enjoy a Wordsworthian "knowledge we do not yet have. Or have forgotten." But as the poem concludes, they know that a different, lapsarian knowledge awaits him: "He is so young."

"American Portrait: Old Style" (published in the August 23,

1976 *New Yorker*) juxtaposes the pre- and postlapsarian identities
that pertain to the same individual. The victim of passage in this
instance is the childhood friend whom the speaker visits after a
sixty-year time span, to find that the trickery of time has reduced
the friend's extraordinary gifts to nothing. Originally, "the best
shot in ten counties," and a lad who "could call any bird note back,"
the friend

> Seemed never to walk but to float,
> With a singular joy and silence,
> In his cloud of bird dogs like angels,
> With their eyes on his eyes like God,
> And the sun on his uncut hair bright. . . .

But then of course the fall came, that lapse into the world of Time
which makes a day from one's prefallen life seem "forever / In
memory's shiningness," whereas one's fallen persona now finds "a
year but a gust or a gasp." The friend's subsequent career in the
Big Leagues thus showed merely "How the teeth in Time's jaw
all snag backward / And whatever enters therein / Has less hope
of remission than shark-meat." Career cut off by his drinking, the
friend's pitching arm and shoulders are now "thinning toward old-
man thin," while that "nameless old skull in the swamp" which they
had found as boys now acquires an increasingly personal significance. As though to practice for eternity, the speaker converts the
trench where they had played soldier in prelapsarian days (now "a
stopped-up ditch full of late-season weed-growth") into his imagi-
nary grave, where he lies deadlike. A representative poem of passage in its seasonal setting (with "late summer's thinned-out sky"),
"American Portrait: Old Style" concludes with a typical emotional
tangle. Resisting his implied death wish (which he underscores by
shifting from past to present tense for the grave scene), the speaker
rises—"I am not dead yet"—to affirm that "I love the world even
in my anger." Perhaps he does. The poem, however, clearly displays
the grounds for his anger more than it does any grounds for love of
the world, and thus it exemplifies our poems of passage psychology.
    "Sister Water," recalling Saint Francis' praise of Sister Water
in Canticle of the Sun, is a poem of passage by virtue of its
imagery of the speaker's solipsism, one of Warren's basic lapsarian

themes. The poem's first lines make mockery of an antidote to solipsism, the "Tell me a story" motif that in other poems (such as *Audubon*) serves as a figure for human connections. After breaking off the "story," the narrator similarly locks himself in against the "old man's / Dragging step" that approaches his door, for fear "he might call me by my name." At the center of the poem is a sexual communion faded now into a memory "stirring your heart to tears. . . . [Is] there a *now* or a *then?*" These images of night and loneliness yield at last, for our insomniac *isolato*, to the dawn light that "defines the bars of your window"—a culminant image of solitary confinement. Alienation from God next haunts the speaker, who "cannot pray" though he wants to believe God "loves us all" and "will not / Let all distinction perish." (This wish is evoked by "the cough and mastication of / The garbage truck in the next block" which does, chillingly, make all distinction perish.) Finally, for our isolated persona, there remains only one connection, that implied in the title "Sister Water." It is a connection with, or even baptism in, natural reality: "You can wash your face in cold water."

"Waiting" (published in the December, 1976 *Atlantic Monthly*) suggests in its title what the only recourse of the fallen soul (here called "you") may be: lifelong endurance. So you sustain insomnia ("dark curdles toward dawn"), the ironies of nature ("Drouth breaks, too late to save the corn, / But not too late for flood"), dread of death ("The doctor enters the waiting room, and / His expression betrays all"), dearth of love ("The woman you have lived with all the years / Says . . . she / Had never loved you"), and loss of religious faith (when "You realize, truly, that our Saviour died for us all" you "burst out laughing, / For the joke is certainly on Him, considering / What we are"). If you can outlast it all, a modest reward awaits you: the knowledge that, even in a ruined world, "common men have done good deeds" and "that, at least, God / Has allowed us the grandeur of certain utterances."

Those grand utterances do not, however, appear to include the great national documents that promulgated the American republic. In "Bicentennial" (published in *Esquire*, December, 1976) a sort of national trauma of passage is implied in the lapse from the Founding Fathers' vision to this portrayal of a decrepit society. Parts 1 and 2 establish the poem's central tactic of shifting abruptly from city-

scape to countryside, with irony directed in surprisingly equal proportions at both. Given Warren's previous rendering of New York
City, we might have expected this opening picture of the metropolis
as a stinking cesspool of noise, sticky heat, congested traffic, and
air pollution, driving everyone out to "his own version of / Walden
Pond . . . / and the font of pure American individualism" on this
Fourth of July weekend. That the great open continent shares this
degeneration is evident in Part 2, where the shepherd signifies the
Warren persona's role as a pastoral poet in fleeting and ironic
fashion. There on Mount Bitterroot (a symbolic name, we might
suppose) the shepherd performs two of Warren's recurrent rites of
passage: "He is trying to recall his childhood," that period before
"his eye got knocked out"; and, from the mountain that "totters in
darkness," he "is staring out of his good eye" at a familiar anima
figure fleeing the shepherd's darkening world below: "the eagle
climbs into the / Invisibility of sky."

To this mood the remainder of the poem conforms perfectly,
interweaving various characters and scenes from across the land
into a collage bespeaking squalor, pathos, and despair. In what looks
suspiciously like a travesty of Whitman, Warren catalogues his
American bicentennial portraits: a middle-aged suburbanite ravishes
his baby-sitter (his sexually starved wife will trim her weight and
seek a lover); a wealthy businessman, after closing his son ("a
prick") and his daughter ("a cunt") out of his will, kills his can-
cerous wife and commits suicide; a fat woman (whose buttocks
"look like two shoats wrasslin' under a rug") waddles through
Yellowstone Park; a Jewish liquor store owner is shot dead during
a holdup; a black youth in the Bronx lies dead of an overdose; a
white youth, winner of a National Merit Scholarship to Harvard,
cannot bear the sight of his widowed mother's hands (it "ties his
guts into . . . a knot of outrage and guilt"); the squalid moss
pickers in a Louisiana swamp get drunk, couple promiscuously, and
ply their trade with "hands . . . like crooked and horny claws"
in a sweltering night-heat alive with moccasins and mosquitoes. At
the end of the poem our persona returns, burdened with insomnia
by his vision, to observe that the Founding Fathers who guaranteed
our pursuit of happiness neglected to tell us what happiness is: "It
all seems a matter of luck." Though they "stood and set us free

from tyranny," they "did not get around to setting us free from ourselves."

As though in revulsion against these images of life in a fallen or ruined world, Warren's "Three Poems in Time" (to appear later in 1977 in the *Atlantic*) evoke with mounting emotional intensity the figure of the escaping anima. Poem I, "Heart of Autumn," casts that vanished part of the psyche in the form of geese fleeing the human spectator's cold gray fall: "How tirelessly *V* upon *V* arrows the season's logic." His dream is to join them, "my face now lifted skyward, / Hearing the high beat, my arms outstretched," until he can feel "tough legs, / With folded feet, trail in the sounding vacuum of passage" while sailing "toward sunset, at a great height." In Poem II, "Dream," the loss of the anima leaves the fallen self to live with only dream and memory, two at least potential sources of meaning. But to get that meaning you must "grapple your dream!" —like Jacob wrestling the angel through the night or Odysseus grappling with Ajax. "Yes, grapple," or else, upon waking, the persona will be "a ghost without history even," trapped in a "desert trackless in sun-glare." But what Poem II gives, Poem III—"Ah, Anima!"—takes away. Here, in a storm-ridden disaster area that serves as "a metaphor for your soul . . . in the hurricane of Time," you find that "sleep / Is a disaster area, too," for after lying down "On shards of Time and in uproar of the wind of Being," you will wake in the dark and listen as "the stream / Gnashes its teeth with the *klang* of boulders." So the fallen self, totally without resource now, resorts in the end to the same fantasy as ended Poem I, that of flying away with the anima self and leaving the vacant earthly self behind:

You may wish that you, even in the old wrack and pelt of gray light,
Had run forth, screaming as wind snatched your breath away
Until you were nameless—oh, anima!— . . .
. . . . to leave
The husk behind, and leap into the
Blind and antiseptic anger of air.

With this image of the fallen self yearning after its lost anima, our study of Warren's poetry of passage ends. Although this important ground theme diminishes somewhat in Warren's poetry since *Incarnations* (1968), it nonetheless runs through the bulk of his poems, even after the "conversion" evidenced in the mid-1940s. The reason for this persistence, even after the "Conversion" and "Mysticism" poems have entered the record, is explained again by recourse to William James, who observed in his chapter on "The Sick Soul" that "When disillusionment has gone as far as this [citing Tolstoy's suicidal despair], there is seldom a *restitutio ad integrum*. One has tasted of the fruit of the tree, and the happiness of Eden never comes again. The happiness that comes, when any does come . . . is not the simple ignorance of ill, but something vastly more complex, including natural evil as one of its elements. . . ." Both Bunyan and Tolstoy, James went on to say, "had drunk too deeply of the cup of bitterness ever to forget its taste." [16] Something similar may be inferred about the lifelong persistence of the trauma of passage as a poetic theme of Robert Penn Warren. Interestingly, however, Warren reflects in his poetry the process of psychic healing which James, in "The Divided Self, and the Process of Its Unification," ascribed to Bunyan and Tolstoy: "The fact of interest for us is that as a matter of fact they could and did find *something* welling up in the inner reaches of their consciousness, by which such extreme sadness could be overcome." [17] What that *something* is for Warren has already been indicated in my opening chapter, but for a more thoroughgoing look at it we turn now to the poetry of the undiscovered self, which in turn becomes an avenue to the subsequent poetry of mysticism.

3

The Undiscovered Self

Up to this point, through what we have called Warren's poetry of passage, the configuration of his thought has assumed a pattern similar to that of poets like Wordsworth and Dylan Thomas in their regret over the loss of a prelapsarian self and in their poetic attempts to eulogize the lost self. Warren departs sharply from such companion spirits, however, in his next stage of development, wherein the psyche in its fallen state is at last compelled to cope with its new and terrible sense of reality. This new sense of reality, reaching both outward into the immensity of time and space and inward toward an innate depravity that Warren calls "Original Sin," typically imposes upon the Warren personae identities that they find unacceptable and seek to evade at all costs. Yet it is this mode of identity alone that can remedy the effects of passage on the Warren persona by reconciling the warring parts of the psyche and making possible redemptive mystic perceptions. Extending through *Eleven Poems on the Same Theme* (1942), "The Ballad of Billie Potts" (1943), and *Brother to Dragons* (1953), this psychological metamorphosis occupies the crucial center of Warren's poetic career, producing major changes in form and carrying his theme into that zone of the psyche which C. G. Jung denoted as "The Undiscovered Self." Marking a path that connects the poems of passage with this theme of an undiscovered self are a series of character portraits that we shall study first as a brief prelude.

THE CLEAN AND THE DIRTY

In our poems of passage discussion we remarked that the first consequence of passage into a fallen world is a bifurcation of the self, with the better part receding back toward paradise like the "sunset hawk" escaping the lower darkness in "Picnic Remembered," the doe fleeing the "fanged commotion rude" in "Eidolon," and the *"alter ego"* gone from "That ground once sweetly tenanted" in "Man Coming of Age." As we proceed toward the center of Warren's poetic vision, we find that this vanishing of the prelapsarian self is prologue to a grander obsession in Warren's total canon—namely, the effort to find or construct some sense of identity that may fill what "The Ballad of Billie Potts" calls "the old shell of self," left behind in the fallen world like the cicada's cast-off casing, "thin, ghostly, translucent, light as air." This effort may never reach a satisfactory conclusion, for the experience of the Fall renders such genuine innocence and total wholeness of self irrecoverable. But the craving to recreate that original felicity is one of mankind's deepest obsessions, in Warren's judgment—it motivates the Happy Valley episode in *At Heaven's Gate* and Jack Burden's Great Sleep, Going West, and Back-to-the-Foetus psychology in *All the King's Men*, to mention two rather grotesque fictional examples.

Since the 1940s, when Warren's poetry first began to manifest such characteristics of short fiction as plot and character, this psychological dilemma has evoked narrative and dramatic elements to add to his already well-developed lyric mode of earlier decades. It is particularly through dramatic characterization—monologues, debates, parts of the self in conflict, dialectical confrontations—that Warren has developed his identity-psychology. At the same time he has relied on extended narratives or sequence-arrangements to effect dramatic development in a large number of shorter poems, several medium length ones ("The Ballad of Billie Potts" and *Audubon*), and one book-length masterpiece, *Brother to Dragons*. Among the diverse characters depicted—biblical, classical, legendary, or historical; and those drawn from personal reminiscence or imagination—the two types most important to Warren's identity-psychology are what we may call the Clean and the Dirty.

These two types, whose dialectical opposition provided much of the structure in *All the King's Men*, carry their warfare to the deepest psychological levels in Warren's poetry. Warren's Clean people—those who refuse passage into a polluted and compromised adult environment—range from mild and harmless eremites, victims perhaps of the fundamentalist Protestantism of the poet's native region, to murderous psychopaths like the prophet Elijah in *A Tale of Time* who "screams" in ecstasy at the spectacle of the Dirty people (the prophets of Baal) being butchered. As a poet of reality, Warren naturally tends to side with the Dirty people, partly because their apprehension of the world correlates more largely with the actual state of things, but most importantly because those who accept passage into the world's stew are empowered thereby to proceed to the subsequent stages of spiritual development represented in this discussion by the phrases "The Undiscovered Self" and "Mysticism."

If the poems of passage constitute, collectively, Warren's "Songs of Experience," we might call his small but fine group of poems on the Clean people his "Songs of Innocence"—with the concept of innocence, as we might expect in Warren's work, heavily drenched in irony. For in the "One Life" perspective there is no such thing as innocence, but only the delusion of one's separateness from the filth of the world or, even worse, the delusion that one must rise up and cleanse the fallen world of its putrid corruption. Warren's career as a prose writer began with his portrait of one such world-cleanser, the redoubtable John Brown, whose truth is lyrically still marching on but whose little known cleansing operations before Harper's Ferry included the deliberate slaughter of several whole families in the Kansas-Nebraska territory. Following the John Brown model, the Clean figure rising up in the holy purity of his ideal to rid the world of its putrefaction has been one of Warren's most recurrent fictional types. He appears variously as Percy Munn in *Night Rider*, Adam Stanton in *All the King's Men*, and Jeremiah Beaumont in *World Enough and Time*, to name a few. Those Clean types who eschew violence and withdraw in sanctimony from the world's filth include Hugh Miller (the attorney general) and Ellis Burden ("I have put away foulness") in *All the King's Men*, Seth Parton (the Puritan) in *Band of Angels*, and Thomas Jefferson in *Brother to Dragons*. Both the world-cleansers and those who merely retire from the world's stew into their private righteousness are making a cardinal error that precludes their glimpsing the one life or osmosis of being vision that is Warren's final answer to the quest for identity. After all, anyone might love the world after it has been purified and transformed by the New Creation of religious prophecy or by its modern secular counterpart of political millennialism. But in Warren's opinion such love fails the first requirement of a realistic religious imagination, which is to love the world and its denizens just as they are, brimming with pain, injustice, and corruption.

Both of Warren's Clean types make their appearance at about the beginning of the middle phase of his poetic career in *Eleven Poems on the Same Theme* and the *Mexico Is a Foreign Country* sequence (in *Selected Poems: 1923–1943*); and both types have continued to figure in all of the subsequent volumes. The world-cleansers being the simplest to dispose of, let us consider three men who represent the effort to purge the world of its dirt by enacting their political, Transcendentalist, or religious ideologies. In each instance what Warren objects to is the tendency of every ideology to interpret the world symbolically. When applied to human affairs this tendency has proved exceptionally catastrophic in our age, leading to terrorism, genocide, and military slaughter of unimaginable proportions.

Our exemplary political millennialist appears in the first poem of the "Mexico Is a Foreign Country" sequence, "Butterflies over the Map." "Butterflies" indicates that this is a guerrilla outfit poring over the map in its rural hideout; but the butterflies also represent the shining ideals that motivate the subsequent action and that correspond to reality on about the same scale as the map corresponds to the actual landscape. After the drive down the highway, while "Butterflies dream gyres round the precious flower which is your head," in the name of those transcendent ideals, "you, . . . wrathless, rose, and robed in the pure / Idea smote, and fled," leaving in the aftermath some burning rubble and a funeral scene attended by other insects:

> But when a little child dies in Jalisco,
> They lay the corpse, pink cloth on its face, in the patio,
> And bank it with blossoms, yellow, red, and the Virgin's blue.
> The pink cloth is useful to foil the flies, which are not few.

Our second Clean figure, also "wrathless" and "robed in the pure / Idea," is the Transcendentalist warrior, a Harvard graduate of 1861 who narrates "Harvard '61: Battle Fatigue," one of the "Two Studies in Idealism" in *You, Emperors, and Others*. As a fighter for Right in the Civil War, this young soldier most earnestly "tried to slay without rancor, and often succeeded," "tried to keep the heart pure, though hand took stain." But the "world's stew"— this is the poem where the phrase appears—rises up to spoil the young man's "Touch pitch, be defiled" sanctimony. "I didn't mind dying—it wasn't that at all," the speaker says; "It behooves a man to prove manhood by dying for Right." The problem lies with the Dirty people, and "the way they proceeded / To parody with their own dying that Death which only Right should sustain." In one of Warren's little gems of dramatic narration, the confrontation between Clean and Dirty proves wretchedly untidy in its moral overtones:

> ... At woods-edge we held, and over the stubble they came with
>   bayonet.
>
> He uttered his yell, he was there!—teeth yellow, some missing.
> *Why, he's old as my father*, I thought, finger frozen on trigger.
> I saw the ambeer on his whiskers, heard the old breath hissing.
> The puncture came small on his chest. 'Twas nothing. The stain
>   then got bigger.
>
> And he said: "Why, son, you done done it—I figgered I'd skeered
>   ye."
> Said: "Son, you look puke-pale. Buck up! If it hadn't been you,
> Some other young squirt would a-done it." I stood, and weirdly
> The tumult of battle went soundless, like gesture in dream. . . .

The poem ends with the speaker dead, too, and "glad to be dead" so as to get beyond "life's awful illogic, and the world's stew, / Where people who haven't the right just die, with ghastly impertinence."

Our third Clean man is the prophet Elijah of the "Holy Writ" sequence in *Tale of Time*. In "Elijah on Mount Carmel" we have the ultimate archetypes of Clean and Dirty, the mighty prophet of the True God pitted against the infamous Ahab and Jezebel. Since history—including biblical chronicles—is written by its victors, Warren treats the I Kings account as unreliable and subjects it to his own psychological bias. That bias finds the ethical waters very muddy indeed. Lifted into psychopathic frenzy by the slaughter of the priests of Baal, Elijah runs barefoot, "Screaming in glory / Like / A bursting blood blister," to hunt down Ahab and Jezebel in their palace:

> His thorn-scarred heels and toes with filth horn-scaled
> Spurned now the flint-edge and with blood spurts flailed
> Stone, splashed mud of Jezreel. And he screamed.
> He had seen glory more blood-laced than any he had dreamed.

Elijah's quarry, the Dirty pair, seem appealingly human by contrast, as King Ahab first reverts to a child mentality in seeking Jezebel's comforting—" 'Baby, Baby, / Just hush, now hush, it's all right' "—and then takes refuge in sexual union and in a prayer that reality (God) cease to exist.

A willingness to shed other people's blood for the sake of an idea marks off these world-cleansers from Warren's other Clean people, whom he treats with a gentler irony that sometimes dissolves into empathy. *You, Emperors, and Others* portrays some jewels in this mode, characters who draw piously aloof from the world's foulness. In "So You Agree with What I Say? Well, What Did I Say?" Warren draws a memorable portrait of one such Clean person, a Bible-reading fanatic whose life of poverty and toil embodies an absolute and lonely rectitude:

> Albino-pale, half-blind, his orbit revolved
> Between his Bible and the cobbler's bench,
> With all human complexities resolved
> In that Hope past deprivation, or any heart-wrench.

Returning in the summer dark to his shack and his book and his can of pork and beans, he would pass oblivious to the townspeople who were getting every drop of pleasure they could squeeze from their existence. "He would move past us all"—past the boys playing baseball till "a grounder out of the gloom / Might knock out your teeth," past "the Cobb family admiring their new Chevrolet," past "Sue Cramm in the swing with her date, / Whose hand was already up under her dress, halfway." Usually Warren treats such models of righteousness with sarcasm; but here looking back many years later ("Mr. Moody is dead long back, and some of the boys / Who played in that ball game dead too, by disease or violence"), the narrator sympathizes with the man who may have wasted his life in self-denying otherworldliness. Indeed, God deserves to be replaced by an IBM machine (its rewards being more perfectly calibrated) if He played such a cruel trick: "if God short-changed Mr. Moody, it's time for Him / To give up this godding business, and make way / For somebody else to try, or an IBM."

A victim of the Protestant fundamentalism of the poet's native region, Mr. Moody evokes Warren's sympathy as do few others of his Clean people. More typical is the tone of "Man in the Street," about a "nice young man I happened to meet, / Wearing gray flannel suit, knit tie, and Brooks Brothers shirt down the sunlit street." Although the street is sunlit, the young man recoils in horror—like many poems of passage people—from the realities forcing themselves upon his attention:

> "Why are your eyes as big as saucers—big as saucers?"
> I said to the man in the gray flannel suit.
> And he said: "I see facts I can't refute—
> Winners and losers,
> Pickers and choosers. . . .
> . . . .
> And God's sweet air is like dust on my tongue,
> And a man can't stand such things very long."

With his eyes big as saucers, his "face flour-white as a miller's," and his body shaking "like wind in the willows," the nice young man reacts to seeing "things that can't help but hurt" by projecting Messianic hope of a world superior to this one: " 'And I go to prepare a place for you, / For this location will never do.' " But as we know from Warren's poetry of passage, this location will have to do. As against the otherworldliness usually ascribed to the Savior's promise "to prepare a place for you," Warren uses his headnote to show Jesus' *this*-worldliness according to the Apocrypha ("The Sayings of Jesus"): "*Raise the stone, and there thou shalt find Me, cleave the wood, there am I.*" In his "clean" desire to escape this world, Warren's man in the street further evokes the religious thought of Warren's mentor, William James, who in "Pragmatism and Religion" uses phrasing notably similar to the young man's

"Winners and losers, / Pickers and choosers": "I find myself willing to take the universe to be really dangerous and adventurous, without therefore backing out and crying 'no play.' . . . I am willing that there should be real losses and real losers, and no total preservation of all that is." [1] Unlike his "nice young man," Warren shares James's religious pragmatism.

By contrast with these Clean folk, Warren's portraits of the Dirty more largely engage his fellow-feeling. "Mad Young Aristocrat on Beach" (Poem XIV in *Promises*) subjects its title character to fits of madness, egotism, sexual turpitude, and self-pity in successive stages; yet all is perfectly justified. His madness, on closer look, is an altogether reasonable wish to make the sea be still by mopping it ("Yes, somebody ought to take steps and stop it"); and his egotism about his smile and his looks—"He is young and sun-brown and tall and well formed, and he knows it"—is balanced off by his painful knowledge that his pedigree and good looks will have to be wasted on an American: "he will marry a passport, / And dollars, of course . . . *Mais l'Amerique, merde!* why it's full of Americans there." As for his sexual turpitude, it was justified by his loneliness, and besides, it gave him good reason for self-pity: "So thinks of a whore he once had: she was dull as a sow, / And not once, never once, showed affection. He thinks he will cry. . . ." Warren's preference for the Dirty is not purely ironic or perverse. Like Hawthorne, Warren feels that in a fallen world some merit attaches even to sin, vice, and guilt. Whereas righteousness separates, guilt unifies the human community. To feel guilty towards someone is to have a genuine, if unhappy, relationship with the injured party; and to commit sin is to share a humiliation—an erosion of the ideal self-image—that exempts very few. Unbeknownst to the Clean in their aloofness, a sense of complicity is finally the true cement of the human bond, ultimately binding all creatures into Warren's "mystic Osmosis of Being." In his folly, weakness, and sin, then, the mad young aristocrat is a vicarious figure—one of us, after all: "We should love him because his flesh suffers for you and for me, / As our own flesh should suffer for him, and for all / Who will never . . . be loved for themselves, at innocent nightfall."

Our next Dirty fellow appears in "Two Studies in Idealism" in *You, Emperors, and Others*. The two main figures in the "Idealism" sequence, the Confederate soldier in "Bear Track Plantation: Shortly after Shiloh" and the Harvard graduate of 1861, make up twin exempla of Norman Mailer's "Cannibals and Christians" dichotomy. In Mailer's usage, concocted with reference to the Vietnam war, Cannibals and Christians comprise the two modes of military psychology. Both types go forth to annihilate the enemy by every means available, but whereas the "Christians" (like the Harvard graduate in Warren's poem) do so in the name of Right, Justice, and Necessity, the "Cannibals" deliver lead, bombs, or napalm while taking frank and simple pleasure in their ancient pastime. Warren's Confederate trooper is the Cannibal type whose only complaint is that before dying he failed to kill all the Yankees allotted him by his leaders: "hell, three's all I got, / And he promised me ten, Jeff Davis, the bastard. 'Taint fair."

We end our preliminary look at the Dirty with the poems in "Two Pieces after Suetonius" (*You, Emperors, and Others*). "Tiberius on Capri" tells of the Roman's withdrawal to the famous pleasure island where he lived out the last years of his tyrannical reign, but whereas Suetonius disapproved of the emperor's sexual perversion, Warren does not judge the aging sybarite adversely. As a man of modern temper Warren understands that Tiberius's "Eastern lusts and complex Egyptian fantasies" were a justly sought solace for a mind too much aware of the sovereign Nothing to which even a deified emperor is subject: *"All is nothing, nothing all: / To tired Tiberius soft sang the sea thus. . . ."* So the whores who "titter, yawn, paint lip, grease thigh" really avail nothing, as "darkward he stares in that hour." Some nineteen centuries later, in his characteristic autumn setting, Warren's persona likewise stands on this "goat island" and stares darkward, towards a Europe where "Many were soon to die— / . . . not knowing the reason, in rank / On rank hurled. . . ." And he too protests "the paradox of powers that would grind us like grain, small and dry" by throwing a stone into the sea: "I could do that much, after all."

The other emperor, Domitian, is a pathological case, and hence all the more to Warren's liking: "He was not bad, as emperors go, not really— / Not like Tiberius cruel, or poor Nero silly." So the rabid fits of ill behavior that Suetonius reproved—madness, sexual acrobatics, pulling wings off flies—merely display the underlying humanness that we and Domitian hold in common: "Suppose you were proud of your beauty, but baldness set in? / . . . Wouldn't you, like Domitian, try the classic bed stunt . . . ?" With this reference to *you* ("Let's stop horsing around—it's not Domitian, it's you / We mean") we have a convenient transition to the true subject of all Warren's Dirty portraits. Even so repulsive a sadist as Lilburn Lewis in *Brother to Dragons* evokes for Warren the classical insight that "Nothing human is foreign to me." And it has been a leading purpose at the heart of his poetry to establish that nothing human is foreign to *you* either—*you* being the "Clean" part of the self that comprises every man's consciously contrived identity, combining his social self and what Freud would call the private superego. What Domitian's frenzied antics prove is that "virtue comes hard in face of the assigned clock"; given great enough pressure, such as Domitian's omens of death (" 'Fear the fifth hour' "), *you* might well lapse from the Clean to the Dirty as he did, or perhaps undergo total loss of identity.

So we come to the central subject of Warren's poetry and the most dramatic and original thing in it, to which the poems of passage form but an elaborate prelude. Culminating the motif of the Clean and the Dirty, Warren's long and crucial series of *you* poems forms the arena wherein guilt and innocence stage their epic battle for possession of the psyche—bringing us squarely into the Jungian territory that provides the backdrop for the rest of this chapter. Beginning with *Eleven Poems on the Same Theme* and "The Ballad of Billie Potts" (1942, 1943), and continuing through *Brother to Dragons* (*you* being Thomas Jefferson), *Promises* (especially "Ballad of a Sweet Dream of Peace"), and *You, Emperors, and Others* (notably the "Garland for You" sequence), the *you* poems have been Warren's most obscure and for that reason least appreciated body of verse. But they are certainly his most distinctive and probably his most important poetic works.

THE "YOU" POEMS

In Warren's poems of passage, the trauma of passage typically involves recognition of the fallen world "out there," after a knowledge of naturalistic reality has cast the child-self out of his original worldly paradise and forced him irremediably into the realm of time and death and losses. But unlike such other poets of passage as Wordsworth, Housman, and Dylan Thomas, Warren proceeds beyond the self-consoling stance that normally obtains at this point (Wordsworth's attempts to recapture the child-self, Thomas's to eulogize it, Housman's to savor the irony) to deal with a trauma even greater than that of naturalistic loss and oblivion—namely, the humiliating sense of inward pollution that we might call the psyche's fall from the Clean to the Dirty. Beginning as a peripheral subject in *Thirty-six Poems*, this motif swelled to central importance in Warren's second volume, *Eleven Poems on the Same Theme*, and continued to dominate the poetry of the 1940s and 1950s.

The apparent origin of this theme occurs in one of Warren's earliest poems: "The Return: An Elegy." Here we have a clue the size of a man's hand of some dark guilt that is rising to stain the soul beyond any power of will to stop it. Literally a poem of pasage in that it treats that awful rite of passage, the death of a parent, "The Return" interrupts its outpouring of grief—"the dark and swollen orchid of this sorrow"—with subterranean expressions that harshly contradict the youth's surface mood of bereavement: "the old bitch is dead / what have I said! . . . *the old fox is dead / what have I said. . . . the old fox is dead / what is said is said.*" Other poems from Warren's first volume, such as "Cold Colloquy" and "Letter of a Mother," likewise indicate a tragic estrangement between mother and son that might later contribute to the theme of psychic defilement. And in "Revelation," one of the *Eleven Poems*, the son's intense guilt towards his mother is expressible only in what John Ruskin would have to consider stupendous examples of the pathetic fallacy—though psychologically the imagery might be perfectly justified. "Because he had spoken harshly to his mother," the poem begins, "The day became astonishingly bright":

> By walls, by walks, chrysanthemum and aster,
> All hairy, fat-petalled species, lean, confer,
> And his ears, and heart, should burn at that insidious whisper
> Which concerns him so, he knows; but he cannot make out the
>   words.

The peacock screamed, and his feathered fury made
Legend shake, all day, while the sky ran pale as milk;
That night, all night, the buck rabbit stamped in the moonlit glade,
And the owl's brain glowed like a coal in the grove's combustible
　　dark.

In culling out these images of burning guilt, I of course do not mean
to psychoanalyze the poet or to imply that his theme of psychic
pollution derives mainly from this tormented mother-son relationship. On the contrary, "Revelation" itself ends with the boy learning "Something important above love, and about love's grace" from
this episode—namely, that "In separateness only does love learn definition." But these few fragments do provide a clue to Warren's
larger vision of inner darkness by defining its innateness and uni-
versality.

　　Turning now to the remaining ten of the *Eleven Poems on the
Same Theme*, I should like to observe that Warren has seen fit to
break up their original integrity in the 1944 and 1966 collections
and has distributed them in smaller clusters among the other poems.
On examining these clusters, I think it wise to take the poet's hint
and approach them in their revised format. In the 1966 collection
the initial cluster (appearing last in the book) is a group of four
poems that carry over the theme of passage from the poet's earlier
period: "Love's Parable," "Picnic Remembered," "Bearded Oaks,"
and "Monologue at Midnight." These poems, to which we could
add "Question and Answer" (dropped from the 1966 collection),
accordingly have already been discussed in the poems of passage chapter. But they further show the path to and link up with
the crucial remaining cluster at the heart of the *Eleven Poems*
group: "Crime," "Original Sin: A Short Story," "Pursuit," and
"Terror"—to which we may add "End of Season," a poem that
forms a transition from the passage motif implied in its title to
the new awareness of the undiscovered self.

　　This mention of the master theme of Warren's "middle period"
suggests it is time to define terms. In *The Varieties of Religious Experience* William James praises the "wonderful explorations by . . .
Freud, Mason, Prince, and others, of the subliminal consciousness,"
and calls this discovery of a subconscious mind "the most important
step forward that has occurred in psychology since I have been a

student of that science." In James's opinion, which would later be shared by Carl Gustav Jung but not by Freud, this subconscious zone of the psyche is the source of both divine and demonic propensities, of both mystic insight and pathological depravity: "That region contains every kind of matter: 'seraph and snake' abide there side by side." In its positive, "seraphic" operations the subconscious might be, James thought, the only source of authentic religious experience: "If there be higher powers able to impress us, they may get access to us only through the subliminal door." This was especially likely to be the case, James added, when the conscious zone of the psyche—which Warren endows with the designation "You" —finds its resources completely depleted (as happens at the culmination of the Warren persona's passage experience): "In the extreme of melancholy the self that consciously *is* can do absolutely nothing. It is completely bankrupt and without resource, and no works it can accomplish will avail." [2] A soul in this condition, James felt, was ripe for the experience he called "Conversion."

Freud, in his commitment to reason as the sole avenue to knowledge of reality, categorically dismissed the mystic or "seraphic" possibility as illusion. But he readily accepted the "snake" part of James's "snake and seraph" formulation and regarded the subconscious as mainly a repository of bestial impulses deriving from man's savage origins—impulses still dangerously alive and energetic though repressed under the forms of civilized life. Warren does make some recourse to Freudian psychology, as in the Oedipal connection between Lilburn Lewis and his mother in *Brother to Dragons;* and there is no doubt that the Freudian *id* strongly resembles the shadow self that rises horrifically in Warren's "middle period" to replace the lost child-self of prelapsarian innocence. But as a logical rationalist predisposed to atheism, Freud was much too narrowly dogmatic to satisfy Warren's larger imagination of reality. We must remember that in *The Future of an Illusion* Freud declared not only religion but also philosophy and art to be deadly adversaries of his beloved "science"—a position that even Wallace Stevens, himself a man with atheistic leanings, found deplorable.

So we shall turn for further clarification of Warren's undiscovered self motif to a third explorer of subliminal consciousness,

Carl Gustav Jung, who in fact coined the expression "the Undiscovered Self" to describe one of his fundamental archetypes. But first I must make one point clear: Jungian psychology should not be considered a source for Warren's poetry. Publication dates alone refute that possibility: *Eleven Poems* appeared nearly two decades before Jung's *The Undiscovered Self*, which is our chief source of illumination. Nonetheless, Jung's writings provide a relevant means of clarifying Warren's poetry.

Given this qualification, we may study in *Eleven Poems* the developing Jungian dilemma of a subliminal part of the psyche seeking recognition from a surface ego that wants no part of its polluted *doppelgänger*. In the poems of passage cluster among *Eleven Poems* we find prevalent two conditions that we might consider preliminary to this Jungian crisis. First, the speaker in these poems—"Love's Parable," "Picnic Remembered," "Bearded Oaks," and "Monologue at Midnight"—has passed into such dread knowledge of naturalistic reality as to have attained the state James spoke of when "the self that consciously *is* can do absolutely nothing. It is completely bankrupt and without resource, and no works it can accomplish will avail." In "Love's Parable," for example, the speaker has "seen the fungus eyes / Of misery spore in the night," while "within, the inward sore / Of self . . . cankers at the bone." And in "Picnic Remembered," Eden vanished when "darkness on the landscape grew / As in our bosoms darkness, too," leaving "Our hearts, like hollow stones" full of "that brackish tide" of ruinous knowledge: "The jaguar breath, the secret wrong . . . / We know; for fears have fructified." "Bearded Oaks" goes still farther as its speaker spends his time intensely imagining what being dead is like, so as "To practice for eternity." In the submarine silence of this imagined state, "Passion and slaughter, ruth, decay / Descend, minutely whispering down," making hash of all human values: "All our debate is voiceless here, / As all our rage, the rage of stone; . . . And history is thus undone." And finally, "Monologue at Midnight," as its title implies, rounds out the melancholy picture with a profound sense of solipsistic isolation:

> The match flame sudden in the gloom
> Is lensed within each watching eye

> Less intricate, less small, than in
> One heart the other's image is.

These four poems also pose a second condition that seems preparatory to the later Jungian material and that is implied in the prevalence of the pronoun *we* (in contrast to the *you* that prevails later). On an immediate level the four poems use the *we* form because they are "love" poems that describe with regret the decay of a once blissful union. But the poems also lend themselves to an allegorical reading. Howard Nemerov, for example, has proposed that the lovers in "Love's Parable" are man and God.[3] I would suggest the additional allegorical possibility that the *we* in these poems refers to the parts of the united prelapsarian psyche. All four of these poems, after all, are paradise remembered exercises, recollections of "our garden state / Of innocence," as "Love's Parable" describes it. And here too, in "Picnic Remembered," we have that striking instance of bifurcation of the self following the Fall that sends the child-self (or "soul") fleeing back towards paradise like a "hawk . . . / On glimmering wings," leaving the fallen self "unmanned" and "vacant," earthbound in the darkening landscape ("sun is sunk and darkness near"). Such bifurcation, splitting the prelapsarian *we* into postlapsarian *you* and its Jungian shadow self, may also be seen in the "civil broil" metaphor in "Love's Parable," which longingly recalls the inner harmony that prevailed before this civil war got started:

> O falling-off! O peace composed
> Within my kingdom when your reign
> Was fulgent-full! . . .

Since Warren's characteristic embodiment of this bifurcated self is in animal imagery, like the hawk fleeing in "Picnic Remembered," we might add similar images of flight and pursuit from "Bearded Oaks" and "Monologue at Midnight" to complete this rumination: the "doe that, leaping, fled" in "Bearded Oaks" and "the windward hound" whose voice we have heard "Bell in the frosty vault of dark" in "Monologue at Midnight." With such developments taking place deep in the psyche, there is good reason in the latter poem for the speaker's bewilderment over his present identity:

"The hound, the echo, flame, or shadow . . . / And which am I and which are you?"

With the child-self having vanished like the hawk or doe, the fallen self that remains—"unmanned" and "vacant"—is ready for the Jungian illumination. That illumination begins modestly enough in this first cluster of *Eleven Poems*. Consider the following use of the word "shadow," for example, to indicate a subconscious, inexpungable guilt in the psyche (the lines are quoted from "Monologue at Midnight"):

> And always at the side, like guilt,
> Our shadows over the grasses moved,
>
> Or moved across the moonlit snow;
> And move across the grass or snow.
> Or was it guilt? Philosophers
> Loll in their disputatious ease.

Tentative as it here appears, this mild sense of personal guilt foreshadows the worldwide outpouring of depravity that characterizes the later *Eleven Poems*. To grasp this theme as a whole, then, let us turn for a moment to Jung's parallel formulation, noting particularly his use of the shadow metaphor:

> The evil that comes to light in man and that undoubtedly dwells within him is of gigantic proportions, so that for the Church to talk of original sin and to trace it back to Adam's relatively innocent slip-up with Eve is almost a euphemism. . . . The evil, the guilt, the profound unease of conscience, the obscure misgivings are there before our eyes, if only we would see. . . . None of us stands outside humanity's black collective shadow. Whether the crime lies many generations back or happens today, it remains the symptom of a disposition that is always and everywhere present— and one would therefore do well to possess some "imagination in evil," for only the fool can permanently neglect the conditions of his own nature.[4]

"Evil," "guilt," "original sin," "profound unease of conscience," "obscure misgivings," "crime," "humanity's black collective shadow," "imagination in evil"—this terminology strikes to the heart of Warren's "Same Theme" in *Eleven Poems*. But just as James saw both "seraph and snake" in the subliminal self, so Jung also sees in "humanity's black collective shadow"—or collective unconscious, as he more frequently called it—redemptive possibilities. Indeed, given the bankruptcy of the conscious self, Jung called the unconscious "the only accessible source of religious experience." [5] And as we follow the development of Warren's psychodrama in *Eleven Poems*, "The Ballad of Billie Potts," *Brother to Dragons*, and elsewhere, we shall see that Warren also finds both religious insight and savage bestiality in the shadow self, whereas *you*—the Clean conscious ego—are capable of neither.

In what we might call the "middle three" of the *Eleven Poems* the focus shifts away from the external abyss of nature to explore the perilous but nonetheless more hopeful inner darkness. The Warren persona turns from the path opened up by the conscious, rational mind, which leads to time's ocean-bottom, the knowledge of naturalistic reality, to the path of the unconscious or intuitive, which leads to such instinctive knowledge, for example, as draws the entire animal kingdom "home" at the end of "The Ballad of Billie Potts":

> (The bee knows, and the eel's cold ganglia burn,
> And the sad head lifting to the long return,
> Through brumal deeps, . . .
> Carries its knowledge, navigator without star. . . .)

The bee knows, but rational man does not—nor will he until his "sad head" yields to unconscious instinct the way the eel's does. Once again, Jung offers a substantiating judgment: "Separation from his instinctual nature inevitably plunges civilized man into the conflict between conscious and unconscious, spirit and nature, knowledge and faith, a split that becomes pathological the moment his consciousness is no longer able to neglect or suppress his instinctual side." [6] Looking ahead to the final cluster of *Eleven Poems*, we see precisely this Jungian split as the central issue, as the shadow self is locked out of the house of the psyche in "Original Sin: A Short Story," murdered (only to rise again) in "Crime," or fled from (without success) in "Pursuit" and "Terror."

But meanwhile the three "middle" poems explore the "seraph and snake" dialectic of this journey to the interior of the psyche.

In "Question and Answer" the direction of the search is forced
inward simply because there are no answers anywhere else. After
posing the title question, "*What has availed / Or failed?*," the poem
warns *you* of the futility of demanding the answer from sea or sky
or gull or one's own true love,

> For all—
> Each frescoed figure leaning from the world's wall
>
> . . . .
>
> Demand
> In truth the true
> Answer of you.

In this situation the outer world merely reflects the seeker's question, so that

> . . . all repeat
> In mirrored-mirrored-mirror-wise
> Unto our eyes
> But question, not replies. . . .

At this low point of the inquiry, when the rational consciousness
has reached its dead end of futility, Warren's peculiar synthesis of
psychology and religion begins to operate, bearing out Jung's
contention that the unconscious is the "only accessible source of
religious experience." In "Question and Answer" this "seraphic"
element of the deeper self exists in two manifestations. First, the
poet evokes the example of the Israelites wandering in Sinai, literally
a Waste Land, where they nonetheless unexpectedly drank "the
living stream's delight" after Moses struck the rock in the desert.
Second, for wanderers in the modern Waste Land, Warren's concluding analogy is that of the heart as a bow that shall "let the
arrow fly / At God's black, orbèd, target eye."

   In addition to this mention of "God," even if only a "target"
the heart aims at, other instances of religious diction in *Eleven
Poems* collectively indicate that a "Conversion" experience of
some kind is in the making. This conversion would be a far cry
from T. S. Eliot's entry into the Church of England; but some
rudiments remain similar in Eliot and Warren. Above all, for both
poets passage into a fallen world and revulsion against it set into
motion a resistance to the findings of the naturalistic intellect. In

his chapter on "The Sick Soul" in *The Varieties of Religious Experience*, William James observes that "the purely naturalistic look at life. . . . is sure to end in sadness," but if that view of life proceeds so far as to produce "a pathological melancholy"—as is true in, for example, "The Hollow Men" and Warren's earlier poems of passage—then the individual in question may be ripe for a psychic reaction. James's chapter on "Conversion" describes both conscious and subconscious elements in that reaction:

> . . . the shifting of men's centres of personal energy within them and the lighting up of new crises of emotion . . . [are] partly due to explicitly conscious processes of thought and will, but . . . due largely also to the subconscious maturing of motives deposited by the experiences of life. When ripe, the results hatch out, or burst into flower.[7]

For T. S. Eliot, *Ash-Wednesday* was the "result that, when ripe, . . . burst into flower." But the "subconscious maturing of motives" left a long trail of markers behind it, from the "infinitely gentle, infinitely suffering thing" of *Preludes* to the hopelessly divided self of "The Hollow Men," which gathers its contradictory voices of naturalistic realism and desperate religious desire in close proximity:

> This is the dead land
> This is cactus land
> Here the stone images
> Are raised, here they receive
> The supplication of a dead man's hand
> Under the twinkle of a fading star.
>
>   Is it like this
> In death's other kingdom
> Waking alone
> At the hour when we are
> Trembling with tenderness
> Lips that would kiss
> Form prayers to broken stone.

James would surely have thought this a classic specimen of what, in "The Divided Self, and the Process of Its Unification," he calls the twice-born soul, as opposed to the once-born or "healthy-minded" who find the naturalistic world perfectly satisfactory as is: "The psychological basis of the twice-born character seems to be a certain discordancy or heterogeneity in the native temperament of the subject, an incompletely unified moral and intellectual constitution." [8]

Perhaps even more obviously than Eliot, Warren proceeded from his early lapsarian poems into James's "Divided Self" category, whereby some "subconscious incubation" may be struggling against the naturalistic intellect. In one of the very early poems, "The Last Metaphor," Warren's typical autumnal setting gives over at last to an untypical religious posture:

> Thinking that when the leaves no more abide
> The stiff trees rear not up in strength and pride
> But lift unto the gradual dark in prayer.

For *Thirty-six Poems* (1935) this constitutes an unusual irruption of religious feeling, but as we come to *Eleven Poems* we find much more. "Love's Parable," for example, devotes its final stanza to a prayer for relief from the divided psyche that is addressed (the title implies) to a love that once unified the psyche: "Your power . . . again / May sway my sullen elements. . . . That hope [*hope* is a verb here]: for there are testaments / That men, by prayer, have mastered grace." And in the "middle three" of the *Eleven Poems* we find still more of this diction: "love's grace" being the revelation in "Revelation," and "God's black, orbèd, target eye" being the heart's object in "Question and Answer." The third of these "middle" poems, "End of Season," adds to this undercurrent of conversion material by yearning after what T. S. Eliot called, in *Ash-Wednesday*, "strength beyond hope and despair": "you must think / On the true nature of Hope, whose eye is round and does not wink." James's ripening or hatching process seems to have come far in this image as compared to that in "Aubade for Hope," the early poem where "Hope . . . like a blockhead grandma ever / Above the ash and spittle croaks and leans." But the actual hatching is yet a ways off in "The Ballad of Billie Potts" and later poems, for between here and there lies the "snake" part of William James's "seraph and snake" formulation, or that which Jung called "humanity's black collective shadow." What yet blocks the unification of the divided psyche is the reluctance of *you*—the conscious, individual ego—to accept its brother self that emerges from the inner depths bearing both access to religious experience and loathesome inherent pollution.

"End of Season," as the 1966 ordering of *Eleven Poems* implies, serves as a gathering point of all three motifs thus far mentioned: the passage being touched upon in the title and setting, the impending "Conversion" motif about hope taking up the poem's last line, and the undiscovered self now advancing gingerly from the wings. Herewith *you* and *he*—the shadow self—assume an adversary relationship because *you* have been much too meticulous about your public identity to have it sullied by any such contact. With "Hair frosting, careful teeth," you stand "Bemused and pure among the bright umbrellas," grateful for "that perfect friendship" that you developed here at the beach in preference to any inward questing; and you contemplate gladly the cleansing properties of water: how grandpa "slept like a child, nor called out with the accustomed nightmare" at the hot spring in Arkansas, and how water has set us apart from the fallen world according to precedents in the Bible, in history, and in literature:

> For waters wash our guilt and dance in the sun—
> And the prophet, hairy and grim in the leonine landscape,
> Came down to Jordan; toward moon-set de Leon
> Woke while, squat, Time clucked like the darkling ape;
> And Dante's *duca*, smiling in the blessèd clime,
> With rushes, sea-wet, wiped from that sad brow the infernal grime.

So it is quite natural that as your beach days end, you will "On the last day swim far out" or "deep and wide-eyed, dive / Down the glaucous glimmer where no voice can visit." Regrettably, you will have to come up again where your original identity awaits you—"But the mail lurks in the box at the house where you live"— and for all your "annual sacrament of sea and sun, / Which browns the face and heals the heart," you will wear the usual human "smudge of history" upon your return home. There you will "have to learn a new language" to uphold your newly affirmed sense of purity; for otherwise, "all our conversation is index to our common crime." In contrast to the real "conversion" motif, then, "End of

Season" depicts the phony "conversion" of *you*, baptized and cleansed of the world's dirt and safely aloof from the shadow self's impinging pollution.

But as we approach the final "cluster" of *Eleven Poems* the Jungian shadow looms ever larger, bringing both divine and demonic manifestations towards *you*, the appalled conscious ego. In "Crime" the demonic is represented by the mad killer—so different from *you*—who lies in the ditch trying to remember what he has done. But since his act is of truly subconscious origin ("he nursed it unwitting, like a child asleep with a bauble"), he can remember neither the victim ("An old woman mumbling her gums . . . ? / Or the child who crossed the park every day . . . ?") nor even the longed-for cathartic moment ("Nor the mouth, rounded and white for the lyric scream / Which he never heard . . ."). And that is why the poem's first line tells us to "Envy the mad killer," for despite the foulness of the crime he is blessed with an innocence that *you* lack, though you feel perfectly free of guilt feelings: "a tree for you is a tree . . . / Nor [do] the eyes of pictures protrude, like snail's, each on its prong." A further reason to envy the mad killer—one which touches upon the "seraphic" dimension—is the purity of his motivations, "Happiness: what the heart wants" and "the peace in God's eye": "All he asked was peace. Past despair and past the uncouth / Violation, he snatched at the fleeting hem, though in error. . . ."

The real "Crime" in the poem, then, is not the mad killer's psychotic act, but rather the deliberate slaying by *you* of your Jungian shadow—part of "humanity's black collective shadow." Here, then, is another skirmish between the Clean and the Dirty. What the mad killer did in frenzy *you* did in vanity, as you "made the refusal and spat from the secret side of [your] mouth." Unlike the mad killer, however, *you* are condemned to remember your crime, the other self slain and buried "in the cellar dark." This is the final reason to envy the mad killer, then, "for what he buried is buried / By the culvert there," whereas your victim looks distressingly capable of resuscitation if memory should thaw the corpse a little:

> And envy him, for though the seasons stammer
> Past pulse in the yellow throat of the field-lark,

> Still memory drips, a pipe in the cellar-dark,
> And in its hutch and hole, as when the earth gets warmer,
> The cold heart heaves like a toad. . . .

That buried self is not so dead after all; still, this embarrassment may not be so distressing in the long run, Warren hints in the last stanza, for the resurrected self in the cellar holds the secret of a timeless identity described in a previous stanza as "the object bright on the bottom of the murky pond" and here as "that bright jewel you have no use for now." There will be use for that bright jewel yet; for high in the attic above this cold, wet, "cellar-dark" of the unconscious, something has gone wrong with the surface identity. As long as that deeper self remains unacknowledged, surface identity (the name on the letter) also remains unattainable. In this house of the psyche the "cold heart" in the "cellar-dark" and the letter "despised with the attic junk" are inseparable correlatives of a single, unified identity. So the conscious, rational self in the attic sadly awaits reunion with the buried, unconscious self in the cellar:

> The cold heart heaves like a toad, and lifts its brow
> With that bright jewel you have no use for now;
> While puzzled yet, despised with the attic junk, the letter
> Names over your name, and mourns under the dry rafter.

In "Original Sin: A Short Story" the secret self is not only resuscitated but indestructibly alive and damnably insistent on keeping company with *you*, who have been trying so hard to escape or repudiate it. Far from being dead and buried, this shadow self, with "nightmare" appearance appropriate to its subconscious origin, seemingly cannot be escaped from, repudiated, or exorcized:

> Nodding, its great head rattling like a gourd,
> And locks like seaweed strung on the stinking stone,
> The nightmare stumbles past. . . .
>
> You thought you had lost it when you left Omaha,
> . . . .
> But you met it in Harvard Yard as the historic steeple
> Was confirming the midnight. . . .

Little wonder that *you*, resigned to this predicament, should conclude that "Nothing is lost, ever lost!" But *you* can afford to be resigned now. Murder hardly seems necessary on two counts. First, the shadow self is encouragingly detached from the conscious identity: it will never "shame you before your friends" and has "nothing to do / With your public experience or private reformation." Hence *you* can keep your purity and sanctity intact; you will not be humiliatingly contaminated. Second, the shadow self is thoroughly harmless to *you* after all and, except for its irritating habit of hanging around in the background, is really not worth a thought. Loyal, dull-witted, and gentle, it offers no menace and can be outsmarted in any case—can be locked out, for example, when it comes whimpering for recognition:

> It tries the lock; you hear, but simply drowse:
> There is nothing remarkable in that sound at the door.
> Later you may hear it wander the dark house
> Like a mother who rises at night to seek a childhood picture;
> Or it goes to the backyard and stands like an old horse cold
>   in the pasture.

Here the "old horse" and "mother" references confirm Warren's disposition to identify the shadow self with various beast images and especially with the old people. As in "Billie Potts" and some of Warren's contemporary fiction (think of the old people in *At Heaven's Gate*, and the "judgment of the cows" in *All the King's Men*), the beasts manifest the shadow self by their simple unself-consciousness; and the old people, by virtue of having long since accepted their passage into a fallen world and their place among the Dirty. As here, for example, in "Original Sin: A Short Story":

> You thought you had lost it when you left Omaha,
> For it seemed connected then with your grandpa, who
> Had a wen on his forehead and sat on the veranda
> To finger the precious protuberance, as was his habit to do. . . .

Grandpa's wen, like the jewel on the toad's brow in "Crime," repulses *you* by its reminder of the fallen self; but it too will prove its meaning, for it will eventually confer upon *you* both "original sin" and along with it your true identity. For now, however, *you* can only be moved by deep unease in your rejection of the shadow, for clearly it knows who you are:

> . . . and you have heard
> It fumble your door before it whimpers and is gone:
> It acts like the old hound that used to snuffle your door and moan.

Here again we should note that, as in James's and Jung's formulation, genuine religious feeling is connected with the subconscious self rather than with the conscious ego. In this case, we might even say that a religious *virtue* is connected with the deeper self, for what the "grandpa," "Mother," "old horse," and "old hound" images add up to are four portraits in humility, as opposed to *you* the prideful—"for it stood so imbecile, / With empty hands, humble, and surely nothing in pocket." Thus almost subversively— here adding humility to the mad killer's search for "peace in God's eye" in "Crime"—the unconscious keeps building towards the crucial "Conversion" experience that will culminate in the mystic closing of "The Ballad of Billie Potts." And meanwhile *you* keep vainly trying to maintain your Clean distance from the world's Dirt and Shadow: "You have moved often and rarely left an address, / . . . But it has not died, it comes, its hand childish, unsure. . . ."

"Pursuit" shows *you* beginning to break down at last under the strain of some mysterious psychic illness. Exacerbating this condition is the sense of guilt and estrangement that rises now irrationally within you, somewhat reversing your sense of the Clean and the Dirty. The "hunchback on the corner," for example— one of the Dirty, obviously—"stares from the thicket of his familiar pain, like a fawn / That meets you a moment, wheels, in imperious innocence is gone." And likewise with the old people—"even the feverish old Jew stares stern with authority / Till you feel like one who has come too late, or improperly clothed, to a party." So in stanza two you "Go to the clinic. Wait in the outer room" until "The doctor will take you now." But there seems to be little he can do; though he "bends at your heart," the doctor "cannot make out just what it tries to impart; / So smiles; says you simply need a change of scene." As in "End of Season," you make that change of scene—to Florida resort country—but now you can no longer make recourse to rituals of cleansing. Quite the contrary, you are beginning to suspect that maybe the Dirty are somehow custodians of a secret knowledge required for your healing, and so you "Consider even that girl the other guests shun / On beach, at bar, in bed, for she may know / The secret you are seeking, after all." The "Pursuit" of the title is taking on a double meaning, then, with *you* and the shadow self closing towards each other, each pursued and pursuing. *You* are, to be sure, the more reluctant member of this relationship, but your sense of vacancy is becoming intolerable, as "you sit alone . . . / Behind you the music and lights of the great hotel." And at last you seek out the shadow in one of its typical manifestations, the old people—in this instance, a toad-like "old lady in black, by the wall" who "blinks and croaks, like a toad or a Norn, in the horrible light."

To the undercurrent of this continuing psychodrama, "Pursuit" contributes still another religious element—and the most important one yet—by way of building towards the "mystic osmosis of being." This element is love; and like the other religious elements denoted earlier, it must spring up from the deeper self to be efficacious. So *you* move towards "A change of love: if love is a groping Godward, though blind, / No matter what crevice, cranny, chink, bright in dark, the pale tentacle find." In addition to the subconscious nature of this movement, two further implications of this important passage need underscoring. First, the "groping Godward, though blind" seems to describe perfectly the grand mass movement of the creatures at the end of "Billie Potts." Second, the "change of love," though it may have ironic overtones here (where "the shoulder gleams white in the moonlit corridor"), is in fact precisely the needed prerequisite for Warren's mystic vision, for only through a change of love can *you* come to accept your osmotic connections and so draw your ultimate identity from participation in the whole of nature: Clean and Dirty together. Some such change seems to be in the offing as "Pursuit" reaches its final stanza, for *you* are coming to realize the rudiments of the osmotic vision. First, your sitting alone is recognized as "the beginning of error"; and second, you are starting to intuit the metaphysical need for self-transcending connections: "Solution, perhaps, is public, despair personal, / . . . There are many states, and towns in them, and faces. . . ."

This brings us to the last of the *Eleven Poems*, according to the revised format in the *Selected Poems* volumes: "Terror." Here we shift from the relatively "seraphic" working of the unconscious in "Pursuit" to the decidedly demonic, as evidenced in a worldwide outpouring of depravity (*circa* 1940). This expansion of scope, however, should not delude *you* into imagining yourself separate from the stew of corruption out there. On the contrary, the workings of Jung's "imagination in evil" confirm that all the evil going on "out there"—where "the criminal king . . . paints the air / With discoursed madness and protruding eye," where the "face . . . / Bends to the bomb-sight over bitter Helsingfors," or where "the brute crowd roars or the blunt boot-heels resound / In the Piazza or the Wilhelmplatz"—is directly related to your individual self, which has part ownership of humanity's black collective shadow, though "you now, guiltless, sink/To rest in lobbies." Indeed, here we might well add Freudian support to Jung's "imagination in evil," for Warren appears to view the onslaught of World War II as a manifestation of humanity's dark shadow in the same way that Freud, in his letter of December, 1914, regarded his contemporary scene. Freud concluded "that the primitive, savage, and evil impulses of mankind . . . wait for opportunities to display their activity." [9] By 1940 opportunities galore had presented themselves for those evil impulses to "display their activity," and Warren is no more sanguine than Freud was about the true motivations behind some high political ideologies:

> So some, whose passionate emptiness and tidal
> Lust swayed toward the debris of Madrid. . . .
> . . . .
> They fight old friends, for their obsession knows
> Only the immaculate itch, not human friends or foes.

Given the propaganda-polluted atmosphere of the times, many thus politicized the Clean and the Dirty into good guys versus bad guys, ideologically speaking; but unlike the poem's perpetrators of mass violence, *you* are becoming aware that the shadow self persists, though we kill the "bad" people. This is why *you* are "born to no adequate definition of terror": the age has not prepared you for the ultimate terror, the confronting of the shadow self. That haunting specter that *you* were able to lock out of the house of the psyche in "Original Sin: A Short Story" and whose image still seems so quaintly harmless in "Terror" ("like a puppy, . . . darling and inept") begins to terrify *you* in this poem. For all its innocence and sanctity, the surface self is shocked aware at last that something is missing from the picture, so that *you* must exclaim, as Warren describes this awareness in "Billie Potts," " 'Why, I'm not in it at all!' " The awareness of lack of identity, then, is the central theme of "Terror"—and of *Eleven Poems* as a whole—whose final image leaves us with that awareness; for though in a harmless domestic setting, you are implicated by your isolation. Where you ought to find your identity, that black collective shadow of mankind, "you see an empty chair," and the word "conscience-stricken" implies some complicity making *you* responsible for the empty chair: "But you crack nuts, while the conscience-stricken stare / Kisses the terror; for you see an empty chair."

As *Eleven Poems* concludes, then, the surface ego appears sufficiently moved by its vague sense of guilt, dread, and vacancy to be ripe for the fully developed "Conversion," or self-unification, experience. *Eleven Poems on the Same Theme* thus presents a psychological drama that defines the issues and equips us for understanding Warren's whole body of subsequent poetry. Its antagonists are the conscious against the unconscious self; its setting moves from the fallen naturalistic world of the poems of passage through the interior darkness in the house of the psyche (attic to cellar); and the issue at stake is the possible redemption of man, "the groping Godward, though blind," through the uniting of self, of all selves, in the attainment of identity.

Above all, the development toward a Jamesian "Conversion" through the ministrations of a Jungian undiscovered self gives *Eleven Poems* a crucial place in the Warren canon, for its metaphor of a repressed shadow self that was slain and buried in the dank cellar of the house of the psyche (only to rise again) became a protean master metaphor in the later poems. It would be variously manifested in the hanged lady in *Audubon;* the "face drowned deep under water, mouth askew" in *You, Emperors, and Others;* the skeleton granny who "whines like a dog in the dark" in *Promises;* the monster self loathed and shunned throughout *Brother*

to Dragons; and the "sad head lifting to the long return, / Through
brumal deeps" in "The Ballad of Billie Potts." Although its central
drama awaits resolution in Warren's later verse, *Eleven Poems on
the Same Theme* may be considered a masterful achievement in its
own right: original in its conception, significant in its import, and
striking in its presentation. The emergence of a major new vision
and voice in American poetry dates from this work.

THE BALLAD OF BILLIE POTTS

In "The Ballad of Billie Potts" Warren's three ground themes of
passage, the undiscovered self, and mysticism fuse for the first
time into his single paramount theme of identity. Regrettably,
criticism of this poem has mostly failed to appreciate this masterful
effect and has focussed instead on critics' adverse reactions to the
poem's experimental technique of interweaving narrative ballad
with meditative verse in parenthetical stanzas. But since the eight
meditative stanzas make up the very heart of the poem and would
leave only an entertaining yarn if omitted, we shall concentrate
intensively upon them. Far from comprising an extraneous gloss,
each of the eight makes its own distinctive and important contribution to the poem's central theme of identity; thus if Warren had
been obliged to write a "Pure" poem—and his essay on "The
Ancient Mariner" prefers the Impure as more meaningful—he
would have been better advised to drop the narrative ballad and
keep the poetry of meditation. But the narrative and the commentary upon it together constitute an effective complementary
whole.

In fact, the basic structure of "Billie Potts" follows the principle, common since Whitman's time, of patterning a poem after
a musical composition. Like Whitman's "Lilacs" or Pound's *Cantos,*
Warren's "Ballad" unfolds in a fugue-like arrangement, its three
ground themes interweaving throughout the poem until they converge to form a most extraordinary terminal crescendo. The theme
of passage, to begin, renders both setting and characters in such a
way as to underscore appropriate mythical allusions. Although
Warren sets his story in the frontier country of America, he evokes
the image of a very ancient time through his setting "in the land

between the rivers." Mesopotamia, which translated means "the land between the rivers," has long been regarded in Semitic myth, including the Garden of Eden story, as the birthplace of mankind. So Warren subtly implies as early as line 2 of this poem the origin and outcome of the myth he is recreating in the context of New World innocence and its Fall. The importance of this phrase ("the land between the rivers") is indicated by the fact that it becomes the recurrent refrain throughout the ballad, and it ties in with the water imagery that later emerges to predominant significance in the poem.

The characters also suggest Edenic analogies. In the first stanza Warren depicts Big Billie Potts as an American Adam—already fallen but not yet aware of the literal death his sin will entail for his posterity—in rough, cheerily fast-moving diction: "his gut stuck out / Like a croker of nubbins. . . . He would slap you on the back and laugh." Big Billie's wife is also described in realistic terms having mythical overtones. Although she may lack the mythical beauty of the first Eve, she has the same feline cleverness as the original ("clever with . . . eyes . . . like a cat") and the same devious secrecy ("Nobody knew what was in her head"). The resemblance between Big Billie's wife and Eve is seen more clearly toward the climax of the narrative, when it is the woman who instigates the murder of their disguised son: "And the old woman gave the old man a straight look. / She gave him the bucket but it was not empty but it was not water." And Little Billie, if lacking Edenic dimensions, is at least a prime candidate for Warren's psychology of passage because of his rather vulnerable adolescent innocence, "with fuzz on his chin / . . . And a whicker when he laughed where his father had a beller." (Regrettably, the *Selected Poems* 1966 version of "Billie Potts" changes this spelling to "bellow." Otherwise, however, I shall follow the 1966 version, which omits some fifteen lines from the original, because I share the poet's feeling that the poem is strengthened by these cuts, and also because this evidently will be the standard version for future editions of Warren's verse.)

As the poem begins Little Billie rests his identity upon his primal family connection: "He was their darling." But of course this prelapsarian state is only prologue. Phase one of Little Billie's pas-

sage into the fallen world ensues as he squats at swamp-edge seeking
initiation into the villainy of his father. In deciding to ambush the
guest himself rather than pass the message to Big Billie's henchman,
Billie thinks of himself as being inducted into true manhood in the
archetypal rite of passage fashion: "How Pap would be proud and
Mammy glad / To know what a thriving boy they had." One of
Warren's standard fetal images follows, as the poem's narrator
imagines Billie's "face green in the submarine light of leaf." During
the wait for the stranger's arrival, Billie's impending loss of innocence further precipitates the bifurcation of the self so typical of
Warren's poetry of passage, with the prelapsarian self disappearing
and leaving, "like the cicada . . . , / The old shell of self, thin,
ghostly, translucent, light as air." And so Billie sits in "the green /
World, land of the innocent bough, land of the leaf," waiting until
the act itself would confirm his inner transformation, and so
resolve his now fluid sense of identity:

> (. . . and you wait for the stranger's hoofs on the soft trace,
> And under the green leaf's translucence the light bathes your face.
>
> Think of yourself at dawn: Which one are you? What?)

The farcical upshot of Billie's plan, which sends him fleeing
"With blood on his shirt and snot in his nose / And pee in his pants,
for he'd wet his clothes," leads to a momentary reversion to his
child's identity of yesterday, as "his Mammy cried" and "wiped
his nose and patted his head." But the deed of passage imposes the
need for a new external identity to go along with Billie's inner sense
of transformation. So he rides west to acquire a "new name" and a
"new face" and the new "innocence" lent by the lapse of time and
distance. But in the fullness of time—a ten-year sojourn out West—
this strategy only serves to bring the fateful phase two of Warren's
psychology of passage into operation, when, "weary of greetings
now and the new friend's smile" and "worn with your wanderer's
wile," the Prodigal returns at last in his "old shell of self" athirst
to recover his original identity. Instigating this search for the primal, prelapsarian self is Billie's reflection in the first of two parallel
Narcissus scenes, this one occurring out West as Billie leans brood-
ingly over his imaged *alter ego:*

> . . . and the stream you gaze into
> Will show the adoring face, show the lips that lift to you
> As you lean with the implacable thirst of self,
> As you lean to the image which is yourself,
> To set the lip to lip, fix eye on bulging eye,
> To drink not of the stream but of your deep identity.

But the stream's coiling waters, like time's flow, refract the image badly—"Under the image on the water the water coils and goes"—and so he comes home in search of a truer image, vaguely intuited from long ago.

So we are led to the second, and climactic, Narcissus scene; to the still waters of the spring where Billie had drunk as a child and where, drinking again, he hopes to glimpse the vanished prelapsarian child-self that once looked back at him from some dim pool of yesteryear:

> (The reflection is shadowy and the form not clear,
> For the hour is late, and scarcely a glimmer comes here. . . .
> . . . .
> But perhaps what you lost was lost in the pool long ago
> When childlike you lost it and then in your innocence rose to go
> After kneeling, as now, with your thirst beneath the leaves:
> And years it lies here and dreams in the depth and grieves,
> More faithful than mother or father in the light or dark of the leaves.

But after the Fall, as we know, there is no recovery of the vanished *alter ego*. Instead, rising to replace that primal innocence is the Jungian shadow, that undiscovered self who is represented here by Big Billie Potts—"the old man / Who is evil and ignorant and old" —and who brings death, not paradise, to the seed of his loins: "What gift—oh, father, father—from that dissevering hand?"

> And there is the spring in the dark of the trees,
> . . . .
> And one star in it caught through a chink. . . .
> . . . .
> Little Billie gets down on his knees
> And props his hands in the same old place
> To sup the water at his ease;
> And the star is gone but there is his face.

> "Just help yoreself," Big Billie said;
> Then set the hatchet in his head.

Although the richly multiple meanings of this scene may escape any redaction, let it suffice for our purposes to observe that herewith the psychology of passage leads to Warren's second ground theme, the undiscovered self. Not the sought after innocence but a terrible knowledge has ended the quest for identity. Not the child-self but the Old Man has answered, in Mephistophelean perversity, the heart's deep summons, its yearning to complete its own definition. Allegorically, then, for Billie as for his Edenic prototypes, passage into the fallen world brings death and the Jungian shadow and subjects the seeker of identity mainly to knowledge of identity's limitations: naturalistic annihilation and inward depravity, twin gifts of the father, "the patrimony of your crime." With the hatchet's fall the theme of passage culminates; having fused sin and death in one sublime stroke, it can go no farther. The narrative part of the "Ballad" therefore unravels to its denouement quickly, with the conniving parents finding to their grief and horror just who was this stranger they have killed for his money.

With the narrative ballad finished and Little Billie dead, Warren is free to move his true subject and his true main character to center stage—namely, the *you* of the poem's parenthetical passages. For it is not Billie Potts, but *you* that he has been talking about all along, *you* being as always the Clean part of one's identity that William James called the ideal self and Freud called the superego. In fact, one of the subtlest and finest things in the poem is the shifting identity of *you*. Like Billie, *you* began the poem as a Clean fellow with primal innocence safely intact, as befits the conscious ego that is unaware of its connection to the Jungian shadow. To further bait the trap, Warren's narrator initially aligns *his* identity with *you*, both personae being mere innocent observers who scrutinize the scene of this crime of time past from the safely sanitized shelter of time present:

> The oak leaf steams under the powerful sun.
> "Mister, is this the right road to Paducah?"
> The red face, seamed and gutted like the hill,
> Slow under time, and with the innocent savagery

> Of Time, the bleared eyes rolling, answers from
> Your dream: "They names it so, but I ain't bin."

Even this early on, however, in the poem's first parenthetical passage, we may glimpse some sinister implications in the landscape's savageness and something profound in the beast imagery (later to become the poem's most powerful motif):

> (It is not hard to see the land. . . .
>   . . . The fetid bottoms where
> The slough uncoiled and in the tangled cane,
> Where no sun comes, the muskrat's astute face
> Was lifted to the yammering jay; then dropped.)

The setting in place and time, a seemingly peripheral but always important identity factor, continues to preoccupy the narrator in the second parenthetical stanza, with both the narrator and *you* still immunized from any personal connections with the past by the impassable time gap that separates people of long ago from the present: "Their lips move but you do not hear the words, / Nor trodden twig nor fluted irony of birds. . . ." In the third parenthetical passage, however, the tone noticeably intensifies as *you* begin to get emotionally drawn into the story, somewhat like a chorus character in Greek tragedy who wants to warn the tragic victim but cannot: "They will not turn their faces to you though you call, / Who pace a logic merciless as light." That merciless logic, moreover—the sense of past actions deterministically finished and fixed forever—now begins to affect the identity of *you* adversely, since your own life will assume, in its lapsing, a similar profile; and in your ignorance, there is nothing *you* can do to change your fate:

> There was a beginning but you cannot see it.
> There will be an end but you cannot see it.
>
> . . . .
> And speculation rasps its idiot nails
> Across the dry slate where you did the sum.
>
> The answer is in the back of the book but the page is gone.
> And Grandma told you to tell the truth but she is dead.

By the time we reach the fourth parenthetical stanza the distance between Little Billie and *you* has mostly vanished, as Billie and *you* squat at swamp-edge together, waiting for the ambush victim and for the fateful change in identity that is now pending. "Think of yourself riding away from the dawn, / . . . And toward *hello*, toward Time's unwinking eye," the passage begins, and— with the "old shell of self" left behind—it concludes: "under the green leaf's translucence the light bathes your face. / Think of yourself at dawn: Which one are you? What?" Following the mishandled shooting, then, *you* share Billie's exile out West in the fifth parenthetical passage and also his "Cleansed" new identity: "The name and the face are always new. / And they are you." Continuing his water imagery, Warren depicts time as the cleansing agent, the "healing flood" and "redeeming blood" that produce— like a baptism signifying true conversion—a new man. But unlike the true convert, Billie/*you* senses deeply a loss of identity in Time's gift of a "new man" status: "For Time is always the new name and the new face, / And no-name and no-face."

In the sixth parenthetical passage, accordingly, Little Billie/*you* comes home, "Drawn out of distance, drawn from the great plateau / Where the sky heeled in the unsagging wind and the cheek burned." Now *you* loom as the larger part of the Billie/*you* compound, as the problem of something wrong with the identity becomes more pressingly urgent. The problem here, as in *Eleven Poems on the Same Theme*, is that the Clean surface ego (*you*) increasingly appears to represent the whole self very incompletely, if indeed one's real being is in it at all:

> Though your conscience was easy and you were assured of your
> innocence,
> You became gradually aware that something was missing from
> the picture,
> And upon closer inspection exclaimed: "Why, I'm not in it at all!"
> Which was perfectly true.

If, as Jack Burden thought in *All the King's Men*, knowledge is both the end of man and the justification for his being, it becomes really quite insupportable to know oneself so poorly. Worsening the problem, furthermore, is the growing awareness of *you* that death is an onrushing express train whose approach makes desperate the need to resolve the question of identity. One of the finest mood pieces in the poem is Warren's set of metaphors for the diminishing time span within which the surface self must seek out and acknowledge its missing shadow; quite clearly, *you* have now supplanted Little Billie as the poem's target figure:

> And the clock ticked all night long in the furnished room
> And would not stop
> And the *El*-train passed on the quarters with a whish like a terrible
>   broom
> And would not stop
> And there is always the sound of breathing in the next room
> And it will not stop
> And the waitress says, "Will that be all, sir, will that be all?"
> And will not stop
> For nothing is ever all and nothing is ever all,
> For all your experience and your expertness of human vices and of
>   valor
> At the hour when the ways are darkened.

By the end of this sixth parenthetical passage *you* are as bankrupt of any meaningful identity as is Little Billie, for "Though the letter always came and your lovers were always true," and "Though your hand never failed of its cunning and your glands always thoroughly knew their business," such modes of surface identity do not begin to encompass your deepest being. So, "Though your conscience was easy and you were assured of your innocence," *you* found something missing from the picture and exclaimed, " 'Why, I'm not in it at all!' " And *you* accordingly bend homeward with Little Billie to witness the fatal hatchet blow.

With that "gift" of the father in the seventh parenthetical passage, Little Billie vanishes from the text and leaves *you* fully to assume his quest and his identity, and so to carry them into the eighth and final parenthetical passage which concludes the poem. This passage—surely both one of the finest things Warren has written and one of the landmarks of modern poetry—resolves the theme of identity by dovetailing the undiscovered self with a pantheistic mysticism. So far as the undiscovered self is concerned, *you*

now at last head back to the father figure whose fallen condition—
shabby, malodorous, even perhaps depraved—represents the missing
element of your identity: "And the father waits for the son." Bowing in humility to that loathsome figure and acknowledging consanguinity with him, *you* will thereby complete your knowledge
of who you are. In *Eleven Poems* and later in *Brother to Dragons,*
the theme of the undiscovered self is likewise resolved only when
the Jamesian ideal self or Freudian superego submits in this fashion
to acknowledge its id or animus or shadow. But it is doubtful
whether Warren ever again captured that moment of fearsome
though necessary psychic integration with such perfect clarity,
economy, and power as he did at the end of "Billie Potts":

> And you, wanderer, back,
> After the striving and the wind's word,
> To kneel
> Here in the evening empty of wind or bird,
> To kneel in the sacramental silence of evening
> At the feet of the old man
> Who is evil and ignorant and old. . . .

This passage thus serves as the culmination for Warren's theme
of the undiscovered self and also provides a convenient bridge to
the poem's third ground theme of mysticism through religious diction and imagery. The devoutness of tone and setting ("in the
sacramental silence of evening"), the hushed imminence of eternity
("evening empty of wind or bird"), the son's humble posture of
genuflexion, the archetypal connotations of the father and son
motif—echoes and allusions like these strike deeply into the Western
religious consciousness. Above all in the tableau of Son bowing his
head to the hatchet in the silence of evening we have overtones of
Christ in Gethsemane. So the time has come when we must define
Warren's religious position.

Inevitably, Warren's native religious heritage has figured importantly in his subsequent thinking. As a son of the Kentucky-
Tennessee border country, Warren was sufficiently impressed by
the area's Protestant fundamentalism to have drawn upon it for
some very important "minor" characters, like Ashby Windham
in *At Heaven's Gate,* Ellis Burden in *All the King's Men,* and

Brother Potts in *Flood*, each of whom conveys a key idea of his novel (conversion, theodicy, and life's "blessedness," respectively). Warren also has borrowed the area's idea of Original Sin, as is evident in his undiscovered self theme and in Willie Stark's grandiloquent affinity for dirt in *All the King's Men* (e.g., "Come to think of it, there ain't a thing but dirt on this green God's globe except what's under water, and that's dirt too. . . . Man is conceived in sin and born in corruption and he passeth from the stink of the didie to the stench of the shroud").[10] Most notably, a full generation before it became known to and diffused throughout the mainstream of Christianity, Warren made references to the then most distinctive feature of his native region's backwoods fundamentalism: its genuinely mystical practice of glossolalia, or "speaking in tongues." In *Night Rider* (1939), Willie Proudfit describes an Indian Ghost Dance that produces something very like a Pentecostal seizure: "and them Indians move-en round and a-singen. Then somebody starts to feel hit a-come-en and starts a-shaken and a-shudderen. . . . Till that-air feller gits the jerks, lak a man when the gospel hits him."[11] And in *Brother to Dragons* (1953), R.P.W. speaks of the "Truth-dazzled hour when the heart shall burst / In gouts of glory—hallelujah! . . . the hour of the Pentecostal intuition."[12] So for all the Yale, Berkeley, and Oxford overlay, Warren retains something of the Kentucky fundamentalist. As Warren himself has so often averred, "Nothing is ever lost."

Yet we would be greatly mistaken to conclude that he endorses the whole fundamentalist—or even Christian—view. He parts company with the orthodox in his designation of the Old Man to whom the Son knelt in the darkness: "the old man / Who is evil and ignorant and old." For Warren, God is identified with all of reality, not just the Clean part of it; to accept God as sovereign is to accept reality absolutely. Perhaps the clearest analogue to Warren's position is that of John Updike, another quasi-orthodox writer who moved out of his Lutheran heritage to later conceive of a God quite similar to Warren's. "I've never really understood theologies which would absolve God of earthquakes and typhoons, of children starving," Updike says, "so that, yes, it certainly *is* God who throws the lightning bolt."[13]

For a Clean person, a God so identified with all of reality might well appear "evil and ignorant and old"; and even the soul that completely accepts passage into the world's stew rarely bows head to the hatchet easily. "The Mango on the Mango Tree"—the last of the "Mexico Is a Foreign Country" sequence—thus lodges a religious protest. Here, speaking of God as "the Great Schismatic," Warren's persona vents his grievance against the deity's fragmentation of reality into solipsistic or even hostile elements:

> For God works well the Roman plan,
> Divide and rule, mango and man,
> And on hate's axis the great globe grinds in its span.

This, we might say, is a poem of theological passage, which, by identifying God with all of reality, implicates Him in all the world's crimes and sufferings. And the "son," Warren's indignant speaker, is not about to kneel in submission to such a "father." Instead, like Warren's other Clean people, he seizes the opportunity to exculpate himself by pointing to the much greater turpitude of his Maker:

> I do not know the mango's crime
> In its far place and different time,
> Nor does it know mine committed in a frostier clime.
>
> But what to God's were ours, who pay,
> Drop by slow drop, day after day,
> Until His monstrous, primal guilt be washed away,
>
> Who till that time must thus atone
> In pulp and pit, in flesh and bone,
> By our vicarious sacrifice fault not our own?

Yet, if "The Mango on the Mango Tree" seems loudly impious, it points the way to the reconciliation still to come in "Billie Potts," for this poem ends in a wish for cosmic unity:

> For, ah, I do not know what word
> The mango might hear, or if I've heard
> A breath like *pardon, pardon*, when its stiff lips stirred.
>
> If there were a word that it could give,
> Or if I could only say *forgive*,
> Then we might lift the Babel curse by which we live,

> And I could leap and laugh and sing
> And it could leap, and everything
> Take hands with us and pace the music in a ring. . . .

In "Billie Potts" we find this wish turned into reality, as Warren's earliest and perhaps most powerful version of his "osmosis of being" vision blooms suddenly vast as Dante's celestial rose. This irruption of what James and Freud called "cosmic consciousness" provides the poem's final resolution for Warren's ground theme of identity, a resolution that endures as the "One Flesh" idea— akin to Coleridge's "One Life" theme in *The Ancient Mariner*— throughout Warren's subsequent poetry. What binds the "One Life" into unity is precisely the intuition that, as Warren has said elsewhere, all life lifts towards its own definition. Ultimate identity comes from participation in that great quest shared alike by all creation, from the humblest creatures undersea to "you, wanderer" returning like them to a "home" that is definable only in some primal intuition that permeates the "One Life" from the depths of the unconscious:

> The bee knows, and the eel's cold ganglia burn,
> And the sad head lifting to the long return,
> Through brumal deeps, in the great unsolsticed coil,
> Carries its knowledge, navigator without star,
> And under the stars, pure in its clamorous toil,
> The goose hoots north where the starlit marshes are.
> The salmon heaves at the fall, and, wanderer, you
> Heave at the great fall of Time . . .
>
> . . . .
> Back to the silence, back to the pool, back
> To the high pool, motionless, and the unmurmuring dream.

For its power of imagery, its remarkable richness of sound texture, and its profundity of theme, these closing stanzas of "Billie Potts" must rank as Warren's very finest achievement in verse. They bear out James's contention that "lyric poetry and music are alive and significant only in proportion as they fetch these vague vistas of a life continuous with our own." Certainly Warren seems to have fulfilled James's definition of mystic insights as entailing passage "from out of ordinary consciousness as from a less into a more, as from a smallness into a vastness, as from an unrest into a rest. We feel them as reconciling, unifying states." [14] Such reconciliation—of "son" and "father," of life and death, of the solipsistic fragments of reality—holds true even if, in "Billie Potts," the movement from "unrest to a rest" is from time to eternity, from the "thunderous stream" of Time's fall back to the "silence . . . the high pool, motionless, and the unmurmuring dream," also called "the homeland of no-Time."

In becoming "Brother to pinion and the pious fin that cleave / Their innocence of air and the disinfectant flood," Warren's "you, wanderer" also gathers through his osmosis of being with these creatures a type of Blakean "higher innocence" about his deepest identity, as the religious diction implies. Such final innocence becomes possible, in Warren's paradoxical system, only after the ordeal of passage has done its worst and the foul undiscovered self has displaced the phony "Clean" image of individual aspiration in the interior of the psyche. The religious diction here and in the subsequent scene of father and son "in the sacramental silence of evening" evokes a last comparison with James's *Varieties of Religious Experience*, in that Warren's "you, wanderer" has in the end achieved a religious state similar to that recorded in one of James's testimonies: "I . . . knew now what prayer really is: to return from the solitude of individuation into the consciousness of unity with all that is." [15]

Some such return from "individuation" to unity with others has been a basic pattern in most of Warren's work, fiction and poetry alike; but in "Billie Potts" the individuation process is more subtly rendered than elsewhere because its false modes of identity are all gathered under the name of "luck." Warren is not so foolish as to deny that such identity as pertains to the conscious ego does have importance; for it is true that, for the outer world, "the name and the face are you," and similar modes of identity which depend on "luck"—age, sex, health, family or regional origin, economic and social status, vocation, etc.—have their place. Hence the little black mark over Billie's nipple—"Which is your name, / Which is shaped for luck"—and hence too the ironic references to luck elsewhere in the poem, such as Billie's taking West "yore Pappy's luck." But the luck that *you* enjoy proves the weakness of "luck" in general. For although luck is satisfactorily upholding your conventional identity, *you* are eventually driven by some sense of its insufficiency to seek out that mode of identity which transcends all forms of "luck" and gathers you into the osmosis of being that ends the poem.

In binding "you, wanderer" to the whole animate creation Warren establishes an appealingly reversible flow of identity between man and brute creation. First, he humanizes the world's beasts by giving them human expression—"the sad head lifting to the long return"—and conversely, he depicts human history in such a way as to cast our anonymous forebears, moving west, in the mold of the salmon, geese, eel, etc., moving blindly but implacably into their destiny:

> (Leaning and slow, you see them move
> In massive passion colder than any love. . . .
>
> .   .   .   .
>
> [But you do not] hear the rustle of the heart
> That, heave and settle, gasp and start,
> Heaves like a fish in the ribs' dark basket borne
> West from the great water's depth whence it was torn.

Like Dylan Thomas's "force that through the green fuse drives the flower," the force that drives the world's beasts at the end of "Billie Potts" also drives its human agents, "Sainted and sad and sage as the hairy ass, who bear / History like bound faggots, with stiff knees," so that they may fulfill some inconceivable destiny for which they are but means to its end:

> Their names are like the leaves, but are forgot
> —The slush and swill of the world's great pot
> That foamed at the Appalachian lip, and spilled
> Like quicksilver across green baize. . . .
>   . . . seed
> Flung in the long wind: silent, they proceed
> Past meadow, salt-lick, and the lyric swale;
> Enter the arbor, shadow of trees, fade, fail.)

The essential feature of Warren's osmosis of being is that it is, like Whitman's, an "inverted mysticism"—that is, it binds us to worldly and natural reality absolutely rather than pointing an escape from it, either in a heavenly city or the city of art or otherworldliness.[16] As a poet of reality Warren thus adds a further synthesis to his dialectical gathering of opposites in this poem: a fusion of life and art. Whereas writers from Keats to Wallace Stevens, in poetry, and from Poe to Nabokov, in fiction, have seen in Art a refuge from life, Warren binds them in visceral unity. As soon as it is lived, Warren says, life becomes art, a story; but through the osmotic connection the story opens into the "One Life" of any present moment. And so we have the rather remarkable juxtaposition of the following lines, which connect the people of frontier days—locked now in their eternal "Grecian Urn" stasis—with our present "One Life" through a startling biological image:

> [They] breathe the immaculate climate where
> The lucent leaf is lifted, lank beard fingered, by no breeze,
> Rapt in the fabulous complacency of fresco, vase, or frieze:
>
> And the testicles of the fathers hang down like old lace.)

We may reasonably conclude that—leaving *Brother to Dragons* out of the reckoning—"Billie Potts" is probably Warren's best poem, and almost certainly his most important. Its brilliant imagery, its wide-ranging command of sound texture, and its novel synthesis of Warren's three master themes—passage, the undiscovered self, and mysticism—render the "Ballad" analogous to *Tintern Abbey* as the crucial poem in its author's maturation as a poet. From this point on Warren would be a "finished" artist, capable of very substantial technical innovations in later decades, but having essentially completed his formation of a fully developed point of view. Perhaps it was this sense of poetic self-completion that lay behind the ten year lapse between the "Ballad" and Warren's next publication in verse, *Brother to Dragons*.

TWO LATER "YOU" POEMS

Brother to Dragons should be considered here as the chronological successor to "The Ballad of Billie Potts," but its peculiar form ("A Tale in Verse and Voices") and proportions (230 pages) require that we bypass it for the moment to complete our study of Warren's "You" poems. It will then be appropriate to turn to *Brother to Dragons* as Warren's masterwork on the undiscovered self.

The two "You" poems—actually brief poem-sequences—that conclude Warren's work in this form are "Ballad of a Sweet Dream of Peace" in *Promises* (1957) and "Garland for You," in *You, Emperors, and Others* (1960). Since "Ballad of a Sweet Dream of Peace" conveys Warren's most succinct statement of his osmosis of being vision, we shall leave it for larger analysis in our chapter on mysticism; but we must note here its correlations with the "You" poems. "You" in this case is a brash young fellow reluctantly being initiated into the otherworldly mysteries—the mysteries of Warren's osmosis, to be exact. Aghast and appalled at the connections that keep linking him to the various "Dirty" figures he meets—old granny who "whines like a dog in the dark," a former sex partner "who to your bed came, lip damp, the breath like myrrh," and even some hogs that you "slopped . . . in dear, dead days long past"—the young fellow keeps telling his guide (a modern Virgil to his Dante) that he has nothing to do with these forlorn creatures: his grandma is "the old fool" and "old bitch," and as for the hogs, *"Any hogs that I slopped are long years dead, / And eaten by somebody and evacuated."* So he must learn of his connections the hard way. To his question *"Out there in the dark, what's that horrible chomping?"* the answer comes that the hogs will shortly make "one Flesh" of him, as they have just done with granny:

> *But look, in God's name, I am me!*
> If you are, there's the letter a hog has in charge,
> With a gold coronet, and your own name writ large,
> And in French, most politely, "Répondez s'il vous plaît."

In this surrealistic, black humor setting the last we see of the initiate, accordingly, is the pose that we saw in a more tragic mood at the end of "The Ballad of Billie Potts": "when you are ready, our clients usually say / That to shut the eyes tight and get down on the knees is the quickest and easiest way."

Counterbalancing *you* in this poem are not only the hogs, representing the undiscovered self, but also some other spectral seekers of identity: old granny, in Poems 1 to 3; the "cranky old coot" in

Poem 4, and the initiate's sex partner in Poem 5. Of these, old granny's role is the most important, for although reduced to a skeleton whose "bones let the wind blow through," she is one of Warren's heroic people actively trying to recover her lost identity. She searches in Poems 1 and 2 by polishing up and rummaging through the old Victorian bureau, which contains in its bottom drawer—though she has not reached it yet, since she is sifting the rubbish of the "top drawer"—the symbol of her child-self of pre-lapsarian times:

> For asleep in the bottom drawer is a thing that may prove
>   instructive to you:
> Just an old-fashioned doll with a china head. . . .
> .   .   .   .
> For she's hunting somebody to give
> Her the life they had promised her she would live,
> And I shudder to think what a stink and stir will be made
> When some summer night she opens the drawer and finds that
>   poor self she'd mislaid.

But that summer night will never come, for as we have seen, the vanished child-self may never be recovered by those who have passed into a fallen world. Granny's search for identity aptly ends with her absorption into the "one Flesh" that is Warren's ultimate mode of identity, while the horrified initiate watches in "Go It, Granny—Go It, Hog!"

> But they're mannered, these hogs, as they wait for her creaky
>   old tread.
> .   .   .   .
> Then old bones get knocked down with a clatter to wake up the
>   dead,
> And it's simply absurd how loud she can scream with no shred of
>   a tongue in her head.

Chastened by this spectacle, *you* are well on the way to enlightenment in the poems that follow, though understandably reluctant about your initiation.

Warren's last major work in the *you* poem mode was "Garland for You," an eight poem sequence divided almost evenly between *you* and your old adversary, the undiscovered self. Poem 1, "Clearly about You," resumes where *Eleven Poems on the Same Theme* left off, with scathing irony concerning the primary characteristic of *you*, your Cleanness:

> Your mother preferred the more baroque positions.
> Your father's legerdemain marks the vestry accounts.
> So you didn't know? Well, it's time you did—though one shuns
> To acknowledge the root from which one's own virtue mounts.

Little wonder, then, that like Billie Potts and your predecessor in *Eleven Poems,* you sense an impending identity crisis from which there seems to be no exit: "You will try the cross, or the couch, for balm for the heart's ache— / But that stranger who's staring so strangely, he knows you are you."

Following in your role as a Clean man is the "Man in the Street," who finds this whole fallen world really quite intolerable: " 'And I go to prepare a place for you, / For this location will never do.' " But of course this location will have to do, in Warren's eschatology; and so *you* will settle for whatever worldly paradise this life may offer. Switzerland, for example, in the poem of that title (Poem 4), is a *"world-mecca for seekers of pleasure and health,"* according to the "Travel agency brochure" in the poem's subtitle. Unfortunately, however, it looks on closer inspection to be just the Old World, for among those seekers of pleasure and health are the resort's old people with "half-destroyed bodies" and others who are half-destroyed psychologically—"The aging alcoholic you once knew in San Diego. / Or the lady theologian . . . for therapy now trying a dago." So by the time we reach Poem 5, "A Real Question Calling for Solution," *you* are beginning to fear that your self-concept is "only a dream you are having," after which, "on your awaking, identity may be destroyed." The ideals of self-improvement that *you* once lived by—running a mile before breakfast, reading Virgil for two hours after lunch, practicing "moral assessment"—have faded into nothing. Replacing them, a strange streak of perversity has sometimes possessed you: "When you slept with another woman you found that the letter / You owed your wife was a pleasure to write, gay now and teasy." In short, *you* are now becoming readied, like the initiate in "Ballad of a Sweet Dream of Peace" and his predecessors, to move towards the undiscovered self after discovering the bankruptcy of the conscious ego.

Recognition, pursuit, and capture, if possible, of the shadow self accordingly form the main substance of the other four (of eight) poems in "Garland for You." Characteristically, both the "seraphic" and demonic dimensions of the shadow are set forth in alternate order. "Lullaby: Exercise in Human Charity and Self-Knowledge" takes up the seraphic dimension with its dismissal, in successive stanzas, of name, face, and sex—three modes of identity important to the conscious ego—in favor of the deeper identity afforded during sleep. The headnote, in quoting Walter Winchell's radio phrase "Mr. and Mrs. North America," may give a flavor of irony to the ensuing poem; but in fact, Warren's osmosis of being thesis actually depends on the intuition of such a collective identity as Winchell's phrase denotes. And here an apprehension of collective identity through intuitions of the unconscious provides the only answer to the conscious ego's fear of naturalistic annihilation. For it is the unconscious, not the conscious self, that during sleep may feel perfectly at one with the cosmic immensity of time and space:

> Sleep, my dear, whatever your name is:
> Galactic milk spills down light years.
> Sleep, my dear, your personal fame is
> Sung safely now by all the tunèd spheres,
> And your sweet identity
> Fills like vapor, pale in moonlight, all the infinite night sky.
> You are you, and naught's to fear:
> Sleep, my dear.

In this unconscious state, the narrator affirms, "you to yourself, at last, appear / Clearly, my dear." And the identity that does obtain here, as in Whitman's similar poem "The Sleepers," is potentially redemptive precisely because of its leveling, extrapersonal dimension: "All the same, and all the same are blest. . . . / Whoever I am, what I now bless / Is your namelessness."

The shadow's demonic dimension, on the other hand, is the subject of the most curious and experimental poem in this sequence, "The Letter about Money, Love, or Other Comfort, If Any."

Here the identity crisis has proceeded so far that *you* are given over to frenzied and utterly bestial behavior. But before talking about *you*, we should say a word about this poem's narrator, whose role—something unusual in Warren—seems to be that of the artist: one who, having "accepted the trust so many years back" out of a "small knack / for honesty" and "a passion, like a disease, for Truth," is now hell-bent to deliver the Letter ("By Hand Only") to *you*, its rightful recipient. By rendering the whole poem in a single sentence that comprises four pages Warren underscores the doggedness of the narrator's pursuit of *you* through the long "metaphysical runaround / which my life became, and for which I / have mortgaged all." Warren's own sense of mission may be guessed in this portrait, which gains strength from the poem's headnote, a favorite biblical allusion for writers: "In the beginning was the Word." And the poem's ending rounds off this portrait of the artist motif with the narrator's enormous sense of satisfaction at having delivered the Letter as contracted. Having at last "fulfilled / The trust," he descends the dark mountain until, "breath-bated and lame," he gets his reward of absolute vindication:

> [I] see, in first dawn's drench and drama, the snow peak go gory,
> and the eagle will unlatch crag-clasp,
> fall, and at breaking of wing-furl, bark glory,
> and by that new light I shall seek
> the way, and my peace with God, and if in some taproom
>   travelers pry into this story,
> I shall not reduce it to a drunken marvel, assuming I know the
>   tongue they speak.

An interesting epiphany, but the triumph of the artist is not the true subject of this poem. The true subject is *you*, who have paradoxically become much more human and appealing now that you have lost your Cleanness and gone over to stark bestiality. To be sure, our narrator cannot approve the way "you had blown, your rent in arrears, your bathroom a sty" from your place in Nashville, nor your leaving Dubuque "With a church letter, / Episcopal, High" while your Llewellin setter starved to death in the woodshed; and you ought not to have "fooled with the female Fulbrights / at the Deux Magots and the Flore, / until the police caught you dead to rights." But even the narrator admits "it's all so human and sad . . . / and nobody blames you much, not even I, despite all the trouble I've had." Quite the contrary, now that *you* have become one of the Dirty, you are by that fact entitled to our poet-narrator's fullest sympathy, for he knows that behind your bestial acts lies only the primordial human struggle to realize your true identity. Particularly touching to our poet-narrator was your momentary reversion, during your search, to the child-self of your prelapsarian period:

> . . . I was moved nigh to tears
> myself by the tale you'd been caught
> crouched in the dark in the canna bed that pretties the lawn
>   of the orphanage where it appears
> you were raised—yes, crooning among the ruined lilies to a
>   teddy bear, not what a grown man ought
> To be doing past midnight. . . .

So it does not matter much that *you* are devolved now into "one who by dog and gun / has been hunted to the upper altitudes," nor that, given over completely to your shadow self now,

> . . . you, like an animal,
> will crouch among the black boulders and whine under knife
>   edge of night-blast,
> waiting for hunger to drive you down to forage
> for bark, berries, mast,
> roots, rodents, grubs, and such garbage,
> or a sheep like the one you with teeth killed,
> for you are said to be capable of all bestiality. . . .

All that matters is that at last *you* are what you really are, without pretense or illusion, and the artist who has delivered the truth to you may now go forth to his closing vindication.

"Arrogant Law" and "The Self That Stares" conclude "Garland for You" with melancholy observations about the schism that separates *you* from the unconscious identity. In "Arrogant Law" a solipsistic isolation of the conscious ego results when *you* plunge into the underwater (unconscious) realm "to break the anchor's deep hold / On rock, where undercurrents thrill cold"; and that isolation deepens in the final two stanzas where *you*, lying next your sleeping love, "desolate, desolate, turned from your love, / Knowing you'd never know what she thought of," and when, in your dying father, "life retired from the knowledgeable head / To hole in some colding last lurking-place." "The Self That Stares" shows this schism working internally, setting off "that brute trapped in your eye" from the conscious self gazing into the mirror. If anything, the animal self has the upper hand in this confrontation— "Yes, pity makes that gleam you gaze through— / Or is that brute now pitying you?"—for its function is merely to *be*, not vainly to seek knowledge from "Time's school," as the conscious mind is condemned to do: "No, nothing, nothing, is ever learned / Till school is out and the books are burned." The one "lesson" that Time's school may profitably teach in the meantime is some kind of self-acceptance, regarding that deeper self, or "To recognize / The human self naked in your own eyes."

With "Garland for You," Warren effectively completed his statement, begun some twenty years earlier with *Eleven Poems on the Same Theme*, on the relationship between the conscious and unconscious zones of the psyche, or between *you* and the Jungian shadow. For his culminating work on this theme, we turn now to his most extensive and ambitious poetic undertaking, *Brother to Dragons*.

BROTHER TO DRAGONS

It may surprise the reader, since Warren nowhere tells the source of his allusion, to find that the title of his most celebrated poetic achievement comes from the Book of Job (30:29): "I am a brother to dragons and a companion to owls." On second glance, however, this reference seems most apt. The occasion of Job's complaint is his feeling of resentment towards his Maker for bringing intolerable humiliation upon him. Loss of wealth and family and even his physical torment he could possibly abide, but humiliation is another matter: "But now they that are younger than I have me in derision, whose fathers I would have disdained to set with the dogs of my flock" (Job 30:1).

It is most revealing that Warren's attention is focused not on

Job's suffering and loss and endurance, but upon the one thing he could not endure—his loss of pride. Being a brother to dragons and a companion to owls, after all, is a fate singularly undeserved for a man who had always (like Thomas Jefferson) walked "upright and perfect . . . and eschewed evil." Job puts the question bitterly: "Did I not weep for him that was in trouble? was not my soul grieved for the poor?" (30:25). And all Job gets for a lifetime of high-minded service tendered in innocence is ridicule at the hands of "base men . . . viler than the earth":

> They were children of fools, yea, children of base men:
> they were viler than the earth.
> And now I am their song, yea, I am their byword.
>
> (Job 30:8–9)

Job's bitterness at finding himself a "brother to dragons" (a condition he actually refuses to admit until the very end of the Book of Job) provides a most satisfactory analogy to the attitude of Warren's Thomas Jefferson. Both men lacked, in Warren's estimation, that sense of limitation which is essential to the religious attitude. Both thought themselves freed, by means of their virtue, from common human contamination. Even Divinity must recognize their triumph, their disentanglement from the influence of the Fall, they would contend. Surely a just and true God could not fail to distinguish the righteous from "base men . . . viler than the earth."

But, of course, Warren does not grant such a distinction. Humanity's black collective shadow belongs as much to a Job or a Thomas Jefferson, for all their innocence and virtue, as to all the rest of mankind. Warren's answer to Job's complaint of injustice, then, is to fling Job's own protest back at him shorn of its original sarcasm: You are indeed a brother to dragons, Brother Job (and Brother Jefferson). And so we have the poem's master metaphor, its dominant and most recurrent image.

The exact meaning of this master metaphor has not been completely or properly understood. Critics have been inclined to lean too heavily on one occurrence of this beast image, while ignoring others. Such an approach would be useful if the beast image meant the same thing each time it appears, but it does not: like Melville's whale, Warren's beast has a different meaning for each of his characters. Thus I believe that George Palmer Garrett and Frederick McDowell err when they agree in viewing "the birth of the minotaur and the creation of the Labyrinth" as "a symbol which dominates the poem." [17] This is actually only Thomas Jefferson's view of the beast within the self, a view badly distorted by an excess of outrage and revulsion. For this reason the minotaur image, though in itself a masterpiece of poetic brilliance and power, is only briefly handled. After the first few pages it gives way to something more akin to the dragon image of the title—the serpent R.P.W. sees with startled fright, but without outrage or revulsion.

Because R.P.W. lacks Jefferson's outrage and revulsion—because, that is, R.P.W. has, like Melville's Ishmael, the most comprehensive and objective perspective of anyone in the story—we must consider his vision of the beast image the most accurate and crucial of all. The actual dominant symbol of the poem, then—to which the minotaur image is related but subordinate—initially appears as R.P.W. describes his first visit, in the heat of summer, to the ruined home site on the hill:

> I went up close to view the ruin, and then
> It happened. . . .
>
> In some black aperture among the stones
> I saw the eyes, their glitter in that dark,
> And suddenly the head thrust forth, and the fat, black
> Body molten flowed, as though those stones
> Bled forth earth's inner darkness to the day.[18]

We have seen this fellow before. He first appeared in *Eleven Poems on the Same Theme*, where in such poems as "Crime" and "Original Sin" he lay toad-like in the "hutch and hole" of the "cellar-dark," and was later repudiated altogether by the conscious mind. He reappears in *Brother to Dragons*, however, in truly awesome magnitude, for in this tale of subconscious depravity he can no longer be ignored by even so high-minded a consciousness as Jefferson's. His existence, as this tale drawn from history proves, is real. The "fat, black" serpent represents the unconscious self, which "haunts beneath earth's primal, soldered sill, / And in its slow and merciless ease, sleepless, lolls / Below that threshold where the prime waters sleep" (p. 33).

Because of its central importance in the poem, Warren devotes several pages to this first encounter of R.P.W. and the serpent. The poet's highest powers of imagination go into this attempt to describe the emergence of inner self from "earth's inner darkness to the day." Transmuted by the viewer's imagination, this perfectly natural serpent ("just a snake") attains a mythical superstature appropriate to its symbolizing of the unconscious self:

> Thus it flowed forth, and the scaled belly of abomination
> Rustled on stone, rose, rose up . . .
> I saw it rise, saw the soiled white of the belly bulge,
> And in that muscular distension I saw the black side scales
> Show their faint flange and tracery of white.
> And so it rose and climbed the paralyzed light.
> On those heaped stones it was taller than I, taller
> Than any man, and the swollen head hung
> Haloed and high in light. *(p. 33)*

"Taller than any man," R.P.W. called it, as his "natural tremor of fatigue converted to the metaphysical chill" and his "soul sat in [his] hand and could not move." But being a representative of modern man, R.P.W. quickly assures himself that "after all, the manifestation was only natural." This was not, surely, the serpent whose archetype appears throughout the history of religion in various civilizations: "Not Apophis that Egypt feared . . . Nor that Nidhogg whose cumbrous coils and cold dung chill / The root of the world's tree, nor even / Eve's interlocutor by Eden's bough." It was not even a "Freudian principle": "Nor symbol of that black lust all men fear and long for / Rising from earth to shake the summer sky."

But if the snake is not a traditional religious image or a Freudian principle of sexuality, neither is it "just a snake." Its rising "taller than any man" evokes too many parallels in other parts of the poem for us to dismiss its appearance so easily. The first parallel, the beast image rising "taller than any man," appears with Jefferson's minotaur image at the poem's beginning. At that time, however, the image of man's innermost self seemed to Jefferson, rapt in his folly of joy, not a beast but an angel:

> I was nothing, nothing but joy,
> And my heart cried out, "Oh, this is Man!"

> And thus my minotaur. There at the blind
> Blank labyrinthine turn of my personal time,
> I met the beast. . . .
>   But no beast then: the towering
> Definition, angelic, arrogant, abstract,
> Greaved in glory, thewed with light, the bright
> Brow tall as dawn.
>
> *(p. 9)*

As we shall see, Jefferson will have plenty of time to correct his mistaken impression of the nature of man's innermost self. This revision, in fact, will constitute the main substance of Jefferson's commentary until his last speech of the poem, where he finally accepts the beast within the self as neither minotaur nor angel, but deeply human.

The third major occurrence of this beast image in *Brother to Dragons* arises in connection with the third major character, Lilburn. What distinguishes Lilburn's version of the beast "taller than any man" from R.P.W.'s or Jefferson's is that he does not *see* the horrendous inner self; he *is* that darksome entity. I do not mean to oversimplify Lilburn's position in the poem, for Warren takes great pains to emphasize throughout the work that Lilburn is not merely the monster-self which Jefferson tries so hard to exorcize. Lilburn is, as R.P.W.'s consistent sympathy with him is intended to show, a real, recognizable, commonplace human being, motivated by an understandable though horribly perverted love for his mother. It is clear, however, that Lilburn does embody personally that dimension of unconscious evil which the serpent symbolizes and which is present in every man, whether acknowledged or not, whether active or latent. Our authority for this identification of Lilburn with R.P.W.'s serpent and Jefferson's minotaur is the hapless Laetitia, seer and (aware or unaware) exponent of truth in the poem.

Laetitia's vision occurs in the scene where Lilburn persuades her to describe in words, and wickedly to relish the telling, the "awful thing"—something unspeakably carnal—he had done to her the previous night. ("Then he did it. And it was an awful thing / I didn't know the name of, or heard tell"—p. 75.) After she finally "said the words," and Lilburn answered, "Now didn't you like it some, and even to tell me?" this is what she saw:

And sudden rose up from my side,
And stood up tall like he would fill the room,
And fill the house maybe, and split the walls,
And nighttime would come pouring in like flood,
And he was big all sudden, and no man
Was ever big like that, and way up there
His face was terrible and in its dark . . .
His eyes were shining, but they shone so dark.

(p. 79)

Like the serpent "taller than any man," Lilburn assumes a symbolic superstature ("no man / Was ever big like that") that identifies him with the monster-self in the subconscious and foreshadows the greater "awful thing" around which the story is woven, the incident in the meat house.

The image of the beast within the self recurs at least a dozen additional times within the poem, the recurrence in each case being colored by the speaker's individual perspective. Jefferson always speaks of it in bitterness and sarcasm, his voice filled with loathing for both the conscious self that aspires futilely for sainthood or heroism and the monster-self within that thwarts such aspiration:

    And as for the heroes, every one, . . .
The saints and angels, too, who tread, yes, every
And single one, but plays the child's play
And old charade where man puts down the bad and then feels good.
It is the sadistic farce by which the world is cleansed.
And is not cleansed, for in the deep
Hovel of the heart that Thing lies
That will never unkennel himself to the contemptible steel,
Nor needs to venture forth ever, for all sustenance
Comes in to him, the world comes in, and is his,
And supine yearns for the defilement of his slavering fang.

(p. 42)

On one very important point Jefferson is wrong about the nature of "that Thing" within the "Hovel of the heart." He claims it will "never unkennel himself" to the "contemptible steel"; but the truth is that the monster-self continually unkennels itself (as its prototype did in "Original Sin" and others of the *Eleven Poems*), even at the risk of repudiation and destruction (both befall Lilburn), in the hope of attaining acknowledgement and definition. It is only Jefferson's excess of revulsion which blinds him, until the poem's resolution, to the redemptive possibilities of the deeper self.

By far the most frequent and most significant references to the beast image come from R.P.W., the spokesman for modern man and the chief advocate of reconciliation in the poem. In his desire to effect a reunification of the divided self—conscious and unconscious (Jefferson and Lilburn)—R.P.W. always speaks temperately, urging understanding, acknowledgement, and acceptance, even though he clearly identifies the inner self with that monstrous collective guilt of mankind which theologians call "original sin":

> And there's always and forever
> Enough of guilt to rise and coil like miasma
> From the fat sump and cess of common consciousness
> To make any particular hour seem most appropriate
> For Gabriel's big tootle.
>
> *(p. 64)*

Probably the most obscure and complex version of the "beast within" metaphor is that of the catfish with "the face of the last torturer" underneath the Mississippi ice:

> The ice is a foot thick, and beneath, the water slides black like
>   a dream,
> And in the interior of that unpulsing blackness and thrilled
>   zero
> The big channel-cat sleeps with eye lidless, and the brute face
> Is the face of the last torturer, and the white belly
> Brushes the delicious and icy blackness of mud.
>
> *(p. 94)*

We have frequently seen Warren use water imagery as an archetype for time flowing into the sea of eternity, but here the meaning of the river is quite different. Its primary meaning is one which the metaphysical poets were so fond of exploring in comparisons of macrocosm and microcosm. John Donne comments in "Meditation Four" that "the whole world hath nothing, to which something in man doth not answer"; and in filling out the details of this comparison Donne makes, in passing, the exact analogy which Warren is driving at: "If all the Veines in our bodies, were extended to Rivers."

In the "catfish" passage Warren does extend the collective "Veines" of mankind into a River at the bottom of which is the familiar face of our collective unconscious, the bestial, never sleeping ("with eye lidless") inner man wantonly delighting in the "delicious" muck and ooze of the channel bottom. The "unpulsing blackness" where he makes his home, far beneath the starlit world of the conscious mind above the ice (the "pulsing" world of time), should remind us of the "blind dark" wherein Jefferson's minotaur dwelt and of "earth's inner darkness" from which R.P.W.'s serpent appeared.

The distinctive feature of the catfish image which elevates its significance above most recurrences of the master metaphor is its extension from the psychological realm into the theological. In its perfect adjustment to its environs, primeval as they are, the unconscious self has attained absolute identity and, thereby, oneness with God:

> . . . there is no sensation. How can there be
> Sensation when there is perfect adjustment? The blood
> Of the creature is but the temperature of the sustaining flow:
> The catfish is in the Mississippi and
> The Mississippi is in the catfish and
> Under the ice both are at one with God.
> Would that we were!
>
> *(p. 94)*

Repugnant as it appears, the inner self has something which the conscious self lacks and wants desperately. Its being "at one with God" ("Would that we were!") finally obviates its disreputableness. In this synthesis of psychology and theism we are reminded of C. G. Jung's contention that "the unconscious [is] the only accessible source of religious experience." [19] The way to God is not onward and upward but backward and downward, until the conscious self besmirches its sanctity in the primeval slime, "the delicious and icy blackness of mud" where our catfish brother awaits our brotherly embrace. There, incredibly, unreasonably, may be found oneness with God, that state in which the unified self finds its absolute identity, which is all the surface self has ever longed for.

Here we need to clarify the major point about the master metaphor. That point concerns the relationship between the conscious and the unconscious self which was the central subject of *Eleven Poems on the Same Theme* (1942) and which continues to be the central theme in *Brother to Dragons*, where the drift of events hangs about the efforts of Lucy Lewis and R.P.W. to reconcile Jefferson to Lilburn.[20] Until the very end Jefferson stoutly maintains his individual sanctity, for after all, *he* had not wielded any meat-ax:

> Jefferson:
>> But I know this, I'll have no part, no matter
>> What responsibility you yourself wish.
> Lucy:
>> I do not wish it. But how can I flee what is nearer
>> Than hands or feet, and more inward than my breath?
>>> *(p. 188)*

Even near the point of his exit from the poem, Jefferson can still recoil in indignation at the suggestion that he take Lilburn's hand ("take it, and the blood slick on it?"—p. 191); but he breaks down at last and begins to see the truth as Lucy and R.P.W. see it. This final vision of universal complicity, which espouses Warren's characteristically tragic view of the human condition, sees all human good not as "given" in the manner presumed by the Romantic utopians, but as earned out of the general human "wrath" and "guilt" and suffering "in the midst of our coiling darkness":

> We must strike the steel of wrath on the stone of guilt,
> And hope to provoke, thus, in the midst of our coiling darkness
> The incandescence of the heart's great flare.
> And in that illumination I should hope to see
> How all creation validates itself.
>
>> *(p. 195)*

"Nothing . . . / Is lost," Jefferson goes on to say, and he follows that fundamental Warren premise with another: "All is redeemed, / In knowledge." That such knowledge includes acceptance of the monster-self within is clear enough, for Jefferson adds that "knowledge . . . is the bitter bread." But bitter or not, Jefferson partakes at last of that communion symbol—"I have eaten the bitter bread" —and so in his final speech of the poem he earns access to lasting joy: "In joy, I would end" (pp. 195, 196). This joy, which stands in contrast to the delusory jubilation when Jefferson thought man an angel, comes from his two part reconciliation, which involves on one hand an acceptance by the conscious self of the darker self, the beast in the labyrinth (Lilburn), and on the other hand a return of the awakened, self-knowing individual to the group.

This reconciliation of Jefferson to his darker inner self paves the way for R.P.W.'s lengthy synthesis that ends the poem. Here the serpent self, his recognition accomplished at last, sinks back into "earth's dark inwardness" and is imperturbable (like the catfish) in his timeless dark:

> Down in the rocks . . . looped and snug
> And dark as dark: in dark the white belly glows,
> And deep behind the hog-snout, in that blunt head,
> The ganglia glow with what cold dream is congenial
> To fat old *obsoleta*, winter-long.
>
> *(p. 208)*

(The serpent's scientific name is ironically suited to Warren's purpose, for the whole scheme of the poem shows that "old *obsoleta*," as a symbol of something innate in human nature, is not really "obsolete" after all, even in an age which has repudiated the notion of original sin.) Here, too, in his concluding synthesis, R.P.W. specifically identifies himself and his age with Lilburn's crime ("We have lifted the meat-ax in the elation of love and justice"—p. 213), and he apprehends, like Jefferson, something redemptive in such painful awareness of guilt: "The recognition of complicity is the beginning of innocence" (p. 214). "And our innocence needs, perhaps, new definition," Warren had said at the end of "The Ballad of Billie Potts" (original version). At the end of *Brother to Dragons* our innocence has achieved that "new definition," paradoxically, through descent to the ooze at the river's bottom, through acceptance of guilt and complicity, through reconnecting the lines of communication between the conscious self and the unconscious.

This matter of communication between the conscious self and the unconscious is the crucial issue in *Brother to Dragons*, as it is in much of Warren's earlier verse. Here also, and with particular reference to *Eleven Poems on the Same Theme*, the initial overtures are made by the deeper self, the serpent-self which the conscious mind tries so hard to repudiate. In contrast to the aloof and prideful surface self, the deeper self appears not so monstrous after all. Instead, it comes forward in shy, sad humility, begging and giving forgiveness simultaneously, asking only to be reunited with its brother self, the conscious identity. R.P.W. had seen this redemptive aspect of the deeper self in his first encounter with the serpent:

> ... he reared
> Up high, and scared me, for a fact. But then
> The bloat head sagged an inch, the tongue withdrew,
> And on the top of that strong stalk the head
> Wagged slow, benevolent and sad and sage,
> As though it understood our human pitifulness
> And forgave all, and asked forgiveness, too.
>
> *(p. 35)*

This remarkable passage may well be the most important key to the poem, for it anticipates the moral and thematic resolution of the tale. All that remains after this vision, this "moment of possibility" (as Warren was to call it in "Gull's Cry," in *Promises*), is to get Jefferson and all he stands for in the modern world to see it too, and thus to restore the broken lines of communication. The deeper self, "benevolent and sad and sage" under its brute countenance, patiently awaits the necessary, redeeming embrace throughout the remainder of the poem. Because of this redemptive humility and need, the monster-self transcends its loathsomeness. The "sad and sage" head thereby takes its place alongside similar brute faces we have seen in Warren's earlier verse—the "sad head lifting to the long return / Through brumal deeps" at the end of "The Ballad of Billie Potts," and the even sadder face in "Original Sin: A Short Story" (in *Eleven Poems*) that "whimpers and is gone" like "the old hound that used to snuffle your door and moan."

Of the remaining recurrences of the master metaphor, two in particular deserve mention. The first of these shows that Jefferson's darker self, Lilburn, has his own inner self as well; and that both Jefferson and Lilburn are finally guilty of the same butchery, though Jefferson's act of mutilation is spiritual while Lilburn's is physical. It is Lucy Lewis who calls her brother's attention to the damaging analogy:

> He saw poor George as but his darkest self
> And all the possibility of the dark that he feared,
> And so he struck, and struck down that darkest self. . . .
> And . . . in your rejection you repeat the crime.
> Over and over, and more monstrous still,
> For what poor Lilburn did in exaltation of madness
> You do in vanity.
>
> *(p. 189)*

The other reference to the monster-self is the face whose "red eye" glares in spontaneous hatred at R.P.W. on the highway (p. 15). The occasion of this apparition is the ironic contrast Warren sets up between Jefferson's idyllic vision of the West as Promised Land and the actual waste land on which R.P.W. urinates (making appropriate answer to Eliot's prayer, "If there were only water"). Jefferson's vision of the West, "great Canaan's grander counterfeit," was originally paradisiacal:

>   . . . like the Israelite,
> From some high pass or crazy crag of mind . . .
> I saw all,
> Swale and savannah and the tulip-tree
> Immortally blossoming to May,
> Hawthorn and haw,
> Valleys extended and prairies idle and the land's
> Long westward languor lifting toward the flaming escarpment
>   at the end of day.
>
> *(p. 11)*

Through the handiwork of Jefferson's protege, the Common Man, the Promised Land has become a waste land by the time R.P.W. comes ripping over the highway a century and a half later and encounters the unforgiving red eye of New Canaan's present inhabitant:

> We ripped the July dazzle on the slab—
> July of '46—ripped through the sun-bit land:
> Blunt hills eroded red, stunt-oak, scrag-plum,
> The ruined coal-tipple and the blistered town,
> And farther on, from the shade of a shack flung down
> Amid the sage-grass by the blasted field,
> A face fixed at us and the red eye glared
> Without forgiveness, and will not forgive.
>
> *(p. 15)*

The ferocity of hatred in this red glare, casual, anonymous, and impersonal as the hatred is, carries forward the beast image into a permanent time present—into the "any time" Warren speaks of in his headnote. And though R.P.W. says, "But touch the accelerator and quick you're gone / Beyond forgiveness, pity, hope, hate, love," he knows very well that he cannot really escape the red eye's pitiful malediction. As a matter of fact, R.P.W. himself helps to perpetuate the general cursedness of things when he spatters the parched earth with hot urine, while the sunlight screams and a million July-flies voice their "simultaneous outrage" at what he has done:

> So we ripped on, but later when the road
> Was empty, stopped just once to void the bladder,
> And in that stunning silence after the tire's song
> The July-fly screamed like a nerve gone wild,
> Screamed like a dentist's drill, and then a million
> Took up the job, and in that simultaneous outrage
> The sunlight screamed, while urine spattered the parched soil.
>
> *(p. 15)*

There are those who take exception to such passages, which are not unusual in Warren's poetry, on the grounds that such coarseness and crudity is offensive and unnecessary. But in my opinion most of the time Warren's humor, whether coarse or delicate, is entirely functional; the passage above, as I read it, is a case in point. And even aside from its organic function in any particular context, Warren's irony deserves our gratitude. His broad, generous, manly irony gives his work a refreshing quality, by comparison with which even the work of so great an ironist as T. S. Eliot seems frequently lacking. Warren's irony, unlike Eliot's, is never petty, cruel, or superior. More than that, it is never (except in his very early poems) self-pitying. Although a greatly serious artist, Warren does not commit the fundamental error of taking himself too seriously.

Up to now, I have considered the master metaphor, the motif of the beast within the self, largely on its own terms. I think this has been the proper approach to the poem, for it is a work that deals primarily with that sense of debasement which led Job to complain about being a "brother to dragons." The title allusion clearly indicates that Warren's central concern is what we might describe as the inner dimension of the dark night of the soul: a sense of moral anxiety. Here, as in previous poems, the search for identity begins with a journey inward and downward through fearsome pollution and darkness.

It is important to note, however, that Warren places this central theme within, ultimately, the largest possible perspective. That largest perspective is the external dimension of darkness, that part of the dark night of the soul which considers the individual man in relation to final reality—an immensity of time and cosmos leading finite, transient man to despair of his own significance. This perspective is the main substance of R.P.W.'s lengthy concluding statement which follows resolution of the poem's main issue—Jefferson having acknowledged his darker self and the serpent having withdrawn into his primal, subterranean drowse.

Warren begins to develop this larger perspective quite early in the poem. R.P.W.'s first long speech, in fact, places the story's events in the vast, minimizing perspective of time. Speaking of the vanished Ohio boatmen, who represent the generations of man on the river of time, Warren recapitulates the time perspective we saw in "The Ballad of Billie Potts." The narrator is particularly moved by the hearty strength with which our forefathers undertook their one-way river journey:

> Haired hand on the sweep, and the haired lip lifts for song,
> And the leathery heart foreknows the end and knows it will
>   not be long,
> For a journey is only a journey and only Time is long,

And a river is only water. Time only will always flow . . .

. . . .

The last keel passes, it is drawing night.

(p. 17)

We see this river image several times again in the poem. One instance is the passage about the catfish in the Mississippi mud. Another is R.P.W.'s vision of "All men, a flood upon the flood," as the poem ends (p. 210). Still a different variation is the glimpse R.P.W. has, near the end of his first long speech, of a "lost clan feasting" at nightfall by the sea of eternity. This image parallels T. S. Eliot's vision of his ancestors' merriment in "East Coker." Whereas Eliot saw "Feet rising and falling. Eating and drinking. Dung and death," Warren sees "a lost clan feasting while their single fire / Flared red and green with sea-salt, and the night fell— / Shellfish and artifact, blacked bone and shard, / Left on the sea-lapped shore, and the sea was Time" (p. 21).

In addition to these images suggesting the immensity of time, there are a number of passages in *Brother to Dragons* evoking the vastness of space, the purpose here also being to place "the human project," as Warren later calls it, in its proper perspective. Jefferson introduces this motif when he says, "I was born in the shadow of a great forest" (p. 37). Although this forest may be a biblical allusion, most likely to the myth of Adam and Eve, it also probably has naturalistic connotations suggesting the vast unconquerable wilderness of nature against which the encroachments of human civilization seem negligible. R.P.W. takes up this motif a few pages later when, commenting on "the massive dark of forest," he observes that "the forest reaches / A thousand miles in darkness beyond the frail human project" (p. 45).

This sense of nature's all-encompassing vastness reaches its consummation toward the middle of the poem when R.P.W. describes the coming of winter in the *annus mirabilis*. The lyric power of this passage and its breadth of imagination make it one of the most moving reading experiences in the book. Even the great forest appears small and submissive under the onslaught of "the unleashed and unhoused force of Nature, / Mindless, irreconcilable, absolute: / The swing of the year, the thrust of Time, the wind." Primal forces of nature move in over the planet as "far north the great

conifers darkly bend." Whereas the summer journey to the site of
the Lewis house (the summer connoting the high noon of human
life and energy) had afforded R.P.W. a glimpse into man's inner
darkness, the winter setting here and at the end of the poem serves
to dramatize man's relationship to the outer darkness. In the "glittering infinitude of night" the arctic stars' "gleam comes earthward
down uncounted light-years of disdain" as the wide empty land lies
waste and frigid in a scene deathlike and static as eternity: "in radius
of more than a thousand miles the continent / Glitters whitely in
starlight like a great dead eye of ice" (p. 95).

The fullest expression of this sense of time-space immensity
comes significantly at the end of the poem, when R.P.W. makes his
winter visit (December 1951) to the Lewis homesite. As R.P.W.
stands near "the shrunken ruin," watching the "last light of December's, and the day's, declension" and thinking "of the many dead
and the places where they lay," he sees how "winter makes things
small. All things draw in" (p. 215). Underscoring this feeling of
diminishment, as R.P.W. looks at the pathetic decay and rubble of
what was once a "human project," are the vast "emptiness of light,"
or "cold indifference of light," and the great, vacant hush of afternoon in which faint sounds of living creatures ("Some far voice
speaking, or a dog's bark") wane into nothingness. Even the river
of time has a "cold gleam." Thinking how "the grave of my father's
father is lost in the woods" and "how our hither-coming never
knows the hence-going," R.P.W. sees that river for the last time
as "that broad flood" on which men move and are moved together:
"The good, the bad, the strong, the weak, all men. . . . All men,
a flood upon the flood" (pp. 204, 209).

These images of the immensity of time and space that seem to
dwarf the "frail human project" effectively culminate the "naturalistic considerations" R.P.W. mentioned early in the poem (p. 29).
These "naturalistic considerations" first applied to the inner darkness of man and the psychological theory of determinism which
would render virtue nonexistent, and which, consequently, R.P.W.
rejects, though he has seen man's inner darkness: "But still, despite
all naturalistic considerations, / Or in the end because of naturalistic
considerations, / We must believe in virtue" (p. 29). This qualification of the "naturalistic considerations" applying to man's inner

darkness has a counterpart in the naturalistic darkness exterior to man. Though he has seen both the inner and outer darkness, Warren does not accept the premises of naturalism as the final truth of existence. Just as "we must believe in virtue," despite inner darkness, so, too, Warren would say, we must believe in an ultimate meaning to our existence despite the all-enveloping oppressiveness of external darkness.

Warren's answer to the problem of cosmic darkness is, in a Jungian sense, theological. Since the inner darkness is his main concern in this poem, the theological implications are not very profuse in number or obvious in meaning, but clearly they do exist. There is, first of all, the concept of being "at one with God" already discussed. In ascribing deific connections to the catfish, Warren is restating his intuition—first stated in his essay on *The Ancient Mariner* and first illustrated in "Billie Potts"—that "Nature participates in God." As an embodiment of this conception, the catfish denotes a kind of immortality not available to the conscious psyche.

The most explicit theological content of the poem, and that which most closely approximates religious orthodoxy, is the series of Christian paradoxes that form the thematic resolution of the work. Both the style and the content of these lines resemble the resolution of *Four Quartets,* but the ideas antedate the modern period. These paradoxes formed a favorite theme of metaphysical poets and preachers, such as John Donne and Lancelot Andrewes, and their ultimate source goes all the way back to the sayings of Jesus. The inner and outer darkness come together here, as Warren considers virtue and a permanent identity ("the beginning of selfhood") ultimately interrelated:

> Fulfillment is only in the degree of recognition
> Of the common lot of our kind. And that is the death of vanity,
> And that is the beginning of virtue.

> The recognition of complicity is the beginning of innocence.
> The recognition of necessity is the beginning of freedom.
> The recognition of the direction of fulfillment is the death of
>   the self
> And the death of the self is the beginning of self-hood.
>
> *(p. 214)*

We may note in passing, by way of explaining the prosaic style of this passage (poetry of statement, one might call it), that all these ideas were implicit in "The Ballad of Billie Potts"—there was the "recognition of complicity" and of "necessity" and the "fulfill-ment" through the "death of the self"—but critical understanding of that poem was very scant. Thus I believe Warren undertook in *Brother to Dragons* to restate these fundamental premises of his art in explicit, prosaic terms, since subtler modes of communication had apparently failed in his earlier poetry.

Having discussed both the inner and the outer darkness in *Brother to Dragons,* I would like to conclude with a comment about the relationship between those dual dimensions of the dark night of the soul. The relationship between inner and outer darkness is rendered, as I see it, by means of an intermediary image—the "house" of the human psyche. We saw this image elaborately worked out in "Crime," one of the *Eleven Poems,* where the con-scious self sat in the attic amid rubbish suggesting temporal identity while the deeper self lay buried in the "hutch and hole" of the "cellar-dark." It may be fanciful to attach similar connotations to Lilburn's house, but there is some evidence that Warren intended such a meaning.

Jefferson first broaches this use of the "house" image when he speaks of "that sweet quarter of the heart where once . . . faith / Her fairest mansion held" (p. 24). The lines following this one, where Jefferson tells Lucy, "Sister, we are betrayed, and always in the house!" strongly imply the concept of the house of the psyche. R.P.W.'s subsequent comment, "If you refer to the house Charles Lewis built . . . [it's] nothing but rubble," could be taken both literally and metaphorically. If taken both ways, it ties to-gether the motifs of inner and outer darkness, for Lilburn and Nature between them have indeed reduced a nation's proudest household to "rubble," morally and physically.

If we assume that the Lewis house is indeed the house of the psyche, then R.P.W.'s first look at the ruins in his July visit has some very interesting, though not immediately apparent, overtones. First of all, there is the contrast between the "huddled stones of ruin," the remains of the surface self, and the underground burrow where the serpent-self still endures (p. 32). This contrast is repeated in R.P.W.'s second visit—his December trip at the end of the poem—where we picture the serpent "looped and snug" underground, safely beyond the reach of naturalism's winter. What these images add up to, we may surmise, is Warren's concept of individual immortality: the conscious self dies away in time, leaving the human hope for survival to reside in the collective unconscious, the inscrutable bedrock identity which renders us "all one Flesh, at last." A number of obscurities come clear as a result of this reading. It explains, for example, the urgent, repetitious insistence on accepting the inner self that is the central theme in much of Warren's poetry. Only the deeper, unknown self can hope to transcend time's decay; the conscious, temporal self is doomed to naturalistic oblivion. And such oblivion is hardly hope-inspiring if we may rightly infer that Warren's description of the ruined house extends to the house of the psyche:

> And there it was: the huddled stones of ruin,
> Just the foundation and the tumbled chimneys,
> To say the human had been here and gone,
> And never would come back, though the bright stars
> Shall weary not in their appointed watch. . . .
>
> *(p. 32)*

The concept of the house as an extension of human identity appears elsewhere in the poem with similar implications. R.P.W. evokes his lyrical depiction of winter in the middle of the poem for the specific purpose, he says, of escaping the human house, dominated now by the dark psyche of Lilburn:

> . . . we also feel a need to leave that house
> On the dark headland, and lift up our eyes
> To whatever liberating perspective,
> Icy and pure, the wild heart may command,
> To escape the house, escape the tightening coil.
>
> *(p. 95)*

The perishable self is again identified with the house in the scene, late in the poem, where R.P.W. thinks of his vanished ancestors of only one or two generations ago. Riding with his father under the "lemon light" of December, R.P.W. looks out over "the land where once stood the house of his [father's] first light," and observes, "No remnant remains. The plow point has passed where the sill lay" (p. 204). The conscious, temporal identity, it appears, has disappeared into nothingness—"I do not know what hope or haplessness there / Inhabited once"—and so R.P.W. concludes that "the house is a fiction of human possibility past."

Warren's feeling that "nothing is ever lost," an idea that Jefferson affirmed after his conversion ("It would be terrible to think that truth is lost"—p. 194) is tenable, I think, only because of the potentiality of the deeper, undiscovered self, the serpent serenely "looped and snug" under the ruins of the house above ground. This mysterious, undefinable self, our collective unconscious, is the sole hope of transcending temporal limitations. This is the final significance of the beast-metaphor: there is not merely shame but hope in acknowledging oneself a brother to dragons.

4

Mysticism

WITH the resolution of the undiscovered self theme after his "middle" period in the 1940s and 1950s, Warren was free to leave a Jungian and return to an essentially Romantic sensibility. He could proceed, that is, past the quasi-Romantic trauma of the Fall in the poems of passage into a Blakean or Wordsworthian "higher innocence" that might yet redeem the fallen creation. The sign of that higher innocence is the ability of the Warren persona, his inner being unified now by a reconciliation between the conscious and unconscious zones of the psyche, to connect himself vitally to the outer world, unclean and ruined as it may be, in "such a sublimation that the world which once provoked . . . fear and disgust may now be totally loved." [1] The essence of Warren's mysticism is an unqualified love of the world *just as it is*, not as it might be if cleansed and made perfect by the New Creation of religious orthodoxies or by any form of secular ideology, such as Marxism or the Palace of Art, which aims at its own New Creation. Such love is long in coming, but like the T. S. Eliot of *Ash-Wednesday* who says "I rejoice that things are as they are," Warren gives increasing evidence in his later verse of achieving this total love of the natural world.

Since we have already gotten well into the subject of Warren's mysticism in earlier chapters, we can now complete the journey through a larger discussion of the osmosis of being concept and of Warren's recently proliferating epiphanies. The osmosis theme and the epiphanies make up the redeeming knowledge that Warren spoke of in his essay on "Knowledge and the Image of Man," which postulates that "only by knowledge does man achieve his identity." [2] Since identity is widely recognized as Warren's most compulsive theme—and beyond that, according to Ralph Ellison, "the search for identity . . . is *the* American theme"—it is desirable to examine the osmosis concept as Warren's final answer to the identity problem.[3] Thereafter a concluding look at Warren's epiphanies will close out this chapter on our poet's mysticism.

THE OSMOSIS OF BEING

For all his many voices, with verse forms and styles multiplying over the years, Warren's central themes and preoccupations have remained largely consistent. Questions of man's place in the total scheme of time and nature, of his relationship to the other beings with whom he shares existence, and of his guilt and complicity in the evils that surround him—those questions, in short, that make up the problem of the search for identity—recur from Warren's earliest work to his latest. Because the search for identity becomes, necessarily, an attempt to define reality, and because reality presents itself to us ambiguously—in men's heroism and depravity, in nature's beauty and horror—Warren's work most often assumes a dialectical configuration: the Clean versus the Dirty, the One versus the Many, Solipsism versus Synthesis of Being, Time versus no-Time, Consciousness versus Dream and Intuition. Given this dualistic perception of things, Warren's poetry must try to reconcile opposites, as in Coleridge's or Shelley's classic formulation (*A Defence of Poetry*, 1821): "[Poetry] marries exultation and horror, grief and pleasure, eternity and change; it subdues to union . . . all irreconcilable things."

Warren's agreement with Shelley's conception is evident everywhere in his writings, but probably the most direct and articulate statement of his reconciling synthesis appears in his essay "Knowledge and the Image of Man," published in 1955. Essentially, this essay advances two propositions: first, that the end or purpose of man's existence is knowledge, particularly self-knowledge; and second, that this knowledge—of one's ultimate identity, as it turns out—comes through a vision or experience of interrelationships that Warren calls "the osmosis of being": "[Man is] in the world with continual and intimate interpenetration, an inevitable osmosis of being, which in the end does not deny, but affirms, his identity."[4]

In all his writings Warren's most negative characters are those who reject the osmosis of being, while his spiritual guides are those who accept it, like Blanding Cotshill in *Flood,* who adds the word *mystic* to the key phrase: "Things are tied together. . . . There's some spooky interpenetration of things, a mystic osmosis of being, you might say." [5] An awakening to this truth typically provides the structure for Warren's fiction and poetry alike. Osmosis of being affords the central vision of *Audubon: A Vision;* requires Jack Burden in *All the King's Men* to accept responsibility for history; causes Thomas Jefferson in *Brother to Dragons* to acknowledge complicity in murder; leads a long series of Warren characters in all his novels towards acceptance of a father figure, however shabby or tainted; and draws forth the theme of a reconciliation between conscious and unconscious zones of the psyche in Warren's poetry about the undiscovered self. And ultimately osmosis of being imparts whatever meaning the self may have within eternity, absorbing the self into the totality of time and nature with the consoling promise, often repeated in Warren's work, that "nothing is ever lost."

Hence, Warren's osmosis has moral, metaphysical, and psychological ramifications; it is his contribution to modern religious thought, having an ethical and a mystical dimension. Looking back over Warren's career, moreover, we may find that osmosis was there all the time, much like T. S. Eliot's Christianity, implicit in the early works and explicit later on. Like Eliot's Christianity, again, Warren's osmosis appears in the early work mostly through negative implication, the naturalistic fragmentation of the world being so intolerable as to evoke a craving for some sense of oneness. In "Mexico Is a Foreign Country," (a poem written about 1943) the narrator watches some soldiers marching—"And I am I, and they are they, / And *this* is *this,* and *that* is *that*"—with a vain wish that "everything / Take hands with us and pace the music in a ring." And in his fiction likewise osmosis of being is what Warren's characters should be seeking, whereas characteristically they are observed bent towards other ends, narrowing their identity to a basis of fame, sexual prowess, success in business, or membership in a philosophical, religious, or political sect. There are, however, some positive intuitions of the osmosis concept even in Warren's earliest work. "The Garden," one of Warren's typical poems of passage, thus points beyond its imagery of loss towards a "sacrament

that can translate / All things . . . / From appetite to innocence."
This need would later find fulfillment in what Warren called the
"sacramental vision" of Coleridge's "One Life" theme. A similar
irruption of osmotic thought into a grimly naturalistic setting
occurs in "Kentucky Mountain Farm," where the breakdown of
flesh, flora, and even stone into "fractured atoms" evokes the underlying presence of a permeating, pantheistic spirit:

> So that the fractured atoms now are borne
> Down shifting waters to the tall, profound
> Shadow of the absolute deeps,
> Wherein the spirit moves and never sleeps
> That held the foot among the rocks, that bound
> The tired hand upon the stubborn plow,
> Knotted the flesh unto the hungry bone,
> The redbud to the charred and broken bough,
> And strung the bitter tendons of the stone.

Thus adumbrated, the osmosis of being concept was eventually
to claim highest importance in Warren's thought as his answer to
the basic question of identity. In addition to shaping Warren's
metaphysical vision, it has also affected his ethics by shaping his
definition of virtue. As an example, a recent poem, "Interjection
5: Solipsism and Theology" (in *Or Else*), describes a character
who is "wild with ego," and with "world-blame," "grief," "despair," and "weeping" in the poem's successive stanzas, and who
confronts in each stanza a brutal image of isolation: the "enormity
of ocean" (which *"does not even know my name"*), the "antic
small aphid green on the green leaf" (which *"has a home, but I—
I'm the lost one"*), the "glitter of winter stars" (which *"would
grind me . . . small as dust, and not care"*), and "the classic shut
eyelids of his true love sleeping." Culminating this progression, he
at last "stared into the dark pit of self" to find everything worthless;
yet, in the poem's last line, he "yearned after virtue"—which would
be the self-transcending link between the "Solipsism" of the poem's
title and its "Theology," or its imagery of the outer world.

To clarify the meaning and importance of osmosis in Warren's
work, then, I should like to examine in turn its major dimensions:

psychological, social, and metaphysical. Concerning the psychological dimension, or the workings of osmosis within the individual psyche, Warren depicts something missing in the way of self-definition. What is wrong is that the Freudian id or Jungian shadow, this darker, more bestial part of the psyche, has been denied its place in reality. An innocent, idealistic figure like Thomas Jefferson in *Brother to Dragons;* or Tobias Sears, the utopian transcendentalist in *Band of Angels;* or Adam Stanton, the physician to the poor in *All the King's Men*—such high-minded humanists are not about to think themselves brother to dragons or indeed to concede any reality to a monster-self within.

But the reality of evil, though denied for a time, will finally make itself known. Warren's narratives body forth this "original sin" in some of his most memorable characters and episodes: in the two hatchet-wielders, Lilburn Lewis and Big Billie Potts; in the gradually escalating violence of "The Free Farmers' Brotherhood of Protection and Control" in *Night Rider;* in the degrading trip to Big Hump's island in *World Enough and Time;* in the horrific episode of the slave raid into Africa in *Band of Angels;* in the frenzied sexual orgy following Brother Sumpter's preaching in *The Cave;* in the callous butchery of Negroes by whites during the New York draft riots of 1863 depicted in *Wilderness;* in the swamprat animalism of Frog-Eye in *Flood.* (Nor are Warren's "good people" exempt, as the lawyer-hero of *Meet Me in the Green Glen* discovers when he realizes he wanted his client to die.) Actual history, as discussed in Warren's books, adds confirming evidence. Warren's first book, *John Brown: The Making of a Martyr*, shows the famous abolitionist to be a murderous fanatic, an obvious forebear of Warren's fictional killers lifting rifle or meat-ax in an elation of justice. And *Who Speaks for the Negro?* (1965) identifies Malcolm X as the monster-self in the inner dark: "Malcolm X can evoke, in the Negro, even in Martin Luther King, that self with which he, too, must deal, in shock and fright, or in manic elation. . . . Malcolm X is many things. He is the nightmare self. He is the secret sharer." (In writing this, shortly before Malcolm X's assassination, Warren was thinking particularly of the Negro leader's statement at a Harlem rally, "We need a Mau Mau to win Freedom!")[6] John Brown's and Malcolm X's opposite numbers make an appearance in *Or Else* (1974), where in "News Photo" and "Ballad of Mister Dutcher and the Last Lynching in Gupton" two white racists leave their bloody mark on history, always of course in the cause of true justice, as the killer in "News Photo" tells his boy: *"Now I tell you, son . . . / I done right in my heart and in the eyes of God-a-Mighty."* [7]

From the beginning Warren has dramatized the discovery of a beast within the self as a basic structure in his work. In his first novel, *Night Rider,* a piously Bible-quoting Professor Ball is heard to say, "Yes, sir, I'm a man of peace. But it's surprising to a man what he'll find in himself sometimes." [8] What Professor Ball comes to find in himself is a capacity for murder, cowardice, and betrayal, causing the death of the book's main character, Percy Munn. And in the next novel, the masterful *At Heaven's Gate,* Slim Sarrett likewise traces out the melancholy curve of self-discovery. Early in the book, Slim is the artist-intellectual writing of literature and self-knowledge ("Bacon wrote: Knowledge is power. . . . Shakespeare wrote: Self-knowledge is power"). [9] But when his own self-knowledge comes to include the murder-cowardice-betrayal syndrome, Slim writes ruefully not of power but of a dark unbanishable being within the self:

> It came from your mother's womb, and she screamed at the
> moment of egress,
> The family doctor slapped breath in, relighted his bitten
> cigar
> While the old nurse washed it and washed it, without complete
> success.

All the King's Men brims with similar imagery, as nearly all its major characters have to come to terms with a self that is unknown (Willie Stark), forgotten (Judge Irwin), frozen (Jack Burden), buried (Jack's mother), or otherwise unacknowledged (Adam Stanton, Cass Mastern, the lady Abolitionist who whips her slaves mercilessly). The Cass Mastern episode frames the issue in biblical tones, as Cass confesses "with shame what evil has been in me, and may be in me, for who knows what breeze may blow upon the charred log and fan up flame again?" [10] For our studies in Warren's imagery, Willie Stark's deeper self enclosed like a beast in a cage may be most relevant: "and the feet would keep on tramping, back and forth like the feet of a heavy animal prowling . . . in a locked-up room, or a cage, hunting for the place to get out. . . . And listening to it, you wouldn't be so sure for a minute the bar or board would hold." [11] And in *Flood* the main character feels a beast within himself quite literally: "Then, in the inner darkness of himself . . . the black beast heaved at him . . . that black beast with cold fur like hairy ice that drowsed in the deepest inner dark, or woke to snuffle about, or even, as now, might heave unexpectedly at him and breathe upon him." [12]

Whereas Warren's fiction thus hints at a beast—a darker being or pollution of "original sin"—within the self, Warren's poetry describes it much more explicitly. "And our innocence needs, perhaps, new definition," Warren said at the end of his 1944 version of "Billie Potts." It is clear that this new definition of innocence must embrace, like osmosis, the guilt that "always and forever [will] rise and coil like miasma / From the fat sump and cess of common consciousness," as R.P.W. says in *Brother to Dragons*. [13] In all his major volumes of poetry Warren refers to this guilt in the common consciousness by means of animal imagery. *Eleven Poems on the Same Theme* shows the conscious ego, sanctimonious and sure of an innocent identity, unsuccessfully trying to repudiate the animal self variously described as "old horse" and "old hound," octopus, and toad (in "Original Sin," "Pursuit," and "Crime"). In *Brother to Dragons,* Thomas Jefferson also thinks himself guiltless until his sister and R.P.W. finally get him to clasp his murderous nephew's hand and so accept his consanguinity with Lilburn, the emblem (together with minotaur, catfish, and serpent) of man's darker self within. The key embodiment of the shadow self in this poem, though R.P.W. calls it "just a snake," turns out to have suspiciously human characteristics linking it to the "old hound" and "old horse" metaphors of *Eleven Poems on the Same Theme*. Its "benevolent and sad and sage" head suggests what the relationship between the conscious ego and the shadow self should be, but is not (until the very end) in Jefferson's case: "I still reject, cast out, repudiate, / And squeeze from my blood the blood of Lilburn." [14]

In *Promises,* too, man's natural revulsion towards the shadow self is implicit in the slaying of a snake by some men getting hay in "The Snake": "Snagged high on a pitchfork tine, he will make / Slow arabesque till the bullbats wake." Behind this image of a propped pitchfork lifting its burden to the night, the most grievous symbol in Christendom suggests itself, with its theme of vicarious guilt being exorcised. Elsewhere in *Promises*—in "Foreign Shore, Old Woman, Slaughter of Octopus"—the ugly sea-creature takes the snake's role, rising from his "cold coign and dark lair of water, / Ectoplasmic, snot-gray, the obscene of the life-wish," with "Sad tentacles weaving like prayer," to meet the boys' knife-flash. In *Or Else*, the narrator himself goes after the rattlesnakes and is proud of his skill in getting gas-slosh and thumb-struck match to land in unison in "Rattlesnake Country":

> Once I get one myself. I see, actually, the stub-buttoned tail
> Whip through pale flame down into earth-darkness.
> "The son-of-a-bitch," I am yelling, "did you see me, I got him!"

But of course the beast within the self is not exorcised by such impulsive destruction, though men are prone to locate evil anywhere outside the self and then move ahead with the slaughter, whether of snake, octopus, or human enemies. "It is the sadistic farce by which the world is cleansed," says the embittered Thomas Jefferson, "And is not cleansed, for in the deep / Hovel of the heart that Thing lies / That will never unkennel himself to the contemptible steel." [15]

In *You, Emperors, and Others*, the beast in the psyche assumes various faces. The emperors Warren writes of are Domitian and Tiberius, whom the Roman historian Suetonius considered monstrous criminals for using their imperial power to indulge greed, cruelty, incest, and orgiastic pleasures. The "You" in Warren's title, however, is hardly superior to the emperors. He has a tainted ancestry ("Your mother preferred the more baroque positions. / Your father's legerdemain marks the vestry accounts") and a criminal character of troublesome if not imperial proportions as illustrated in "The Letter about Money, Love, or Other Comfort, If Any," in which the narrator pursues a beastly alter ego from place to place ("you had blown, the rent in arrears, your bathroom a sty") and from crime to crime ("your Llewellin setter / was found in the woodshed, starved to death" and "you fooled with the female

Fulbrights / at the Deux Magots and the Flore, / until the police caught you dead to rights—"). In *Audubon* the woman who butchers her guests for their belongings evokes comparison with Big Billie Potts, "Who is evil and ignorant and old," as a female version of that beastly figure. And most recently, in *Or Else*, the "Ballad of Mister Dutcher and the Last Lynching in Gupton" renders the beast in the psyche through the characterization of a drab little man who for a lifetime has walked "the same old round like a blind / mule hitched to a sorghum mill." With his gray face, his "worn-out gray coat," his "small gray house," his "sort of gray smile," and his "small wife whose face was / . . . gray," Mister Dutcher has lived a life in which nothing has happened. But the killing of a posse member by a Negro holdup man activates, "in the fullness of time, and / in glory," the gray man's secret capacity to enjoy committing murder: "It / was the small gray-faced man who, to / the general astonishment . . . , said: 'Gimme / that rope.' "

Assuming that these characters represent the general human proclivity toward evil that Freud and Jung spoke about, we might see Warren's treatment of them as a synthesis between the Clean part of the self and its Shadow. In the "Mister Dutcher" poem above, Warren actually "merges . . . the slayer with the slain," as his *Sewanee Review* essay phrased it, by harkening towards the long-ruined grave sites of both lyncher and victim at the poem's end. In *Audubon*, too, the title character merges his identity with that of his would-be killer in the hanging scene. Thus Warren has pursued a purpose that he had earlier ascribed to Coleridge— namely, to "aim at a glorious synthesis in which all breaches would be healed and all malice reconciled." [16] Insofar as these "breaches" refer to parts of the psyche in conflict, we may conclude that in Warren's work the reality of evil within the self is represented in a long series of vile characters, violent episodes, and beast images; and that acceptance of that reality is the first step toward psychic wholeness in Warren's people—an internal osmosis of being, as it were.

Proceeding from the inner caverns of self to the outer world, we find an equally long series of technical devices—plot, character, imagery, allusion, irony, and so forth—sustaining the idea of osmosis on a family and social level. The repeated summons toward a father figure—felt by Sukie Christian in *Night Rider*, Jerry Calhoun in *At Heaven's Gate*, Billie Potts in the "Ballad," Jack Burden in *All the King's Men*, Jeremiah Beaumont in *World Enough and Time*, R.P.W. in *Brother to Dragons*, Rau-Ru and Amantha Starr in *Band of Angels*, Ikey Sumpter in *The Cave*, Adam Rosenzweig in *Wilderness*, Bradwell Tolliver in *Flood*, and Warren himself in a great many poems since the 1950s—this call to acceptance of a father is especially fundamental in Warren's work because it grounds osmosis of being in physiological fact. As Jack Burden puts it in *All the King's Men:* "The child comes home and the parent puts the hooks in him. The old man, or the woman, as the case may be, hasn't got anything to say to the child. All he wants is to have that child sit in a chair for a couple of hours and then go off to bed under the same roof. . . . This thing in itself is not love. It is just something in the blood. It is a kind of blood greed, and it is the fate of a man. It is the thing which man has which distinguishes him from the happy brute creation. When you get born your father and mother lost something out of themselves, and they are going to bust a hame trying to get it back, and you are it. They know they can't get it all back but they will get as big a chunk out of you as they can." [17]

It follows, then, that the true villains in Warren's work are not hatchet-murderers like Big Billie Potts and Lilburn Lewis so much as those characters who willfully reject the claims of osmosis. Among these truly damned are Ikey Sumpter in *The Cave* and Slim Sarrett in *At Heaven's Gate*, both of whom renounced the father, cut all their human ties, and vanished into the vicious and glittering isolation of New York City (a Gomorrah symbol since Warren's Fugitive-Agrarian days). Sometimes the temptation is subtle and human, as with the rich and powerful substitute fathers Bogan Murdock in *At Heaven's Gate* and Aaron Blaustein in *Wilderness*, glamorous figures who nearly seduce Jerry Calhoun and Adam Rosenzweig from the memory of their real fathers, the stooped and shabby ones. Or maybe the sin of rejection is committed in pride of youth, as with the brash young fellow in "Ballad of a Sweet Dream of Peace" who keeps calling his grandma "old fool" and "old bitch" until some supernatural hogs abruptly appear to chomp them both into "one Flesh." And sometimes osmosis is shunned not because of ignorance or temptation toward wealth or glamour, but out of fear of contamination. Thomas Jefferson's reluctance to shake Lilburn's hand with "the blood slick on it" is a case in point, and similar fear of contamination is delightfully portrayed in "Two Studies in Idealism" in which a Union soldier, a Harvard graduate of 1861, complains bitterly how a filthy old man fighting for the other side had the gall to forgive the graduate for killing him: "Said: 'Son, you look puke-pale. Buck up! If it hadn't been you, / Some other young squirt would-a done it.'" Like the serpent who "forgave all, and asked forgiveness, too," in *Brother to Dragons*, the rebel soldier offers a human communion transcending his loathsome appearance. To be sure, the Harvard graduate is too clothed in the Right of the Union Cause to accept the old man's dying gesture. But such acceptance of human communion beyond right and wrong is what he needs for salvation, as opposed to his dependence on the "Treasury of Merit" (Warren's term for the North's enduring sense of virtue in having fought for Right in the Civil War).

In his *Meditations on the Centennial: The Legacy of the Civil War*, Warren finds American ideologies generally iniquitous, partly for their self-serving hypocrisies, but also because they thwart the workings of social osmosis. In contrast with abstractions like the Legalism and Great Alibi of the pre- and post-Civil War South and the corresponding Higher Law and Treasury of Merit in the North, Warren sees his nation's history as a matter of fleshly realities. Consequently, although they are but anonymous "seed / Flung in the long wind," the pioneers rolling westward in "The Ballad of Billie Potts" relate directly to the poem's narrator, via an image of biological connection: "And the testicles of the fathers hang down like old lace." In "History" (a poem in the 1944 *Selected Poems*), Warren reverses this perspective, so that the pioneers who sacrificed and suffered may look upon their progeny in our time, a generation whose Waste Land mentality seems hardly worth the ancestral effort: "In the new land / Our seed shall prosper" and "cultivate / Peculiar crimes," having not "love, nor hate, / Nor memory," but rather the form of despair that Warren calls "defect of desire," which leads them suicidally to "grope toward time's cold womb." Despite this prevision of bleakness, the pioneers push down into the valley of the future:

> Now at our back
> The night wind lifts,
> Rain in the wind.
> . . . .
> Wind fondles, far below, the leaves of the land. . . .

And so the "people who made us," as Faulkner would say ("in whose living blood and seed we ourselves lay dormant and waiting"), commit their identity to "the big myth we live" (as the foreword in *Brother to Dragons* describes history): "Let us go down before / Our thews are latched in the myth's languor, / Our hearts with fable grey."

In *Promises*, too, Warren gathers the fragments of history into osmotic connections. "Founding Fathers, Nineteenth-Century Style, Southeast U.S.A." runs over a Whitmanesque catalogue of those anonymous people who "died, and are dead, and now their voices / . . . But beg us only one word to justify their own old life-cost." That word may come in the poem's last line, which links us with them as "their children . . . under the shadow of God's closing hand." And while awaiting his own absorption into history—time past, God's closed hand—the narrator in "Infant Boy at Midcentury" lays forth the promise of history for his son, who will learn with his first step "the apocalyptic power to spurn / Us, and our works and days, and onward, prevailing, pass" to his own "dawning perspective and possibility of human good," while (though dead by now) the narrator's "eyes, purged of envy, will follow your sunlit chance." In this same poem a total stranger confirms the narrator's benediction: "And once, on a strange shore, an old man, toothless and through, / Groped a hand from the lattice of personal disaster to touch you," saying "*ciao, bello,* as evening fell." Two decades later, in "Bicentennial," Warren would use the headnote "*Who is my brother?*" to introduce his catalogue of doomed, sordid, or pathetic people.

Warren's osmosis, then, postulates an ethic of community that includes and transcends self and family and tribe. It also transcends the separations worked by time or sin or ignorance. And in the end, the Warren protagonist must accept osmosis even as Jack Burden finally accepts the "Great Cobweb" concept of Cass Mastern in *All the King's Men:* "he learned that the world is all of one piece. . . . that the world is like an enormous spider web and if you touch it, however lightly, at any point, the vibration ripples to the remotest perimeter. . . ." Later, having witnessed a procession of unsatisfactory father figures stream through his life—the Scholarly Attorney, the Tycoon, the Count, the Young Executive, the Judge —Jack Burden comes to accept his first (though not his biological) father: "So now I live in the house which my father left me. With me is my wife, Anne Stanton, and the old man who was once married to my mother. . . . (Does he think that I am his son? I cannot be sure. Nor can I feel that it matters, for each of us is the son of a million fathers)." [18]

Passing beyond these interconnections on the family and social level, Warren's poetry since the 1950s has developed the osmosis of being concept to include all animate creation, much in the spirit of the Romantic vision. As Blake said, "everything that lives is holy," and Coleridge, "He prayeth well, who loveth well / Both man and bird and beast," Warren has asserted, "we're all one Flesh, at last." That Warren considers this "one Flesh" to encompass more than human flesh is clear in many poems, but two grisly episodes from *Promises* may underscore the point convincingly. In one instance, "Court-Martial," the victims are human; in the other, "Boy's Will, Joyful Labor Without Pay, and Harvest Home (1918)," the victim is a black snake. The behavior of the self while confronting extinction is so similar in both instances (human or reptile) as to suggest that ultimately the distinctions are secondary.

> They took shape, enormous in air.
> . . . enormous, they hung there:
>
> . . . .
> Each face outraged, agape,
> Not yet believing it true—
> The hairy jaw askew,
> Tongue out, out-staring eye,
> And the spittle not yet dry
> That was uttered with the last cry.
> *("Court Martial")*

But a black snake rears in his ruined room.
Defiant, tall in that blast of day,
Now eye for eye, he swaps his stare.
His outrage glitters on the air.
Men shout, ring around. He can't get away.
("Boy's Will . . .")

Their "outrage" is not less because the victims are themselves killers and predators. The dying men and dying snake alike represent a principle of self, momentarily externalized and gruesomely offering to the observer an image of his own mortal condition. So the one-ness of Flesh, making an interrelationship of all creatures through-out the entirety of the time continuum, is perceived by Warren with much the same mystic intensity as Robert Frost evinces in his memorable couplet describing evolution in "Sitting by a Bush in Broad Daylight": "And from that one intake of fire / All creatures still warmly suspire."

Osmosis of being is apotheosized most strikingly in a series of lyrics in *Promises* called "Ballad of a Sweet Dream of Peace." Here, in a macabre transition zone between the living and the dead, a brash young initiate is instructed in the mysteries of osmosis. Thanks to the universal guilt implied in Warren's "original sin" motif, the relationship between slaughterer and victim is now seen in a horrify-ing and truth-revealing reverse order, for here some hogs wait to devour their former devourers. In the following exchange, the mysteriously omniscient guide (whose role is much like Virgil's in Dante's *Inferno*) speaks in regular type; the initiate, in italics:

Out there in the dark, what's that horrible chomping?
Oh, nothing, just hogs that forage for mast,
And if you call, "Hoo-pig!" they'll squeal and come romping,
For they'll know from your voice you're the boy who slopped
      them in dear, dead days long past.
Any hogs that I slopped are long years dead,
And eaten by somebody and evacuated,
So it's simply absurd, what you said.

In this otherworldly context, the initiate's protestation of innocence, couched in the logic of the Jew of Malta ("But that was in another country, and besides, the wench is dead"), is so much chaff in the breeze. For the hogs confirm a basic motif in all Warren's art: "Oh, nothing is lost, ever lost!" (in "Original Sin: A Short Story" and elsewhere). Resurrected and ravenous, the hogs that were eaten and evacuated now chomp frightfully close by, forcing the initiate to find some justification besides innocence with which to face them. The initiate's only appeal, the guide makes clear, is to oneness of Flesh, a concept transmitted in what may well be Warren's single most significant line of poetry (comparable in magnitude to Eliot's final synthesis of naturalism and Christianity in *Four Quartets:* "And the fire and the rose are one"): "You fool, poor fool, all Time is a dream, and we're all one Flesh, at last."

Warren's hogs immediately proceed to demonstrate the meaning of this apocalyptic revelation by chomping one and all into the "one Flesh, at last" which their most fleshy bodies symbolize. They begin by devouring the initiate's grandma—the skeleton granny in search of identity whom the initiate had previously called "old fool" and "old bitch":

> . . . all Time is a dream, and we're all one Flesh, at last,
> And the hogs know that, and that's why they wait,
> Though tonight the old thing is a little bit late,
> But they're mannered, these hogs, as they wait for her creaky
>   old tread. . . .
> .   .   .   .
> Then old bones get knocked down with a clatter to wake up the
>   dead,
> And it's simply absurd how loud she can scream with no shred of
>   a tongue in her head.

The implication is that granny's identity has been found at last, with her skeleton form transubstantiated into the universal hog-flesh. For the initiate this metaphysical instruction is providential, for after consuming his granny, the hogs proceed to the initiate himself in a poem called "I Guess You Ought to Know Who You Are":

> . . . *But look, in God's name, I am me!*
> If you are, there's the letter a hog has in charge,
> With a gold coronet and your own name writ large,
> And in French, most politely, "Répondez s'il vous plaît."

In devouring their former devourers, then, these supernatural hogs provide a universal eucharist, a compulsory last supper to which the guest comes to be eaten and thereby to be absorbed into a collective final identity.

Since he enunciated in *Promises* his central concept that "Time is a dream and we're all one Flesh, at last," Warren's subsequent volumes of poetry have been deeply affected by it. This concept has given coherence and direction to his work; it constitutes the "figure in the carpet" that Henry James talked about, "the primal plan" that "stretches from book to book." In *Tale of Time* (1966) and *Incarnations* (1968), Warren pursues the meanings of time and flesh somewhat separately, or at least with the stronger emphasis each title implies, although ultimately these meanings are inseparable. In these books, and in those that come before and after (*You, Emperors, and Others; Audubon: A Vision;* and *Or Else*), Warren's basic premise has been that the meaning of one's flesh is best perceived in the incarnation of other beings. Of paramount importance in this study is the recurrence in book after book of flesh which is dying or knows itself doomed to extinction. For the moment of extinction is when the dream of Time is about to end and the one Flesh concept is to become manifest. In *Promises* the snake propped high on a pitchfork tine and the men being hanged project this image, which the later books underscore increasingly. Some of the most moving poems in *You, Emperors, and Others* fall into this category: "Mortmain," about the death of the poet's father; "Ballad: Between the Boxcars," concerning a youth mangled under a train; and "Prognosis: A Short Story, the End of Which You Will Know Soon Enough," about a woman dying of cancer. And the spectacle of the murderous woman being hanged in *Audubon: A Vision* moves the great naturalist to such a mystical empathy that he sustains sexual excitation (typical in victims of strangulation) and feels suddenly wakened from "Time's dream":

> And in the gray light of morning, he sees her face. . . .
> . . . .
> The dark eyes stare at nothing, or at
> The nothingness that the gray sky, like Time, is, for

> There is no Time, and the face
> Is, he suddenly sees, beautiful as stone, and
>
> So becomes aware that he is in the manly state.

In *Tale of Time: New Poems, 1960–1966,* the spectacle of doomed flesh is pervasive. The book's first cluster of poems, a sequence called "Notes on a Life to Be Lived," has a narrator like one of Hemingway's insomniacs, tormented unto dawn by memories of his father's death, by the present ordeal of a cancer-stricken neighbor, and by a worldwide stew of violence ranging from a cat killing a chipmunk to cannibalism in the Congo. In the next poem-cluster, called "Tale of Time," this tone intensifies to match the subject, the death of the poet's mother. These six poems recall some curiously personal early poems, similarly guilt-haunted and passionate, on the same theme—poems like "The Return: An Elegy," where a son traveling to attend his mother's funeral thinks, "the old bitch is dead / what have I said!"; and "Revelation," where, recalling a bitter quarrel with his mother, the grieving son learns too late (she is now dead—"that irremediable face") that "In separateness only does love learn definition." Later, in *Promises* (Poem I), he has a vision of both his father and mother lying under the cemetery— "their bones in a phosphorous of glory agleam, there they lay, / Ruth and Robert"—from whence they pass him a message related to the osmosis of being: "Child . . . / We died only that every promise might be fulfilled."

In "Tale of Time" the poet again turns to the osmosis process, beginning with its failure in Poem I, "What Happened":

> . . . my mother
> Died, and God
> Kept on, and keeps on,
> Trying to tie things together, but
>
> It doesn't always work, and we put the body
> Into the ground, dark. . . .

So we have another insomniac narrator, troubled when he does sleep by "the dream of the eating of human flesh," who rises after midnight to stare in the mirror and "think of copulation, of / The sun-dappled dark of deep woods and / Blood on green fern frond, of / The shedding of blood. . . ." And he thinks of time. According to Jean-Paul Sartre in *Being and Nothingness*, "Time is that which separates"; through death it separates absolutely. Warren's images of time likewise tend to stress its destructiveness; he speaks of "Time's slow malediction" in *Promises* (Poem IV), of "The Turpitude of Time" in *You, Emperors, and Others* ("Mortmain"), and of "the cold hypothesis of Time" here in "Tale of Time" ("Insomnia," Part 3).

Working against this sense of loss and brokenness, however, are two constructive factors in this poem sequence: first, an appeal to something Warren elsewhere calls the "human fabric," that network of personal relationships which holds our peculiarly human identity in escrow; and second, the poet's imagination reconstructing what is lost in poems like "What Were You Thinking, Dear Mother?" (where he relives an evening from her childhood) and "Insomnia" (where he undertakes through a visionary imagination to communicate with her departed spirit). Among the faces making up the human fabric for mother, two in particular are evoked here. The apothecary in "The Mad Druggist," carried off to the asylum for deliberately killing (by altering prescriptions) some "folks that wouldn't be missed, / Or this God-durn town would be lucky to miss," had liked "Miss Ruth" (Warren's mother) and spared her from his list of victims. He "Had the wit to see that she was too precious to die: / A fact some in the street had not grasped—nor the attending physician, nor God, nor I." The other face in the human fabric is that of the narrator's black mammy in "The Interim." This poem, divided into eight segments, begins and ends with the osmosis of being theme. The interim of the title is that time "Between the clod [his mother's burial] and the midnight" when "the heart cries out for coherence" (Part 1): "Between the beginning and the end, we must learn / The nature of being, in order / In the end to be. . . ." The next six segments of "The Interim" describe the speaker's visit to Mammy to find out what love is; aged and dying, she can only raise her hand feebly and say "*you.*" Part 6 says, "There is only one solution. If / You would know how to live"; and Part 8 defines the solution as an osmotic eucharist similar to the hogs devouring everyone into one flesh in

Promises: "the solution: You / Must eat the dead. / You must eat them completely, bone, blood, flesh, gristle, even / Such hair as can be forced." This accomplished, "Immortality is not impossible, / Even joy."

The human fabric, a metaphor that evokes the social meaning of the osmosis of being theme, appears in "Fall Comes to Back-Country Vermont," a poem about death by cancer in a town so tiny that the death will leave only fifteen voters. Here as elsewhere the osmosis or human fabric motif mitigates losses:

> [He has] died, but for now let us take some comfort
> In the fact that the fifteen surviving voters,
> Remembering his name, feel, in the heart,
> Diminished, for in this section death
>
> Is a window gone dark and a face not seen
> Any more at the P.O., and in the act
> Of rending irreparably the human fabric,
> Death affirms the fact of that fabric. . . .

In addition, the animal imagery in the poem extends the osmotic grasp beyond the human fabric—to a bear calling its mate (like the human widow) in Part 2 ("On the mountain the moon-air will heave with that hunger"), and to a lynx the cancer victim has shot and stuffed in time past: "And the stuffed lynx he shot now all night glares / At the empty room with a feral vindication, / And does not forgive, and thinks with glee / How cancer is worse than a 30.30. . . ."

In *Incarnations* the one flesh concept is, as the title implies, all-pervasive. Working out from his biblical headnote, *"Yet now our flesh is as the flesh of our brethren"* (Nehemiah 5:5), Warren gathers a wide assortment of creatures under scrutiny, from a fish under sea ("The Red Mullet") to a hawk in the air ("The Leaf") to human beings on the point of extinction ("Internal Injuries"). Flesh now extinct also attracts the eye, ranging from a drowned cat riding the sea swells ("Masts at Dawn") to the "clutter of annual bones, of hare, vole, bird" up in the hawk's lair, that "high place of stone" that is Nature's sacrificial altar. Among these extinct creatures are similarly anonymous human beings, nameless "bodies / . . . eaten by dogs, gulls, rodents, ants, / And fish" ("Natural

History"), which are ironically survived by their artifacts: "A handful of coins, a late emperor. / Hewn stone . . ." ("What Day Is"). The main beneficiary of all this decay of flesh seems to be the vegetation: "and the root / Of the laurel has profited, the leaf / Of the live-oak achieves a new luster" ("Natural History"). For a D. H. Lawrence or a Henry Miller, Death's old adversary, Eros, might provide a cheering alternative to this vision of things; but another poem in *Incarnations*, "Myth on Mediterranean Beach: Aphrodite as Logos," shows Love, under time's slow malediction, to be almost as grotesque as death itself. A hump-backed old crone whose "breasts hang down like saddle-bags," Warren's Aphrodite on the beach "passes the lovers, one by one, / And passing, draws their dreams away."

Only osmosis of being remains as a possible alternative to naturalistic loss, as stated in the book's headnote from Nehemiah and restated in "Night Is Personal"—"for we are all / One Flesh." By adding foliage to the one flesh concept, *Incarnations* expands the notion into the one life we all live, with flame imagery used to signify life incarnate in flesh and foliage alike. "The Red Mullet" nicely illustrates both uses of flame imagery: "The fig flames inward on the bough," as the poem begins, while Warren's persona swims undersea to confront one flesh in a different incarnation: "Where no light may / Come, he the great one, like flame, burns, and I / Have met him, eye to eye. . . ." As we read on the dialectic between flesh and foliage becomes cyclical: men eat the figs which have "Flesh like flame, purer than blood," only to become themselves good manure for a root system, giving the live-oak its "new luster." So the flame of one life seems most dangerous in its vegetable incarnation, as when we are warned not to eat a plum in "Riddle in the Garden," for "it will burn you, a blister / will be on your finger." This is why the red mullet mentioned above "sees and does not / Forgive"; for Warren, in Nature's grand eucharist, nothing is innocent and all are cannibals, including the plums, figs, and laurel. The meaning of one's flesh, therefore, can be understood, if at all, only in the light of an osmotic relationship that binds everything into unity and complicity together.

Looking to nature for confirmation of this osmotic vision, Warren has increasingly employed voice imagery to signify uni-

versal connection: not only man's puny inexhaustible voice that
Faulkner spoke of in his Nobel Prize speech, but all the voices in
nature. *You, Emperors, and Others*, for example, concludes with a
poem called "Grasshopper Tries to Break Solipsism." Solipsism is
the obvious enemy of osmosis; and the grasshopper's song, in seeking to establish connections, counteracts solipsism by showing the
humblest creatures' need for each other. In *Incarnations* a crow's
call serves the same function, but with powerfully added force deriving from its contextual imagery of whiteness. Thinking of Melville contemplating the Milky Way in *Moby-Dick*, of Poe's giant
white waterfall threatening Arthur Gordon Pym with oblivion, of
Robert Frost hearing the snow fall in dark woods, or of Wallace
Stevens's "mind of winter," readers of American literature have
been well conditioned for *Incarnations*, where whiteness also means
eternity, annihilation, and solitude. Fog, snow, dry bones, the belly
white of a dead fish floating, a white gull hanging, moonlit faces
"washed white as bone," Paul Valéry watching how "white the far
sail / Heeled now to windward" while "Surf . . . / Boomed, and
clawed white" and "a gull / Wheeled white in the flame of / Air,"
and even the "appalling speed" of Light beyond the stars—such
images have, for Warren as for Melville, a power to affright beyond
that of the redness of blood.

This imagery of whiteness culminates in the closing poem of
Incarnations, "Fog," where a "Blank mufflement of white" envelops
the speaker in deathlike solitude. "White, white, luminous but /
Blind," the fog cuts off all connections: "All, all / Is here, no other
where. . . . The heart, in this silence, beats." In this solipsistic void
an eye foresees death and surrealistically "Screams in the belly,"
seeing "the substance of body dissolving." Once again, the only
appeal is to the osmotic vision, represented in this instance by a
crow call that comes from "fog-height, unseen, . . . the hem of
silence." The closing lines of *Incarnations* rest everything upon this
tentative sense of connection:

> What, in such absoluteness,
> Can be prayed for? Oh, crow,
> Come back, I would hear your voice:
>
> That much, at least, in this whiteness.

The importance of this "voice in the whiteness" motif is further underscored by its recurrence in *Audubon*, where the great naturalist keeps staring at the stiffening face of the hanged woman while "Far off, in the forest and falling snow, / A crow was calling."

Imagery of whiteness also pervades *Or Else*, in poems like "Time As Hypnosis" (about mouse-tracks terminating where owl-feathers have brushed the snow) and "I Am Dreaming of a White Christmas," where the poet imagines his parents returning, mummified, from the dead. Here, however, the voice that contradicts solipsism on behalf of the osmotic vision is the poet's own, intruding upon the poems of passage in the volume by way of a series of lyrics called "Interjections." Placed at strategic points throughout the volume, these "Interjections" contribute apprehensions of delight, reconciliation, and even mystic insight to the whole; they strengthen a dialectical structure that Warren evidently had in mind in saying that *Or Else* "is conceived as a single long poem composed of a number of shorter poems as sections or chapters." An engaging example of this counterpoint is evident in the book's first two poems. Poem I, "The Nature of a Mirror," typifies Warren's poetry of passage, with its theme ("Time / Is the mirror into which you stare") placed against an autumnal setting ("The solstice of summer has sagged") and a sunset that makes the world seem threateningly carnivorous: "the sun, / Beyond the western ridge of black-burnt pine stubs like / A snaggery of rotten shark teeth, sinks. . . ." Given Warren's view of the soul's perversity, not even the good deeds that solaced Everyman can help, for as his theme of the Clean and the Dirty bears out, "Virtue is rewarded, that / Is the nightmare." Counterposed against this poem, "Interjection # 1: The Need for Re-evaluation" opens up a Nabokovian vista of alternatives whereby time (or time's mirror) and identity may be reconstrued completely. (Presumably this choice of perspectives is what Warren had in mind in choosing this book's title.) *"Is this really me?* Of course not, for Time / Is only a mirror in the fun-house. / You must re-evaluate the whole question."

With this decision to "re-evaluate the whole question" of Time and identity, we cross into the most momentous dimension of Warren's osmosis, the metaphysical. That decision first manifested itself, as we observed, in "The Ballad of Billie Potts," which reflects the "sacramental conception of the universe" that Warren discovered in Coleridge. The "imagination shows us how Nature participates in God," Warren wrote in his essay on *The Ancient Mariner*.[19] With "Billie Potts" he showed that nature participates in God by subordinating its individual elements or members to the status of tools to be used and discarded under the sovereignty of Time for the advantage of a larger being that goes on and on. In his earlier "Kentucky Mountain Farm" sequence Warren had identified this larger being as "the spirit that moves and never sleeps" in "the tall, profound / Shadow of the absolute deeps"—there receiving, in "fractured atoms," the broken rubbish deposited by time's stream: "flesh," "redbud," and "stone" whose time in the world had expired forever. There is no evidence that Warren's definition of this pantheistic spirit has changed since "Kentucky Mountain Farm." What has changed, most dramatically, is his persona's attitude toward it. Whereas this early poem evinces a tone full of irony, resignation, and despair, Warren's personae since "Billie Potts" have manifested an ability, like that of Melville's Queequeg or Father Mapple, to accept their annihilation sacramentally.

The immediate price of osmosis, then, is humility, which (as in Thomas Jefferson's case) is not easy to come by; and the ultimate price is death: a permanent consignment of self to the oneness of time and flesh. Death may involve a final annihilation of the conscious ego, that temporary and prideful separation from the larger collective being; but such a condition may prove desirable, and in any case it appears to be inevitable. Part of Warren's concern with the father-son relationship bears upon this need to accept one's extinction, for in the natural world the father always comes bearing the gift of life in one hand and a hatchet in the other. "The father waits for the son," Warren says at the end of "Billie Potts," and so the son comes back, at last, to what looks like prenatal unconsciousness: "Back to the silence, back to the pool, back / To the high pool, motionless, and the unmurmuring dream." And if he understands osmosis of being properly he will come willingly, when he must, to bow his head to the hatchet-blow, kneeling "Here in the evening empty of wind or bird, / . . . in the sacramental silence . . . , / At the feet of the old man. . . ."

By the same token, the father—and the old people generally—

are sacralized in Warren's writing by their acceptance of annihilation in the name of the osmotic process. In *The Cave*, Jack Harrick, stricken with cancer, at first resents the prospect of his wife and son living on while he must die: "Old Jack Harrick wished she were dead, dead so he could love her, and not hate her as he did when he thought of her lying alone in bed on a June night with moon coming in the window, and . . . her struggling against the need for a man-shape, simply a man-shape in the dark, not him, not Jack Harrick"; and "I wanted my own son to die." [20] But he comes to accept his approaching extinction after he learns of his son's death in the cave. And in *Promises*, Warren's own parents, Ruth and Robert Warren, accept the price of osmosis, willing in their deaths that the generations supplant one another. "Child," the two skeletons tell their son in his vision at their gravesite (in "What Was the Promise That Smiled from the Maples at Evening?"), "We died only that every promise might be fulfilled." Later in *Promises* the skeleton granny who is devoured by hogs repeats this acceptance of sacrificial death in the name of the one flesh sacrament: "I died for love." In "A Way to Love God," the first of the "Arcturus" poems, the mountains and sheep contribute to this theme by accepting their annihilation in "the perfected pain of conscience, that / Of forgetting the crime." So the mountains accept their "slow disintegration," though they "moan in their sleep" to indicate the sacrifice they are making, and the sheep accept their absorption into the night's death-mist: "Their eyes / Stared into nothingness. . . . / Their jaws did not move." To accept this lifelessness ("You would think nothing would ever again happen") is, at the poem's end, "a way to love God."

Like his parents, Warren commits his own identity to the one flesh concept in a number of particularly moving lyrics where he accepts his mortality in order that his children's promise may be fulfilled. *Promises* appropriately includes several of these poems. "Brightness of Distance" shows Warren asking his infant son, "as you move past our age that grudges and grieves," to think "How eyes, purged of envy, will follow your sunlit chance" in "the brightness and dwindle of distance" as the youth grows toward the new century. And in "Lullaby: Moonlight Lingers" Warren conveys to his sleeping son the blessing he had himself received in his own infancy from people now supplanted in time by the poet's own generation:

> Moonlight falls on sleeping faces.
> It fell in far times and other places.
> .   .   .   .
> Those who died, died long ago,
> Faces you will never know,
> Voices you will never hear—
> Though your father heard them in the night,
> And yet, sometimes, I can hear
> That utterance as if tongue-rustle of pale tide in moonlight:
> *Sleep, son. Good night.*

As a considerably older man—nearing his seventies, with his son entering manhood—Warren restated this commitment in "Sunset Walk in Thaw-Time in Vermont," one of the concluding poems in *Or Else*. In Section 1 the poet contemplates his mortality as the "Sunset Walk" motif might indicate, with "Eyes fixed past black spruce boughs on the red west," and hearing "In my chest, as from a dark cave of / No-Time, the heart / Beat." "Where / Have the years gone?" he asks. And in Sections 2 and 3 mortality encroaches closer in "the sound of water that moves in darkness" and "the cold exhalation of snow" above the "movement of darkening water." But in the closing section of the poem, the osmosis vision takes over. "When my son is an old man," the poet muses, "what / Blessing should I ask for him?" The answer is "That some time, in thaw-season, at dusk," while staring "Red-westward, with the sound of moving water / in his ears," he

> Should thus, in that future moment, bless,
> Forward into that future's future,
> An old man who, as he is mine, had once
> Been his small son.
>
> For what blessing may a man hope for but
> An immortality in
> The loving vigilance of death?

For Warren himself, then, as for his various personae, a life as a conscious being is a tool to be used up in the service of the larger being that goes on eternally. But if the price of osmosis is high, meaning death for the conscious ego, its rewards are also high, meaning a kind of immortality through the ministrations of that shadow self so often shunned and loathed and locked out of the house of the psyche. For the shadow self, as made known in dream or animal intuition, is perfectly at ease in that infinitude of time and space which smites the conscious mind with the anxiety that man and his earth are bubbles in a cosmic ocean. The indestructibility of this deeper self was implied in its survival through *Eleven Poems*, despite murder and burial in the house of the psyche's cellar, and this immortality seems even clearer in *Brother to Dragons*, with particular reference to the serpent and catfish metaphors. In having "the face of the last torturer," the catfish is clearly associated with the "original sin" aspect of Warren's thought, but it also has redemptive possibilities not given to the conscious ego. Using ice to denote the separation between the world of light and time and consciousness above, and the timeless, totally dark world of unconsciousness below, Warren enviously describes the catfish as having "perfect adjustment" (or we might say osmosis) with its environment and thereby being "at one with God."

In its oneness with the total darkness under ice, the catfish need not fear, as the conscious ego must, the awesome infinitude of time and cosmos above the ice where "The stars are arctic and / Their gleam comes earthward down uncounted light-years of disdain." The catfish's brother image, the serpent, likewise evinces intimations of an immortality transcending the naturalistic winter at the end of *Brother to Dragons*, where the snake, "looped and snug," survives in "earth's dark inwardness" underneath the pitiful ruins of the Lewis house, those "huddled stones of ruin" which "say the human had been here and gone / And never would come back, though the bright stars / Shall weary not in their appointed watch." [21] Jasper Harrick in *The Cave* gives human embodiment to these metaphysical speculations when he describes the cave as a place resembling the catfish's dark and timeless realm under ice: " 'It's a nice temperature down there,' he had said. 'It is not summer and it is not winter. There aren't any seasons to bother about down there,' he had said, and laughed. 'Blizzard or hot spell,' he had said, 'a lot of things don't matter down there.' " And Jasper goes on to state yet another advantage of that dark underworld; it, and only it, can yield forth the secret of final identity: "He had said, 'Well, in the ground at least a fellow has a chance of knowing who he is.' " [22]

"Perfect adjustment," being "at one with God," and knowing at last who you are—such are the final rewards of Warren's osmosis, though its final price is the death of the conscious ego. "And the death of the self is the beginning of selfhood," R.P.W. had stated in *Brother to Dragons*.[23] But the collective selfhood under the aegis of one flesh appears clearly superior to the separate ego, not only because of its gift of immortality but also because of its access to redeeming knowledge. In "The Ballad of Billie Potts" Warren had indicated this supremacy of the unconscious over the conscious self in a pair of memorable passages. The first lists several modes of establishing a conscious identity in a series of subordinate clauses— "Though the letter always came and your lovers were always true, / Though you always received the respect due to your position"— and then proceeds to undermine them with the main statement: "You became gradually aware that something was missing from the picture, / And upon closer inspection exclaimed: 'Why, I'm not in it at all!' " But as against this bankruptcy of the conscious ego in facing the question of identity, the unconscious—as usual, embodied in a series of animal images—shapes the direction and meaning of life through its secret, intuitive knowledge.

> (The bee knows, and the eel's cold ganglia burn,
> And the sad head lifting to the long return,
> Through brumal deeps, in the great unsolsticed coil,
> Carries its knowledge, navigator without star. . . .)

Like these creatures, Billie crosses from the realm of conscious to unconscious direction in coming home to his father and thus to death and eternity ("homeland of no-Time") in the poem's closing synthesis.

In the poetry since "Billie Potts," Warren has increasingly turned to the animal kingdom for models of calm acceptance of the mortal darkness. *Promises* gives us, in "The Flower," one of Warren's typical images used in this fashion. "The *rocca* clasps its height. / It accepts the incipient night," the poem reads, and then it places a gull against this setting:

It hangs on that saffron west.
It makes its outcry.
It slides down the sky.

. . . .

It has sunk from our sight.
Beyond the cliff is night.
It sank on unruffled wing. . . .

Such birds against the sunset recur throughout Warren's poetry. Taken together, they measure—in their acceptance of "the incipient night"—the difference between Warren's post-"conversion" philosophy and his earlier naturalistic cynicism. In a very early poem, "Pondy Woods," buzzards preside; several of them "swing against the sky and wait" for a posse to catch up with a fleeing murderer. Their comment, "Nigger, your breed ain't metaphysical," applies equally to Warren himself in that preosmosis period. By the time he finished *Promises*, however, Warren was "metaphysical" enough to draw upon even inanimate nature for eschatological instruction, for in the book's final poem, "The Necessity for Belief," acceptance of darkness is incumbent upon a nonliving thing: the sky, which "does not scream" although "The sun is red." Later, justifying the sky's "belief," the moon rises—"The moon is in the sky, and there is no weeping"—and so the poet bears out his theme: "There is much that is scarcely to be believed."

Among those things which are "scarcely to be believed," but which are of utmost importance in the dialectic of Warren's poetry, are his intuitive definitions of Time as opposed to the naturalistic definition offered by rational philosophers. Warren himself, in the aforementioned "Pondy Woods," spoke of "Time, the beaked tribe's [buzzards'] astute ally." But that was before Warren decided to "re-evaluate the whole question," as stated in *Or Else*, in this case by portraying Time—"the mirror into which you stare"—as "only a mirror in the fun-house." Here we reach the apex of Warren's mysticism: given the inability of even the most brilliant scientists, philosophers, and religious thinkers to encompass this most mysterious dimension of reality, Warren has permitted his intuitive powers to work freely in their stead, evolving thereby his conception of time as a dream.

The motif of the dream—a perception of reality arising from

the unconscious, as the word dream implies—has probably been Warren's most important new theme in poetry since *Brother to Dragons. Promises* is full of this motif, relating its highest promise— "*All Time is a dream* and we're all one Flesh, at last"—to the whole of Nature. In this light, the previous reference to the sky not screaming though "the sun is red" may become more meaningful, for inanimate nature is also locked in time's dream, according to Warren's vision. "The sky's dream is enormous," says "Colder Fire" in *Promises,* while in "Gull's Cry" in the same book Warren links up an osmotic moment on the human scene, caused by his daughter's laughter, with the "molecular dance" of "the stone's dream": "But at your laughter let the molecular dance of the stone-dark glimmer like joy in the stone's dream, / And in that moment of possibility, let *gobbo, gobbo's* wife, and us, and all, take hands and sing: redeem, redeem!"

The three "Lullaby" poems in *Promises* manifest the power of the dream in the person of the poet's sleeping son. "You will dream the world anew," says "Lullaby: Smile in Sleep," a dream shared vicariously by the child's observer: "Watching you now sleep, / I feel the world's depleted force renew." As against the trauma of passage that awaits the child's conscious personality—"You will see the nestling fall. / . . . see all / The world's brute ox-heel wrong"—sleep will provide "a sunlit meadow / Drowsy with a dream of bees / Threading sun" in which the child may "Dream grace" and "Dream the sweetness coming on." "What if angry vectors veer / Around your sleeping head . . . ?" the poem concludes,

> For you now dream Reality.
> Matter groans to touch your hand.
> Matter now lifts like the sea.
>
> . . . .
> Dream the power coming on.
> Dream, strong son.
> Sleep on.

"Lullaby: Moonlight Lingers" likewise murmurs, "Sleep, son, past grief," and "Lullaby: A Motion Like Sleep" compares the mind during sleep to water that, "under starlight . . . finds the dark of its own deepest knowledge." This "deepest knowledge" available in sleep compares to that which motivated the creatures coming "home" under subconscious direction at the end of "Billie Potts":

> . . . for sleep and stream and blood-course
> Are a motion with one name,
> And all that flows finds end but in its own source. . . .
> And will go as once it came.
> So, son, now sleep.

Climaxing this poetry of the dream in *Promises* is the "Ballad of a Sweet Dream of Peace," whose apocalyptic vision we have already considered under the "one flesh" theme. On closer look, we find further intuitions worthy of our attention, particularly as related to the poem's theism. The first line of this poem, *"And why, in God's name . . . ,"* introduces a recurrent motif that reminds us of Warren's statement about Coleridge's great "dream" poem: that *The Ancient Mariner* manifests "a sacramental conception of the universe, for the bird is hailed 'in God's name.' " [24] In his "Sweet Dream of Peace" Warren substantially exceeds Coleridge's theistic measure, for not only is the phrase "in God's name" repeated some sixteen times in nine pages, but God himself makes two appearances. In Poem 4, "Friends of the Family, or Bowling a Sticky Cricket," He comes in his ethical manifestation as a "cranky old coot" handing down the Law (with "placard proclaiming, 'I am the Law!' "), although He and His Law have been expelled from high society for spoiling their cricket game ("They learned that he drowned his crickets in claret. / The club used cologne, and so couldn't bear it"). Now, in Warren's comic-surrealistic rendering, "Barefoot in dusk and dew he must go." But final vindication of the Old Man is certain, not only because the king will sustain His Law *("But they drown them in claret in Buckingham Palace!")* but more importantly, because His Law is sovereign throughout the rest of Nature: "And at last each cries out in a dark stone-glimmering place, / 'I have heard the voice in the dark, seeing not who utters. Show me Thy face!' "

Even more momentous is God's other appearance in "Ballad of a Sweet Dream of Peace," where He acts in His metaphysical dimension as the Purchaser of the Woods in the poem's final lyric, whose title takes the form of a telegram: "Rumor Unverified Stop Can You Confirm Stop." The rumor unverified—for who can verify dreams and intuitions?—is that the God of reality is moving to redeem his fallen world:

> . . . there's a rumor astir
> That the woods are sold, and the purchaser
> Soon comes, and if credulity's not now abused,
> Will, on this property, set
> White foot-arch familiar to violet,
> And heel that, smiting stone, is not what is bruised,
> And subdues to sweetness the pathside garbage, or thing body
>   had refused.

The supernatural atmosphere of these lines makes a Christian interpretation tempting; but although possible, such a reading is not necessary. Most important here again is the tone of calm acceptance with which physical death (the "thing body had refused") is "subdued to sweetness" under the power of the mystic vision.

You, Emperors, and Others is also very effective in juxtaposing the conscious and the unconscious identities, to the great advantage of the latter. In contrast to the naturalistic anxiety of "You" (the conscious ego) in "Clearly about You," which is the book's opening poem ("Things are getting somewhat out of hand now—light fails on the marshes"), the book's second poem turns to dream and unconsciousness for therapeutic knowledge. This poem, "Lullaby: Exercise in Human Charity and Self-Knowledge," is addressed to a sleeper who, being unconscious, has lapsed out of the false identity provided in his conscious life by name (Stanza 1), face (Stanza 2), and sex (Stanza 3), and who therefore has access to an osmosis of being that blends his identity with the whole universe: "And your sweet identity / Fills like vapor, pale in moonlight, all the infinite night sky." This identity derived from the unconscious self has no name and elicits the speaker's closing benediction for exactly that reason: "Whoever I am, what I now bless / Is your namelessness." Further emphasis on the superiority of the unconscious appears in "A Real Question Calling for Solution," where conscious life is so chaotic that "There is only one way, then, to make things hang together, / Which is to accept the logic of dream" rather than such things of consciousness as "Night air, politics, French sauces, autumn weather, / And the thought that, on your awaking, identity may be destroyed." Warren's headnotes sometimes prove relevant, too, as when he refers to "a Roman citizen of no importance" and to Walter Winchell's radio greeting to "Mr. and Mrs. North America." According to Warren's osmosis of being, all citizens are of historical importance—or else none are—and even Winchell's phrase might hold a meaning its originator never realized.

You, Emperors, and Others is especially concerned with imparting a sense of power and vision through dream or animal intuition. "In the Turpitude of Time: N.D." states overtly man's need for such animal intuition: "Can we—oh, could we only—believe / What annelid and osprey know, / And the stone, night-long, groans to divulge?" And "Prognosis" (the prognosis is that you will die) tells quite plainly the advantage of knowing what annelid and osprey know. Here a woman doomed with cancer sleeps after a horrible day, and "past despair, / Dreamed a field of white lilies wind-shimmering, slow, / And wept, wept for joy. . . ." The horrors of consciousness having lapsed away, she can now "love the world" and hear "the grain of sand say: I know my joy." Here too she might recover the lost child-self of prelapsarian memory: "Time was not Time now—and once as a child she had lain / On the grass, in spring dusk, under maples, to watch the first fireflies. . . ." Fear of death, moreover, is as irrelevant at this level of consciousness as it was to the catfish in his "unpulsing blackness" under ice; thus the woman says of her impending death, "and I do not grieve to be lost in whatever / awfulness of dark." Intuition ventures past the awfulness of dark in some of the "Nursery Rhymes" like "The Bramble Bush" (where the speaker "now saw past the fartherest stars" and there "heard the joy / Of flesh singing on the bone") and "Mother Makes the Biscuits," where after staring "At the black miles past where stars are" the speaker attains the Coleridgean "sacramental conception of the universe":

> For the green worm sings on the leaf,
> The black beetle folds hands to pray,
> And the stones in the field wash their faces clean
> To meet break of day.

Tale of Time concerns mostly the world of time and consciousness that bespeaks the Fall, but here too the realm of dream and animal intuition offers its counterpoint. One such instance occurs in "Composition in Gold and Red-Gold," where the killing of a chipmunk causes the speaker's child to weep, but the focus shifts to a trout and an eagle, both enviably immersed in their environment, at the poem's end:

> Somewhere, in the shade of alders, a trout
> Hangs steady, head against a current like ice.
>
> The eagle I had earlier seen climbing
> The light above the mountain is
>
> Now beyond sight.

The eagle returns in another poem about death, "Fall Comes in Back-Country Vermont," where "Above sunset, above the mountain," it "Shoulders like spray that last light before / The whistling down-plunge to the mountain's shade," and thereby becomes another of nature's models of acceptance—of darkness, or death, or sleep—for the insomniac speaker. Even vegetable life serves the same theme in two poems about the rose. "Does the Wild Rose?" juxtaposes the flower's serenity, wholly immersed in nature (*"Does the wild rose know your secret / As the summer silence breathes"*), against the wintry grubbiness of the city's "black cement" and the speaker's anxiety over his night flight, imaged in his unopened flight insurance policy. And in "Two Poems About Suddenly and a Rose," "The rose dies laughing, suddenly," making an engaging contrast to the way flesh—particularly human flesh—dies in so many of these poems.

Further counterpoint to the traumas of human consciousness in *Tale of Time* comes through recourse to the unconscious mind. "Vision Under the October Mountain: A Love Poem" questions whether, in the preconscious fetal state, reality was prefigured as a gold dream, both world and self being then unfallen, much as in Wordsworth's "Intimations Ode." In "the tide of that bliss unbreathed, bathed in / un-self which was self," reality may have had a perfection that may later be attainable only in random glimpses, like the recollection of looking at the October Mountain: "did we /

once in the womb dream, dream / a gold mountain in gold / air floating . . . ?" Sleep and dream work similar magic in "Dream of a Dream the Small Boy Had," where the boy's conscious modes of identity are blown away during sleep ("Wind has blown me away, all but my bright bones"), leaving a quintessential self (the "bright bones") to imbibe a pure delight of being: "Where I am I don't know now, but hear my own heart / Off somewhere singing. . . . / It sings in a foreign language, like pig-latin, or joy."

Incarnations evinces fewer such mystic touches, but those few are equally intensive. In the "Island of Summer" series that opens the book the difference between the conscious and unconscious is set forth as the difference between day and night, to the substantial advantage of the subconscious / night. The book's opening poem "What Day Is," sees human artifacts since Roman days ("A handful of coins, a late emperor") as so much sawdust heaped by cicadas at the foot of infinity's tree. "That / Is what day is," the poem concludes, for which reason it ends in a warning that men cannot bear too much consciousness of reality: "Do not / Look too long at the sea, for / That brightness will rinse out your eyeballs," and "They will go gray as dead moons." "Mistral at Night," by contrast to "What Day Is," intuits in the subconscious a "knowledge [that] / Is the beginning of joy." The mistral, a strong northerly wind, compares with the working of the unconscious by creating images of "moonlight / To tatters torn, on night-blue the tetter / Of cloud-scud," along with the sound of clashing leaves—all of which resemble the contents of the mind during sleep: "and that / . . . is / In your sleep, and is as / Unforgettable as what is most deeply / Forgotten." Again the eschatological note sounds, as these images "Will be the last thing remembered, at last, in / That instant before remembering is over." And as usual this mystic knowledge cannot be very precisely rendered: "But what / Is it? You must wait / To find out." You must wait until you die, presumably, but meanwhile the mystic's sense of the importance and certainty of his vision rounds off the poem:

> . . . The world
> Is like wind, and the leaves clash. This knowledge
> Is the beginning of joy. I

        Tell you this as explicitly as I can, for
        Some day you may find the information
        Of crucial importance.

If this imagery of sleep gives a knowledge that is the beginning of joy, "The Ivy" (which follows "Mistral at Night") plunges even deeper below the realm of consciousness and returns with "Peace." The dream in this case belongs to the ivy, which is so unconscious as to be perfectly immersed in time's and nature's great dream. For this reason, "Time / is nothing to the ivy," which "Does not sweat at night, for like the sea / it dreams a single dream," and "Peace is the dream's name." The stone wall that the ivy assaults likewise "dreams," leaving the speaker to conclude on a note of mixed hope and envy: "Night comes. You sleep. What is your dream?"

The answer to that question is not very encouraging to judge from the insomniac speaker facing the return of day in "Masts at Dawn." But even here, though kept awake in darkness by images of people "fornicating in their ketches" and a "drowned cat . . . nudging the piles of the pier," the speaker intuits affirmations. The drowned cat, for example, resembles, while floating freely, "An eyelid, in darkness, closed"; and its lapse from the world of consciousness evokes an image of peace inherent in other deaths by water: "When there is a strong swell, you may, if you surrender to it, experience / A sense, in the act, of mystic unity with that rhythm. Your peace is the sea's will."

Audubon also shows the effects of Warren's osmosis, in its dream motif ("The Dream He Never Knew the End Of" is the longest, most crucial section of the poem) and in its hero's fusion of himself with the whole of nature ("Thinks / How thin is the membrane between himself and the world"). But since *Audubon* best serves our discussion of Warren's epiphanies, we shall pass on to his recent book of poems, *Or Else*. Here the counterpoint between Warren's naturalistic poetry of passage and his mysticism gives the book's title its meaning. The mysticism, as always in Warren, implies fusion with this world rather than escape from it. "Interjection # 6: What You Sometimes Feel on Your Face At Night" thus speaks of "God's / Blind hand" groping in the mist "to find /

Your face"—with the mist suggesting death, as in the "whiteness" motifs mentioned earlier. But here the death-mist comes in a Whitmanesque mood of mystical fulfillment: God's mist-fingers "Want to memorize your face"; they "Will be wet with the tears of your eyes"; God "Wants only to love you, perhaps."

Mystic fulfillment also follows death in "Natural History" in the perfect love and knowledge attained by the poem's spectral parents. The song of the "naked old father" dancing amid rain-drops "tells how at last he understands," says the speaker who, being still of this world, does not understand: "That is why the language [of the father's song] is strange to me." The mother counts "her golden memories of love" like money, and "the sum is clearly astronomical." Wakened by their deaths from time's dream—"That is why clocks all over the continent have stopped"—the old couple seem to have realized the "Natural History" of the poem's title by being absorbed into nature: he into the fertile rain, and she into the flowers—"Her breath is sweet as bruised violets, and her smile sways like daffodils reflected in a brook." At the end of the poem the speaker—like the ignorant initiate of "Ballad of a Sweet Dream of Peace" in *Promises*—protests against the illogic of what he has seen: "They must learn to stay in their graves. That is what graves are for."

The other "Natural History" poem, the longest and most ambitious entry in *Or Else*, is called "I Am Dreaming of a White Christmas: The Natural History of a Vision." The dream-vision of the title expands through the poem's dozen sections into one of Warren's grandest osmotic conceptions, rendering the oneness of time and flesh on a scale that binds together the living with the dead, family members with total strangers, densely compacted city-scape with vastly vacant countryside, summer heat and winter snow, past and present converging upon "the future tense / Of joy." By far the most intense part of the vision fastens with "blood greed" upon the mummified figures of the speaker's parents, who materialize for a phantom Christmas gathering with their three small children (including the speaker himself) in the old family parlor. Unlike their "dust-dried" flesh, lipless, eyeless, and tongue-less, the speaker's own flesh sweats in the (aptly-named) Times Square scene that follows. This midsummer scene, bespeaking in its vitality and chaos the high noon of conscious life, yields in turn to the symbolically deathlike quiescence of the first snow in the Montana mountains: "The first flakes, / Large, soft, sparse, come . . . with enormous deliberation, white / Out of unbreathing blackness." Pending his own submission to such "domination of white" (to revise a Wallace Stevens metaphor), the speaker concludes with two modes of identity. The first questions "Will I never know / What present there was in that package for me, / Under the Christmas tree?"; and the other formulates, in a flat poetry-of-statement style, a closing definition of Warren's osmosis:

> All items listed above belong in the world
> In which all things are continuous,
> And are parts of the original dream which
> I am now trying to discover the logic of.

In espousing this "reconciling, unifying" vision—to quote William James on the essence of all mystic perception—Warren also aims in the poem's last words to convert the "pain of the past in its pastness" into "the future tense / Of joy" through his osmotic connections. By implying a love of the world, joy is the surest mark of grace for the Warren persona; it is his sign of a religious redemption—redemption not in the sense of immortality, but in the sense that the world has come to seem permanently meaningful. This feeling of joy is the point at which Warren's two forms of mysticism converge—his osmosis of being and his epiphanies. And, repeatedly, joy affords the "moment of possibility" wherein the fallen persona may recapture his lost anima and dwell again, like the prelapsarian child-self, at least temporarily in paradise.

The turn to the animal kingdom or even to inanimate nature for osmotic wisdom appears to be culminating in Warren's latest poetry, which abounds with voices of nature striving to give utterance. As though reversing Freud's thesis about the inorganic hiding out within the organic, Warren in his "Arcturus" poems shows mountains, trees, and even the severed head of Mary, Queen of Scots, trying to say something. What they say, on one side, is that they share the human agony of limitations; and, on the other, that the human may share their perfect fullness of being. In "A Way to Love God" the human agony of limitations is enacted most graphically by Mary, who had accepted her death saying "In my

end is my beginning" but who kept trying to speak after her be-
heading: "The lips, / They were trying to say something very important." Her analogue in the poem is the mountains that accept
their "slow disintegration" but "moan in their sleep" over the
crime. "Brotherhood in Pain" extends the analogy to "any chance
object" that suffers "the obscene moment of birth" by being torn
from its matrix to experience individuality. To use William James's
terminology, the trauma is equally rending for the object moving
from the Many to the One as for Mary moving from the One to
the Many. But the object may show the human how to sustain
"Its experience . . . too terrible to recount": "Only when it has
completely forgotten / Everything, will it smile shyly, and try to
love you, / For somehow it knows that you are lonely, too."

What the voices of nature say to the human about fullness of
being is best reserved for our discussion of epiphanies, but we may
note here how abundantly the cosmos gives utterance. "All things
lean at you, and some are / Trying to tell you something" says the
most explicit of these poems, "Trying to Tell You Something."
What they mainly declare is their participation in a paradisical
realm of being such as men also enjoyed before their tragic lapse
into self-consciousness. Thus in "Evening Hawk" the bird "Who
knows neither Time nor error" moves "From plane of light to
plane, wings dipping through / Geometries and orchids that the
sunset builds"; and later, under a star that "Is steady, like Plato,
over the mountain," the "last bat cruises in his sharp hieroglyphics.
His wisdom / Is ancient, too, and immense." This combination of
bat's wisdom, hieroglyphics, and Plato evokes comparison with the
wad of gum's "Hellenistic chisel-work" (left by a molar) in
"Brotherhood in Pain." Acquiring the "immense" wisdom is all a
matter of deciphering an ancient language—a pictorial language,
even, since the message so often (as the oak declares in "Trying to
Tell You Something") is one of supernal natural beauty.

In "Three Poems in Time," which are to appear in 1977 in
the *Atlantic Monthly*, the speaker—a fallen soul—seeks redemptive wisdom through recourse to three successive voices of the subliminal consciousness: wild geese, his own dreams, and his "nameless" anima. Each voice, in turn, poses its reply to a question that
the speaker's rational consciousness finds unanswerable: "Do I
know my own story?" (Poem I, "Heart of Autumn"); "What can

you dream to make Time real again?" (Poem II, "Dream"); and "Can you locate yourself / On the great chart of history?" (Poem III, "Ah, Anima!"). Drawing upon their secret recess of knowledge, the geese in Poem I rise to become "Sky-striders, / Star-striders" in their "path of pathlessness," giving "imperial utterance" with "all the joy / Of destiny fulfilling its own name." In Poem II the dream self ("for the dream is only a self of yourself") comes, like Jacob's angel, to yield "a blessing, by dawn"; and in Poem III, the anima summons the fallen self into a sort of psychic apocalypse, "to leave / The husk behind, and leap into the / Blind and antiseptic anger of air." Magnifying the significance of these subliminal utterances is the contrasting inefficacy, in each poem, of conventional human language. Thus the metamorphosis of the speaker into a wild goose, sailing "With folded feet . . . / toward sunset, at a great height" in "Heart of Autumn," leaves his heart "impacted with a fierce impulse / To the unwordable." Confirming this motif in "Dream" is the severed tongue that Ajax suffers after crashing his head on the ground, jarring his teeth so that "blood filled / That mouth from its tongue, like a grape-cluster, crushed." Finally, in "Ah, Anima!" the fallen self is last seen with "mouth, rounded, . . . and utterance gone" in answer to the anima's summons.

In "Dream of a Dream" (published by the Stinehour Press in December, 1976 as a Christmas card for G. K. Hall & Company), the dream is the mode of consciousness within which the cosmic tongue may best be apprehended, for in Warren's osmotic scheme the whole of nature shares a dream of being. "In my dream Time and water interflow, / And bubbles of consciousness glimmer as they go," says the speaker, who, though puzzled at the grand process, yields his identity to it:

> . . . [I] wonder whence my name
> Bubbled forth on a moonlit stream
> To glitter by the singing stones
> A moment before it, whirling, is gone
> Into the braiding texture of dream.

Here the singing stones give utterance to Time's dream, declaring a fullness of being that asks nothing beyond its own lyric immanence:

> What they sing is nothing, nothing,
> But the joy Time plies to feel
> In fraternal flux and glimmer
> With the stream that does not know
> Its destination and knows no
> Truth beyond its moonlit shimmer.

At the end of the poem the speaker sees his conscious life as another dream, "a glimmering dream of the golden air, / Of green and of dapple," following which he may, like Billie Potts, accept his death sacramentally: "till finally, / From the twilight spruce thicket, darkening and far, / A thrush, sanctifying the hour will utter / The glory of diminution." Later, qualifying this tone, "The owl's icy question shudders the air"; but "By this time the moonlight's bright heel has splashed the stream," thus evoking once more the singing stones and their cosmic utterance.

With this look at Warren's most recent poems, our discussion of Warren's osmosis of being ends. Ever since "The Ballad of Billie Potts" this insight has reigned over Warren's verse as his most important idea, greatly imbuing his characters, images, and even verse forms with thematic meaning, while providing the chief remedy for the lapsarian trauma of his earlier work. We turn next to the final phase of Warren's poetic vision, that of epiphanies. But before we do that, a brief last word on Warren's osmosis seems desirable in order to place this concept in context.

It is only just that we conclude this discussion with a few lines from the master of osmosis, Walt Whitman. In a conversation we once had Warren expressed the misgiving that Whitman's work is unduly optimistic.[25] And certainly Warren's own continuing pre-occupation with delusion, betrayal, and depravity makes some of Whitman's ringing affirmations seem innocent and sentimental by contrast. Warren distrusted Whitman, I think, because Whitman's osmosis (in accordance with his Quaker "Inner Light" heritage) lacked the dimension of conflict and reconciliation within the self between conscious ego and humanity's black collective shadow. On the other hand, Whitman *did* preface his grand osmotic vision with the mystic experience that unified body and soul, like passionate lovers, in Section 5 of *Song of Myself,* which might correlate with Warren's fusion of the bifurcated self in his "Undiscovered Self" poetry. For both poets, in any case, the healing of an internal schism, whether between Whitman's body and soul or Warren's conscious and unconscious zones of the psyche, seemed a prerequisite to the osmotic union between the unified self and the outer world.

Few poets have ever proclaimed the osmosis of being with a force and efficacy equalling Whitman's. "And these tend inward to me, and I tend outward to them," Whitman says in *Song of Myself* after embracing all manner of folk in a tremendous catalogue: "The pure contralto sings in the organ loft . . . The deacons are ordain'd with cross'd hands at the altar . . . The lunatic is carried at last to the asylum a confirm'd case, / (He will never sleep any more as he did in his mother's bedroom) . . . The malform'd limbs are tied to the surgeon's table / What is removed drops horribly in a pail . . . The youth lies awake in the cedar-roof'd garret and harks to the musical rain . . . The old husband sleeps by his wife and the young husband sleeps by his wife . . . And of these one and all I weave the song of myself" (Stanza 15). Whitman's osmosis, like Warren's, embraces creatures long dead as well as those of the present time: "In vain the mastodon retreats beneath its own powder'd bones." And most strikingly, Whitman's metaphysics are at one with Warren's in seeing one's cobweb connections to the entirety of past and future time and in accepting the gift of death gracefully, as a welcome fulfillment or release into ultimate identity:

> Afar down I see the huge first Nothing, I know I was even there,
>
> . . . .
>
> Cycles ferried my cradle, rowing and rowing like cheerful boatmen,
>
> . . . .
>
> For it [my embryo] the nebula cohered to an orb,
> The long slow strata piled to rest it on,
> Vast vegetables gave it sustenance,
> Monstrous sauroids transported it in their mouths and deposited it with care.
>
> . . . .
>
> Now on this spot I stand with my robust soul!
>
> *(Song of Myself, Stanza 44)*

Like Warren's creatures under ice or his sleepers who "do not fear whatever awfulness of dark," Whitman is enabled by his osmosis to accept return to the oblivion that bred him:

> A few quadrillions of eras, a few octillions of cubic leagues . . .
> They are but parts, any thing is but a part.
>
> See ever so far, there is limitless space outside of that,
> Count ever so much, there is limitless time around that.
>
> *(Stanza 45)*
>
> And I say to any man or woman, Let your soul stand cool and
>   composed before a million universes.
>
> . . . .
>
> (No array of terms can say how much I am at peace about God
>   and about death.)
>
> *(Stanza 48)*

And as with Warren, this acceptance of death comes through the ministrations of an unconscious self that perceives a pattern and meaning not available to the conscious ego:

> There is that in me—I do not know what it is—but I know
>   it is in me.
> Wrench'd and sweaty—calm and cool then my body becomes,
> I sleep—I sleep long.
> I do not know it—it is without name—it is a word unsaid,
> It is not in any dictionary, utterance, symbol.
>
> . . . .
>
> It is not chaos or death—it is form, union, plan—it is eternal
>   life. . . .
>
> *(Stanza 50)*

Moved by these intuitions from the unconscious, Whitman can bend his will, even as Warren's parents or old granny did in *Promises*, to commit his identity to the osmosis of being. Just as they "died for love," Whitman tenders his corpse to become food for the grass he loves: "I reach"—like a lover—"to the leafy lips, . . . to the polish'd breasts of melons. . . . I bequeath myself to the dirt to grow from the grass I love, / If you want me again look for me under your boot-soles." And as *Song of Myself* ends, still greater oneness is pending: "I stop somewhere waiting for you."

Osmosis of being, in various manifestations, is not a new idea.

It obviously motivated Emerson's conception of an Oversoul, for example, as well as Wordsworth's pantheistic vision of "a spirit that . . . rolls through all things" (*Tintern Abbey*). And it figured largely in the efforts of other Romantic and pre-Romantic thinkers like Blake, Rousseau, and Spinoza to displace both the Deist's mechanistic God and the King- or Patriarch-God of traditional Judaic thought with something innate and vital and this-worldly. Ultimately, the concept dates back to sacred writ. An idea of osmosis underlies the biblical ethic of brotherhood, as preached by Jesus and Isaiah (who foresees his God embracing Israel and its worst enemies alike at one point, saying—Isaiah 19:25—"Blessed be Egypt my people, and Assyria the work of my hands, and Israel mine inheritance"); and it inspired as well the Hindu metaphysics of *Atman* (the soul), as seen in the *Bhagavad-Gita:* "I am the beginning, the life-span, and the end of all . . . I am the divine seed of all lives . . . Know only that I exist, and that one atom of myself sustains the universe" (Part XI—"The Yoga of Mysticism").

In our times the declining influence of such sacred writ has hastened the tendency, predicted by Matthew Arnold, for the poet to supplant the priest in interpreting life's meaning. And in a number of our best modern writers, an irruption of cosmic consciousness corresponding to Warren's osmosis of being has provided a redeeming, self-transcending vision. Hart Crane's *The Bridge* is a prime instance, its theme of oneness culminating in the mystic ecstasy of "Atlantis": "O Thou steeled Cognizance . . . / Within whose lariat sweep encinctured sing / In single chrysalis the many twain." Among Warren's fellow Southerners, cosmic consciousness seems remarkably pervasive, producing some passionate fusions between self and environment. Carson McCullers' Spinozan "science of love," whose major manifestation lies in Biff Brannon's role in *The Heart Is a Lonely Hunter,* works like Warren's osmosis in her short story "A Tree, A Rock, A Cloud": "For six years now I have . . . built up my science: And now . . . I can love anything . . . a street full of people . . . a bird in the sky . . . a traveler on the road. . . . Everything, Son. And anybody. All stranger and all loved." William Styron delivers his protagonist over to a memorable irruption of cosmic consciousness in *Set This*

House on Fire: "Ah my God, how can I describe it! It wasn't just the *scene*, you see—it was the sense, the bleeding *essence* of the thing. . . . It was no longer a street that I was watching; the street was inside my very flesh and bones, you see, and for a moment I was released from my own self, embracing all that was within the street and partaking of all that happened there in time gone by, and now, and in time to come. And it filled me with the craziest sort of joy." [26] Faulkner too evoked osmosis of being in describing Mink Snopes's sleep with "Helen and the bishops, the kings and the un-homed angels" at the end of *The Mansion,* "himself among them, equal to any, good as any, brave as any, being inextricable from, anonymous with all of them," so that "wouldn't nobody even know or even care who was which any more." And in *The Bear,* the antagonists—man, dog, and bear—die into a similar mystical fusion of identities that resembles Warren's collective unconscious, as Ike visits "the knoll which was no abode of the dead because there was no death, not Lion and not Sam: not held fast in earth but free in earth and not in earth but of earth, myriad yet undiffused of every myriad part, leaf and twig and particle, air and sun and rain and dew and night, acorn oak and leaf and acorn again, dark and dawn and dark and dawn again in their immutable progression, and, being myriad, one: and Old Ben too." To judge from such excerpts, osmosis of being should claim serious attention as a possible revelation of life's meaning. Through it Warren fulfills Coleridge's dictum that "Art is . . . the mediatress between, and reconciler of, nature and man." [27] Through it also Warren becomes a prime exemplar of Wordsworth's definition of the poet, "Carrying everywhere with him relationship and love" wherewith to oppose the world's loss and fragmentation: "In spite of difference of soil and climate, of language and manners, of laws and customs; in spite of things silently gone out of mind, and things violently destroyed, the poet binds together by passion and knowledge the vast empire of human society, as it is spread over the whole earth and over all time." [28]

EPIPHANIES

The question of the One and the Many—whether the universe is ultimately one thing or many disparate things—was described by

William James as "the final question of philosophy. . . . the deepest and most pregnant question that our minds can frame." [29] It is characteristic of Warren's dialectical mentality that his response to this question had been to embrace *both* the monistic and the pluralistic alternatives, as James called them, so as to affirm that reality is simultaneously One and Many in its manifestations. This duality means that the collective, communal, or one may even say cosmic, identity intuited in "Billie Potts," *Brother to Dragons*, and the other poems of osmosis is not Warren's only mode of identity. Together with this collective and perhaps unconscious source of identity that comes from a Whitmanesque synthesis of being, there exists—so long as one lives in the world—the identity of the conscious, individual ego, the Wordsworthian or Thoreauvian private man for whom Warren also wishes to speak, most often by using himself as the material for his poems but sometimes by speaking for a historic personage like Audubon, Flaubert, or Dreiser. The essay on "Knowledge and the Image of Man," which gave us the osmosis of being metaphor, carefully marks this distinction: "Despite this osmosis of being to which I have referred, man's process of self-definition means that he distinguishes himself from the world and from other men. He disintegrates his primal instinctive sense of unity, he discovers separateness." Paradoxically, the tragic fact of loneliness thus experienced provides the basis of subsequent human communion, for "once he realizes that the tragic experience is universal and a corollary of man's place in nature, he may return to a communion with man and nature." We thus arrive at Warren's version of the higher innocence, couched in images that remind us of the poems of passage:

> Man can return to his lost unity, and if that return is fitful and precarious, if the foliage and flower of the innocent garden are now somewhat browned by a late season, all is the more precious for the fact, for what is now achieved has been achieved by a growth of moral awareness. . . .
>
> Man eats of the fruit of the tree of knowledge, and falls. But if he takes another bite, he may get at least a sort of redemption. And a precious redemption. His unity with nature will not now be that of a drop of water in the ocean; it is, rather, the unity

of the lover with the beloved, a unity presupposing separateness. His unity with mankind will not now be the unity of a member of the tribal horde with that pullulating mass; his unity will be that of a member of sweet society.[30]

Complementing his osmosis of being, this "unity with nature" that resembles "the unity of the lover with the beloved" is best seen in Warren's epiphanies, which carry his own love of the world to its ultimate expression. "We must try / To love so well the world that we may believe, in the end, in God," the speaker commented in "Masts at Dawn" *(Incarnations)*. By providing "Joy," "Delight," and insight into "The True Nature of Time"—to quote Warren's designations—Warren's epiphanies convey a power that enables men, even after their trauma of passage into a fallen world, to "love the world" and so to love God, the world's otherwise unknowable sustainer. In his definition of the epiphany experience, Warren appears to follow Walter Pater's classic formulation in the last chapter of *Studies in the History of the Renaissance:* "Every moment some form grows perfect in hand or face; some tone on the hills or the sea is choicer than the rest; some mood of passion or insight or intellectual excitement is irresistibly real and attractive to us,—for that moment only. Not the fruit of experience, but experience itself, is the end. . . . To burn always with this hard, gemlike flame, to maintain this ecstasy, is success in life."

In his epiphanies, Warren obviously shares Pater's thirst for "getting as many pulsations as possible into the given time"; in *Audubon* he goes so far as to say, "what / Is man but his passion?" (and: "what is your passion?"). But unlike Pater and his latter day exponents of the hard gemlike flame—Joyce, Wallace Stevens, Hemingway, Nabokov, Fitzgerald—Warren attaches religious significance to the experience, leading to love of the world and thus (possibly) belief in God. In this conception Warren shares an attitude that William James noted in Havelock Ellis, who (James said) "identifies religion with the entire field of the soul's liberation from oppressive moods," such that (James quoted Ellis here) " 'Even the momentary expansion of the soul in laughter is, to however slight an extent, a religious exercise.' " [31] John Updike, too, has shared this feeling in his most "religious" novel, *The Centaur. "All joy belongs to the Lord"* (Updike italicizes the point): "Wherever in the filth and confusion and misery, a soul felt joy, there the Lord came and claimed it as his own; into barrooms and brothels and classrooms and alleys slippery with spittle, no matter how dark and scabbed and remote, in China or Africa or Brazil, wherever a moment of joy was felt, there the Lord stole and added to his enduring domain. And all the rest, all that was not joy, fell away, precipitated, dross that had never been." [32] Perhaps Warren's clearest statement of this feeling occurs in "Switzerland" in *You, Emperors, and Others.* Here the speaker marshals a half-dozen stanzas of corrosive irony towards this "world-mecca for seekers of health and pleasure," noting among his fellow resort dwellers the "half-destroyed bodies" of the old, the boring routines of the young ("So it's three by the time one's adjusted one's darling, and pressed her"), and the panic of middle age ("the lady theologian . . . for therapy now trying a dago"). But counteracting all this, the last stanza utters a prayer to the "God of the *steinbock's* great sun-leap" to "Let down Thy strong hand to all whom their fevers destroy" and "Deliver them all, young and old, to Thy health, named joy."

  Like his osmosis of being, Warren's epiphanies seem to have come into play only after his "conversion" experience made them possible, and they have become a predominant note only in his recent volumes—flooding in as the undiscovered self theme was tailing off in the late 1950s. The early poems contain almost nothing of the epiphany experience. In *Selected Poems* (1944) only "Resolution" gives a small hint of it: "Time's secret pulse / The huddled jockey knows. . . . / The pitcher on his mound, / Sun low, tied score." Otherwise what might pass for epiphanies, like the "Picnic Remembered" episode, collapse into the ruins of passage. For this reason the function of the epiphany as a final source of meaning in *Promises* constituted something new in Warren's poetry, an incursion of Pateresque thought set off in counterpoint against the long travail to wrest meaning from history in Warren's earlier writing. Jack Burden's venture into "history and the awful responsibility of Time" at the end of *All the King's Men* now yields to the ecstatic intensity of the moment, which may offer the best understanding of the meaning of Time, in poems like "The Flower," "Colder Fire," and "Gold Glade." "Time's irremediable joy" (a phrase from "Lullaby: A Motion like Sleep") gives a permanent sustenance that would develop more largely in *Tale of Time, Audubon,* and *Or Else.* Thus we should consider the epiphany experience in *Promises* rather closely.

In the Rosanna sequence "The Flower" marks the major turning point in Warren's epiphanies. Through the earlier three poems the girl, in her prelapsarian state, had enjoyed a continuous paradisical condition, while the speaker slumped into postlapsarian despair, thinking of the defective child next door, of "how empires grind, stars are hurled," and of beauty destroyed "in the ruck of the world's wind." In "The Flower," however, the absorption of the speaker into the girl's perspective permits not only a remembrance but a partial possession of paradise, and a way of transcending time's ruins after the Fall. Since this is an important turning point, let me quote the speaker's incantation at length:

> Let all seasons pace their power,
> As this has paced to this hour. . . .
> Let the future reassess
> All past joy, and past distress,
> Till we know Time's deep intent,
> And the last integument
> Of the past shall be rent
> To show how all things bent
> Their energies to that hour
> When you first demanded your flower.

The essence of the epiphany is an intuition of Time's oneness that corresponds to the "One Flesh" doctrine developing elsewhere in Warren's poetry:

> And in that image let
> Both past and future forget,
> In clasped communal ease,
> Their brute identities.

In a passage like this we have come a very long way indeed from the image of time's fragmentation in "Picnic Remembered" *(Selected Poems,* 1944): "The *then,* the *now:* each cenotaph / Of the other, and contains it, dead."

Epiphanies of time past are captured to perfection in "Gold Glade" and "Boy's Will . . . ," but we shall end our look at *Promises* with what may be the best of these epiphanies, "Colder Fire." As in Wordsworth's "Resolution and Independence," this poem begins in morning rain-sadness that yields to a later sun-joy suitable for the epiphany experience: "Now sun, afternoon, and again summer-glitter on sea. / As you [Rosanna] to a bright toy, the heart leaps. The heart unlocks / Joy. . . ." In this mood the "colder fire" turns out to be a metaphor for Wordsworth's "emotion recollected in tranquillity," the emotion in this instance stemming from the poem's "collocation / Of memories" that "defines, for the fortunate, that joy in which all joys should rejoice." The mountain-climbing episode at the heart of the poem thus becomes a paradigm for the epiphany experience generally, providing at mountaintop an emotional lift and visual perspective whose effects are permanent:

> Pine-blackness mist-tangled, the peak black above: the glade
>   gives
> On the empty threshold of air, the hawk-hung delight
> Of distance unspooled and bright space spilled—ah, the heart
>   thrives!
> We stood in that shade and saw sea and land lift in the far
>   light.

A descent from this splendid vista into the (emotional) valley is of course inevitable, but through the "colder fire" of memory (or poetry) the epiphany retains its power, for "Height is not deprivation of valley"; it rather imparts, to returning valley-dwellers, "that joy in which all joys should rejoice."

You, Emperors, and Others is a book given over largely to poems of passage and the undiscovered self, but it too has its counterpoint of epiphany-mysticism. In addition to the prayer in "Switzerland" for "Thy health, named joy," there is a poem named "Joy" that points up the ineffability of the experience:

> If you've never had it, discussion is perfectly fruitless,
> And if you have, you can tell nobody about it.
> To explain silence, you scarcely try to shout it.
> Let the flute and drum be still, the trumpet *toot*less.

At the end of *You, Emperors, and Others* the grasshopper singing its epiphany—"Sing *summer, summer,* sing *summer* summerlong"— affirms the relegous meaning of joy. The world proclaims itself, Warren is fond of saying, and all its separate creatures must proclaim themselves in a joy that shows "how Nature participates in God." Here, in "Grasshopper Tries to Break Solipsism," Warren's osmosis and his epiphany-mysticism converge in just such a religious expression, with the insect's song manifesting both its connection with the outer world and its innate Blakean joy of being: "For God is light, oh I love Him, love is my song." From such song, in a sense, God himself derives the world's meaning—"I sing, for I must, for God, if I didn't, would weep, / And over all things, all night, His despair, like ice, creep." (Here Warren seems to reflect William James's view, in "Pragmatism and Religion," that God depends on the world's agents to help Him perfect the world, rather than ordering such perfection: "Suppose that the world's author put the case to you before creation, saying: 'I am going to make a world not certain to be saved, a world the perfection of which shall be conditional merely, the condition being that each several agent does its own level best . . . !' ") [33]

In the poetry of the 1960s and 1970s Warren's epiphanies have gained increasing ascendancy in counterpoint with the poetry of passage that continues its tenure. *Tale of Time* renders some striking examples. "Patriotic Tour and Postulate of Joy" lays out the setting for this development by showing the narrator rising to the sound of the mockingbird late at night, and crying out "in my need / To know what postulate of joy men have tried / To live by, in sunlight and moonlight, until they died." The following poem, "Dragon-Tree," answers that need somewhat in its counterpoint of opposites. After developing images of nocturnal anxiety—a faucet dripping all night, icy black water rushing through the gorge nearby, news of cannibalism in the Congo, geese flying over insomniac ears "in dawn-light"—the poem ends with the narrator asking "to just sit with the children and tell a tale ending in laughter," for although "your heart is the dragon-tree," its "new leaf flaps gilt in the sunlight. Birds sing." "Insomnia," the final entry in the "Tale of Time" sequence about mother's death, likewise synthesizes emotional contraries. A poem in four segments, it first conjures up in a broken style a night-visit to mother's grave, followed by an eerie communion with the departed. The final section consummates the epiphany in a dialectic of pain and joy (his mother's ghost is the "striker from darkness"):

> Come,
> Crack crust, striker
> From darkness, and let seize . . .
>
> . . . .
>
> The heart till, after pain, joy from it
> Spurt like a grape. . . .

After this, as T. S. Eliot says, our exile: the vision collapses like the heat lightning in the last stanza, as the visionary eye, returning to ordinary reality, "Adjusts to the new dark, / The stars are, again, born." But again the epiphany's effects are lasting: "Truth / Is all," the speaker confirms, "I must learn to speak it / Slowly, in a whisper."

Tale of Time concludes strategically with a cluster of eight poems under the heading, "Delight." Here the lyric note decidedly predominates through mostly short lines, much rhyme, and pyrotechnical sound effects, as in Poem II, "Love: Two Vignettes": "How instant joy, how clang / And whang the sun, how / Whoop the sea" and "Now, now, the world / All gabbles joy like geese," for "Look! / All leaves are new, are / Now, are / Bangles dangling and / Spangling, in sudden air / Wangling. . . ." A gift unearned and unreasoned (*"Nor can it be guessed"*), delight strikes "suddenly," strikes *"now"* in these poems, walking "on soundless foot / Into the silence of night, / Or into broad daylight" and provoking emotions that range from the philosophically serene ("Delight may dawn, as the day dawned, calmly, today"—Poem III) to the orgasmically intense ("Look! In that bush, with wolf-fang white, delight / Humps now for someone: *You*"—Poem VI). Sometimes delight comes through the unconscious, during sleep, as in "Dream of a Dream the Small Boy Had" ("my heart a bird singing / . . . in a foreign language, like pig-latin, or joy"). Often it emanates from childhood, as in "Two Poems About Suddenly and a Rose," where the speaker learns delight from his children ("In hands of *now*, they hold / Presents of *is*") and a Keatsian moment ensues: "Now

. . . I see / Forever on the leaf the light. Snow / On the pine-leaf, against the bright blue / Forever of my mind." Having lived in delight, "The rose dies laughing, suddenly," at the end of "Intuition," which is presumably how delight itself dies, between epiphanies.

"Finisterre" concludes *Tale of Time* with something like an artist's delight, perhaps a painter's perspective of San Francisco Bay at day's end, when the sun may "stab gold to the gray sea, and twist / Your heart to a last delight—or wonder." A far cry indeed from "Pacific Gazer," its analogue in *Thirty-six Poems* ("A gazer of saddest intent / . . . Stares where light went"), "Finisterre" is in the tradition of Poe's or Wallace Stevens's belief that beauty is the sole province of poetry, because beauty helps us to live our lives by giving them pleasure and meaning. The "Delight" sequence as a whole likewise stands at the opposite pole from Jack Burden's "history, and the awful responsibility of Time"; but its joyous *carpe diems* nonetheless constitute, like *All the King's Men*, an expression of their author's moral sense. "The truth is implicit *in the poetic act as such, that the moral concern and the aesthetic concern are aspects of the same activity*," said Warren in his *Ancient Mariner* essay (emphasis his), and this seems to be where his epiphanies are leading, to culminate in the "new dimension of beauty" witnessed by Audubon.[34]

Incarnations, although devoted largely to poetry of passage, nonetheless terminates like *Tale of Time* in a few pages of richly textured poems, called "Enclaves," about some epiphanies recollected in tranquillity. Written in an elegant, sound-rich style, full of long vowels, inverted syntax, and trochaic cadences, these poems evoke a tradition reaching from Dylan Thomas to the old epics. "Once over the water, to you borne brightly, / . . . I, / Riding the spume-flash, by gull cries ringed, / Came." So begins "The Faring." Later, in "The quiet place," the lovers learn "The True Nature of Time" (the subtitle of "Enclaves") as time seems to decelerate for them. A sunset ray "Came gilding a track across the gray water from westward," fingering the yellow wall-roses: "One / Petal, yellow, fell, slow." "High beyond roses, a gull, in the last light, hung," while down below, "The sea kept slopping the rocks, slow." Poem 2 renders "the true nature of Time" in its title metaphor of "The Enclave," which fixes the eye of memory upon the moment the lover spotted his sweetheart waiting on shore: "Wind / Lifts the brightening of hair."

"Skiers" brings on the notion that "The human / Face has its own beauty" as the supreme evocation of Warren's epiphanies. If the world's chief function—and that of each separate thing in it— is simply to declare its own being, then the human face would be the world's highest manifestation of this principle. For this reason Schopenhauer in *The World as Will and Idea* had conceived of portrait painting as the highest form of visual art, since the portrait of a human face would best capture that essence of self-declaration wherein each living thing reflects the Will-to-Exist emanating from Schopenhauer's God. Unlike Schopenhauer, Warren does not see this deific Will-to-Exist as something depraved, amoral, perhaps insane. To the contrary, when simply accepted it makes possible a state of grace like that attained at last by Audubon, who was, "In the end, himself and not what / He had known he ought to be. The blessedness!" Audubon acquired this perfected Will-to-Exist (simply to be himself) from its presence in the face of the hanged woman. Her refusal to pray at the moment of death is her first assertion of this principle:

> They are asked if they want to pray now. But the woman:
> "If'n it's God made folks, then who's to pray to?"
> And then: "Or fer?" And bursts into laughing.
>
> . . . .
>   . . . She waits,
> And is what she is.

This recalcitrance in itself suffices to produce in the observer a sure sign of epiphany emotion or "passion" (his erection) and the woman's second assertion of the Will-to-Exist in absolute self-integrity transmits what Audubon considers "a new dimension of beauty":

> The affair was not quick: both sons long jerking and farting,
>   but she,
>
> . . . .
> In a rage of will, an ecstasy of iron. . . .
>   The face,
> Eyes a-glare, jaws clenched, now glowing black with congestion

Like a plum, had achieved,
It seemed to him, a new dimension of beauty.

This scene in *Audubon* climaxes a series of "face-epiphanies"
going back to Nick Pappy's discovery, in Warren's 1959 novel *The
Cave*, that Mrs. Harrick's "was the first human face . . . he had ever
looked into. Really looked into, just for its humanness. At that, some
bone-shaking happiness broke over him. . . ."[35] The "Homage to
Emerson" sequence *(Tale of Time)* likewise ends in the image of a
face, with "muted glitter" of tears in the eyes but "lips about to
smile"—the only image in the whole sequence that bears out Emerson's "thought that significance shines through everything." And
coming back again to "Skiers" *(Incarnations)*, we see the faces
"slowly enlarge to our eyes" as the skiers "swoop, sway, descend,"
and "Cry their bright bird-cries" while coming "With the motion
of angels, out of / Snow-spume and swirl of gold-mist." Returned
to the "Trodden and mud-streaked" bottom, the old world of
"Time and Contingency," they convey in their faces their joy of
being. "They smile. The human / Face has its own beauty."

Or Else is suffused with epiphany-magic. In addition to reprint-
ing here some poems from *Incarnations* and *Tale of Time*, Warren
has stitched a full dozen new epiphany-poems into the warp and
weave of this book, "conceived as a single long poem," his preface
says. Through these epiphanies he pursues the poetic purpose implied in the book's headnote, quoted from Psalms 78:15: "He clave
the rocks in the wilderness, and gave them drink as out of the great
depths."

In "Interjection # 2: Caveat," Warren himself cleaves the rock
figuratively. Looking down a highway where "Crushed rock has /
been spread for miles," his persona asks us to "fix your eyes firmly
on / one fragment of crushed rock," which first "glows a little,"
then evinces "a slight glittering," and soon thereafter, "a marked
vibration." Now it declares its being in a blaze of mystic glory:

> . . . suddenly, the earth underfoot is
> twitching. Then, remarkably, the bright sun
> jerks like a spastic, and all things seem to
> be spinning away from the univer-
> sal center that the single fragment of
> crushed rock has ineluctably become.

A poem that synthesizes the One and the Many, this "Interjection" begins with the osmosis of being—"Necessarily, we must think of the / world as continuous"—and concludes with the rock fragment metaphor of individual identity. The poem culminates with a warning: "Not all witnesses / of the phenomenon survive unchanged / the moment when, at last, the object screams / in an ecstasy of / being."

The ecstasy of being finds its most articulate expression among human beings, particularly if they are artistically gifted. Even poor Dreiser in "Homage to Theodore Dreiser" was momentarily lifted from his naturalistic weltschmerz by moonlight, or so the famous song about the Wabash implies, leading to Warren's image of "the moonlit continent" in the "tearless and unblinking distance of God's wide eye." "Flaubert in Egypt" shows the French master consumed entirely by his sexual and aesthetic epiphanies, finding a joy so intense that not even his chancre sore can dampen the love of the world caused by such beauty:

> . . . on the river at Thebes, having long stared
> at the indigo mountains of sunset, he let
> eyes fix on the motion of three wave-crests that,
> in unison, bowed beneath the wind, and his heart
> burst with a solemn thanksgiving to God for
> the fact he could perceive the worth of the
> world with such joy.

Years later it is this aesthetic religion, rather than faith or works, that ushers him into eternity, when, "death near, he remembered the palm fronds— / how black against a bright sky!"

The major experience of epiphanies in *Or Else* belongs to the Warren persona, who brings them back from "A Place Where All Is Real," according to "Interjection # 3"—a high country "somewhere / northwest of Mania and beyond Delight." Specific epiphanies range from the simple recording of "one thing that is not important but simply is" (a child playing in red dust) in "Forever O'Clock" to the moonlight swim and the wranglers crying "I-yee!" ("That thin cry of joy from the mountain") in "Rattlesnake Country." Turning *"was"* into *"is,"* such memories sustain the "unsleeping principle of delight" in "Interjection # 8"—a principle that

"Declares the arc of the apple's rondure; of, equally, / A girl's thigh," and "brackets, too, the breaker's crest in one / Timeless instant, glittering. . . ."

Among these perceptions of beauty and meaning one poem stands out as rather different from the others. "Folly on Royal Street Before the Raw Face of God" derives its mystic insight from what for Warren the poet is an uncommon source: booze. Flanked by two "skunk-drunk" drinking buddies, our speaker launches the poem with a comic effect by converting Milton's "dark, dark, dark, amid the blaze of noon" (*Samson Agonistes*, lines 80-81) to "Drunk, drunk, drunk, amid the blaze of noon, / Irrevocably drunk, total eclipse. . . ." What happens in this drunken state, however, has real significance for our theme of epiphanies. Once again William James, in the amazing scope of his inquiry, renders a crucial judgment: "The sway of alcohol over mankind is unquestionably due to its power to stimulate the mystical faculties of human nature. . . . Sobriety diminishes, discriminates, and says no; drunkenness expands, unites and says yes. It is in fact the great exciter of the Yes function in man. . . . The drunken consciousness is one bit of the mystic consciousness. . . ."[36] In "Folly on Royal Street" the Yes function of booze displays its power twice: first, when "God's / Raw face stared down. And winked" at the drunkards three; and second, when they "Mouthed out our Milton for magnificence" in the public streets of New Orleans. Given the Eliotic and New Critical bias against Milton's epic style and its underlying vision of human importance, this "magnificence" would have been inaccessible to our drinkers in their sober state. But years later, recollecting that emotion in sobriety ("For what is man without magnificence?"), the speaker intones in verse what James had prosaically asserted: "let / Bells ring in all the churches. / Let likker, like philosophy, roar / In the skull. Passion / Is all. Even / The sleaziest."

Given such a passion, the speaker of "Interjection # 7" notes in his "Remarks of Soul to Body" "how glory, like gasoline spilled, / . . . may flare, of a sudden, up, / In a blinding blaze, from the filth of the world's floor." Two poems on the true nature of time close out our look at this book's epiphanies. "Birth of Love" shows a man watching a nude bather; "all / History dissolving from him," he "is /

nothing but an eye. Is an eye only. Sees. . . ." This alone is meaningful
time, says the speaker: "This moment is non-sequential and absolute," for "it / Subsumes all other, and sequential, moments," much
as happened in the crucial epiphany-poem of *Promises*, "The
Flower." "There's a Grandfather's Clock in the Hall" confirms
this judgment by listing a number of life's most intense experiences
(having sex, lying abed as a child seeing morning sunlight, observing your mother's wedding or death) as instances of "no-Time,"
those intervals between jumps of the minute hand on Grandfather's
clock. To burn in those moments with Walter Pater's hard, gemlike
flame is to know how "Time / thrusts through the time / of no-
Time" as this poem ends—a formulation similar to Eliot's "point of
intersection of the timeless / With time" in *Four Quartets*. Precisely
contrary to the poetry of passage—"it is too late / to pretend we
are children . . . ," concludes the "Dr. Knox" sequence in *Tale of
Time*—Warren's epiphanies assert "the truth, which is: *Seize the
nettle of innocence in / both your hands, for this is the only /
way*." This done, joy may burst insanely from the world's wounds,
and "*every / Ulcer in love's lazaret may . . . sing—or even /
burst into whoops of . . . holiness*" (emphasis Warren's, in
"There's a Grandfather's Clock in the Hall").

In the "Arcturus" poems, epiphanies emanate out of nature in
quasi-Romantic splendor. In "A Way to Love God," the "silence /
Blows like wind by, and . . . the sea's virgin bosom [is] unveiled / To give suck to the wavering serpent of the moon." And
in "Old Nigger on One-Mule Cart" the spectacle of "white night
and star-crackling sky over / The snow-mountain" precipitates the
speaker's fantasy of immersion in nature—"through drifts flounder-
ing, white / into whiteness, among / Spectral great beech-boles,
birch-whiteness. . . ." The most important poem about nature declaring its meaning is "Trying to Tell You Something," which says
"All things" are "Trying to tell you something, though of some /
The heart is too full for speech." Here the object striving to give
utterance is an ancient oak tree, braced now by rods and cables,
which themselves "sing"—in the wind—"Of truth, and its beauty."
What the oak wants to declare is an epiphany of transcendent
beauty, when perfect fullness of being becomes manifest in the
natural world:

> ... It wants,
> In its fullness of years, to describe to you
> What happens on a December night when
>
> It stands alone in a world of snowy whiteness. The moon is full.
> You can hear the stars crackle in their high brightness.

For the lapsarian human, the effects of such a vision could be transforming: "And no one can predict the consequences."

Audubon: A Vision is especially serviceable as our final study in Warren's mysticism because it fuses the osmosis of being theme and Warren's epiphanies into the "Vision" declared in the poem's subtitle. Published in 1969, this is a book whose genesis reaches back for a quarter of a century. In an interview with *The Vanderbilt Alumnus* Warren stated, "I read Audubon's journals twenty-five years ago when I was reading a lot about early America. Well, over these twenty years lines came and went. About three years ago, I started rereading the journals, and the poem began to come." [37] This genesis in the middle of the 1940s explains what might otherwise seem a curious anomaly: the fact that the poem about Audubon centers not upon the bird paintings, but rather upon a brutal frontier episode of attempted murder followed by a hanging. The narrative's plot thus resembles that of "The Ballad of Billie Potts" (published in 1944): Audubon puts up as a paying guest in a back-woods shack, inflames the avarice of his hostess by displaying a fine gold watch before retiring, and awakens to find the woman and her two sons about to kill him. After being saved by three men who burst into the cabin at this moment, Audubon lingers to watch the woman and her two sons hanged the next morning.

Up to this point the narrative seems to bear out the theme of lapsarian knowledge announced in Part II-B: "The dregs / Of all nightmare are the same, and we call it / Life. He knows that much, being a man." But this knowledge is followed by an "Or Else" proposition: "Unless. / Unless what?" Unless an irruption of mystic insight decrees otherwise: that is *Audubon's* answer to the question, as it has been the answer to the trauma of passage ever since "The Ballad of Billie Potts." We have already considered the poem's climactic mystic insight in connection with the "face-epiphany" of the hanging scene. Now it is time to contemplate that mystic moment in the light of the poem's overall structure.

Audubon begins, as is typical of Warren's writings, with an identity problem. The book's first poem, "Was Not the Lost Dauphin," dispels the most famous legend about Audubon—that he was the missing son of Louis XVI and Marie Antoinette. Quite the contrary, Warren's headnote tells us that Audubon was not only common-born but the bastard child of Jean Audubon (then a slave dealer in Santo Domingo) and his mistress, though he passed himself off as the legitimate child of his father and the wife his father had left back in France. Since he was not the person whom legend or even his own imposture declared him to be, the question properly arises, who *was* he? This first poem, and the whole book, proffers the answer that he "was only / Himself, Jean Jacques, and his passion—what / Is man but his passion?" Part B of "Was Not the Lost Dauphin" points to the man's true identity by showing him in his passion, wholly absorbed by a Wordsworthian immersion in nature while watching a bear eat blueberries. Warren's command of sound texture nicely corroborates the richness of the epiphany: "The bear's tongue . . . out-crisps to the curled tip, / It bleeds the black blood of the blueberry," while "Bemused, above the fume of ruined blueberries, / The last bee hums." Its "wings, like mica, glint / In the sunlight." Osmosis with nature seems quite easy and inviting in this setting: "He leans on his gun. Thinks / How thin is the membrane between himself and the world."

What follows this pleasant experience is the harrowing tale of Audubon's encounter in the cabin, which also, however, shows "how thin is the membrane between himself and the world." Continuing for some fifteen pages (about half the book), this episode constitutes Poem II, "The Dream He Never Knew the End Of." Part A of "The Dream" (it consists of segments headed A to M) describes Audubon's first look at the cabin, "a huddle of logs with no calculation or craft: / The human filth, the human hope." Its inhabitants are not only poor but shiftless, too lazy even to chop clean wood, as the foul smoke from their fireplace testifies: "thinks: 'Punk-wood.' / Thinks: 'Dead-fall half-rotten.'" As he raises his hand to knock on the door, the theme of identity passes over to the woman who will answer: "The nameless face / In the dream of some pre-dawn cock-crow—about to say what, / Do what?" (Part

B). Though still nameless (she remains so in fact), she is defined more clearly in Part C. Here and in the later hanging scene, Audubon observes her face with the clarity of one of his bird paintings:

> The face, in the air, hangs. Large,
> Raw-hewn, strong-beaked, the haired mole
> Near the nose, to the left, and the left side by firelight
> Glazed red, the right in shadow, and . . .
> . . . under the coarse eyebrows,
> The eyes, dark, glint as from the unspecifiable
> Darkness of a cave. It is a woman.

In Part D Audubon witlessly precipitates the contingencies that follow by displaying his gold watch, a symbol not only of time but also of the woman's lifelong deprivation:

> It is gold, it lives in his hand in the firelight, and the woman's
> Hand reaches out. She wants it. She hangs it about her neck.
> . . . her eyes
> Are fixed downward, as though in shyness, on that gleam, and her
>   face
> Is sweet in an outrage of sweetness, so that
> His gut twists cold. He cannot bear what he sees.
> Her body sways like a willow in spring wind. Like a girl.

When the time comes to take back the watch and she, "sullen and sunken," turns to fix the food, Audubon catches a warning from an Indian who is also putting up at the cabin: "the Indian / Draws a finger, in delicious retardation, across his own throat." In Part E, after the woman's two sons have come in from the night, the guest pretends to sleep but is disturbed by the sound of the woman honing a knife by the fire; and in Part F she and her sons rise toward him, acting out "the dream he had in childhood but never / Knew the end of, only / The scream." In Part G, rather than defend himself, Audubon seems transfixed by a death wish: " 'Now, now!' the voice in his head cries out," but "now a lassitude / Sweetens his limbs" and "Everything seems far away and small." Like a man convicted of sin—as perhaps he should be, because of the watch—Audubon almost welcomes his immolation: "He cannot think what guilt unmans him, or / Why he should find the punishment so precious." (This undefined guilt marks Audubon as an "aware" character, like Jack Burden or R.P.W. in *Brother to Dragons;* it is part of the osmosis of being theme.) How this dream, or nightmare, might have ended we will never know, as Part H complains, because a band of men burst into the cabin at this climactic moment and truss up the woman and her two sons to await hanging in the morning.

This hanging episode imparts to Audubon his vision of identity, which derives from his discovery while witnessing the woman's death that the human soul—no matter how lowly or wretched its contingent circumstances—is capable of a transcendent grace and dignity. "In heroism, we feel, life's supreme mystery is hidden," said William James of this phenomenon; and in *Audubon* Warren aligns himself with writers like Hemingway and Faulkner who share this feeling.[38] The woman's final heroic stance, as unpredictable as that of Faulkner's Mink Snopes or Wash Jones, points up the Faulknerian verities of the heart—honor, courage, endurance, and the integrity of simply being oneself. Part I shows the woman ready to die bravely, refusing the anodyne of whiskey (as she later refuses the anodyne of prayer); and Part J—the most crucial passage in the book—describes her stoic confronting of death ("She waits, / And is what she is") which precipitates Audubon's greatest epiphany and even kindles his erotic passion. Her nameless face now expresses its innermost identity—"the face / Is, he suddenly sees, beautiful as stone"—as it reveals the woman's "rage of will, an ecstasy of iron" in her dying. In the poetry of years past this woman would probably have figured as one of Warren's beastly people, like Lilburn Lewis or Big Billie Potts, acting out in animalistic style a drama of "Original Sin" or natural depravity. Here, however, because of the osmotic vision that "merges the slayer with the slain" (and the Clean with the Dirty), her face declares to the artist-spectator the "new dimension of beauty" which it is this book's purpose to transmit. Rather like Eliot looking into the "heart of light" in the Hyacinth Girl episode of *The Waste Land*, Audubon enters a state of transcendent emotion (Part L):

> There are tears in his eyes.
> He tries to remember his childhood.

He tries to remember his wife.
He can remember nothing.

Throat parched, hand clutching the gold watch, he yearns at this moment "to frame a definition of joy." In Part M Audubon stands studying the woman's face long after the others have gone, with only a crow call to break the deathlike silence:

> He thought: "I must go."
>   But could not, staring
> At the face, and stood for a time even after
> The first snowflakes, in idiotic benignity,
> Had fallen. Far off, in the forest and falling snow,
> A crow was calling.

Although the modern mind tends to think of death as the extinguishing of identity, Warren appears to believe that death—the end of time's dream—releases the secret of identity or confirms it somehow. Thus the aftereffects of the hanging are short lyrical poems of serenity and affirmation. And in the same way that Warren's figure of grace comes to accept the world and even to "love it" just as it is, he now comes to accept himself just as he is. Part III of *Audubon*, "We Are Only Ourselves," states this insight (the woman's legacy to Audubon) as baldly as its title; but Part IV, "The Sign Whereby He Knew," states it symbolically. In a reversal of Warren's early poems of passage, the vanished *ur*-self (a vanished doe in "Eidolon") now materializes in the hunter's sights—"The quarry lifts, in the halo of gold leaves, its noble head"—and "the self that was, the self that is" coalesce into unity. Reversing this poems of passage motif, too, is Audubon's serene immersion in his autumn and sunset settings (Part IV, B and C), which have their own ingathering beauty. Immersed in nature almost like one of his birds ("After sunset, / Alone, he played his flute in the forest"), he sometimes hears "The jay, sudden as conscience." This call, reminiscent of the crow's call when the woman died, is presumably the sign referred to in the poem's title ("The Sign Whereby He Knew"). In "The Sound of That Wind" he reflects on his life both in nature and in human society. Then he dies easily and naturally, as befits one who has glimpsed the osmosis of being and who therefore has "merged the ugly with the beautiful, the slayer with the slain" until "the world which once produced fear and disgust . . . may now be totally loved":

> His mind
> Was darkened, and his last joy
> Was in the lullaby they sang him, in Spanish, at sunset.
> He died, and was mourned, who had loved the world.
> Who had written: ". . . a world which though wicked enough
> in all conscience is *perhaps* as good
> as worlds unknown."

Audubon's death, like that of the woman, is attested by a cluster of death-images, with Warren himself now the impassioned artist-spectator thinking how when Audubon died, "Night leaned, and now leans, / Off the Atlantic, and is on schedule . . . [and] with no sound sweeps westward" across the Mississippi, where a wrecked tree, "white as bone," is "reflected in dark water, and a star / Thereby." Replacing Audubon's bird against the dawn in Poem I is a plane now "winking westward" in the upper darkness.

In "Love and Knowledge" Warren finally mentions Audubon's celebrated artistic achievement; but again he is more interested in Audubon's soul, or his "passion," than in the paintings: "He slew them . . . with his gun. / Over a body held in his hand, his head was bowed low, / But not in grief." What bowed Audubon's head was not grief but love, which Warren here defines as knowledge ("What is love? . . . / One name for it is knowledge"). In his essay "Love and Separateness in Eudora Welty" (1944), Warren describes Welty's Audubon (in "A Still Moment") as "one who does 'love' the bird, one who can innocently accept nature" (unlike the evangelist Lorenzo who shouts "Tempter!" at a white heron). But he finds "an irony here. To paint the bird he must 'know' the bird as well as 'love' it, he must know it feather by feather, he must have it in his hand. And so he must kill it. . . . He loves the bird, innocently, in its fullness of being. But he must subject this love to knowledge; he must kill the bird if he is to commemorate its beauty, if he is to establish his communion with other men in terms of the bird's beauty." [39] For Audubon, then, as Jack Burden had earlier ruminated, the price of the only kind of knowledge worth having is blood. But blood is also a communion symbol, binding the slayer and the slain—the birds, the hanged woman, and Audubon himself —in their osmotic relationship of passion and knowledge. In Poem I Warren had anticipated this nonorthodox use of communion symbolism by having Audubon witness a heron's flight against a sunrise "The color of God's blood spilt." In the light of Warren's osmosis of being, all blood is "God's blood" in that "Nature participates in God," and Audubon, with "head . . . bowed low," therefore kneels over the "body held in his hand" in a natural eucharist.

The final poem in this book moves from Audubon's forte, painting, to Warren's, which is writing; but in both cases the driving motive is the yearning for knowledge. One thinks again of Wordsworth's *Preface* of 1800: "Poetry is first and last of all knowledge— it is immortal as the heart of man." "Tell Me a Story" concludes *Audubon* with two vignettes of Robert Penn Warren himself. The first, Part A, recalls an evening in early spring when Warren was a boy in rural Kentucky listening to the geese hoot northward in the dark. We are reminded here of the first poem of *Audubon* ("what is your passion?"): "I did not know what was happening in my heart." In Part B Warren advances his notion that life is ultimately a story. After time's dream has unfolded its design, what we have left is a story, the immense tale of Time whose particles the artist gathers. Especially in the light of the osmosis of being, every particle is precious, worthy of passion, worth preserving.

For all the pain and loss in the story's unfolding, *Audubon* terminates in "Delight"; its last line reads, "Tell me a story of deep delight." That, in the "Love and Knowledge" made possible by Warren's mysticism, is the final meaning of the story. It is not the *only* meaning, for the poems of passage continue to provide bass counterpoint, as it were, to this lyric melody. But in Warren's late poetry delight is a final meaning, as it was in Yeats's late poems or Melville's. A passage from Hawthorne's *American Notebooks* best describes Warren's achievement in this respect, I think, for Warren's long poetic odyssey, from the Fall through his undiscovered self period to his mysticism, resembles nothing so much as Hawthorne's "human heart to be allegorized as a cavern":

> . . . at the entrance there is sunshine, and flowers growing about it. You step within, but a short distance, and begin to find yourself

surrounded with a terrible gloom, and monsters of diverse kinds; it seems like Hell itself. You . . . wander long without hope. At last a light strikes upon you. You . . . find yourself in a region that seems, in some sort, to reproduce the flowers and sunny beauty of the entrance, but all perfect. These are the depths of the heart, or of human nature, bright and peaceful; the gloom and terror may lie deep, but deeper still is the eternal beauty.[40]

Whether Hawthorne ever made it through the heart's cavern may be doubted. But to judge from his poems of mysticism, Warren's arrival at the sunlit haven seems more surely attested.

5

Postscript: An Appreciation

LOUISE BOGAN selected "Pacific Gazer" as one of the "very fine" entries in *Thirty-six Poems;* John L. Stewart thought it "probably his worst" in that collection. Stewart, in turn, bestowed the epithets "magnificent poem" and "superb poem" upon "Love's Parable" and "The Return: An Elegy," whereas F. W. Dupee found "The Return" to be "mildly embarrassing" and W. P. Southard called "Love's Parable" the "only flat silly poem" in *Selected Poems* (1944). Skipping over the controversy about "Billie Potts," we find Delmore Schwartz admiring *Brother to Dragons* as "a work which is most remarkable as a sustained whole," and John McCormick contending that "it fails as a formal whole" despite being "superb for lines, pages, and scenes at a time." Concerning its style, Hugh Kenner said "its characteristic voice . . . resembles that of a Kentucky preacher hypostatizing Sin," whereas Leslie Fiedler said, "I . . . praise the skill and courage with which Warren has pursued a difficult, improbable, heartbreaking rhetoric." Reviewing *Selected Poems* (1966), Peter Davison preferred Warren's narrative style to his lyrics, which "often sound windy and portentous"; in the same book Louis Rubin, Jr., focused on the most lyrical cluster of them all, the "Delight" sequence, as illustrating a "poetry of much excitement and movement, filled as always with striking images and a keen ear for rhythmic cadences." To George Core, *Incarnations* proved how Warren's poetry has "slipped noticeably" in recent years, its only good entry being "Myth on Mediterranean Beach"; to Louis Martz, the book was an exciting reading experience: "This volume has a total integrity of great power." [1]

The inference to be drawn from this passel of contradictions is obvious enough: appreciative judgments of however reasonable a tone must lead at last to the subjective cul-de-sac of each reader's personal taste. That being the case, it is best that my own appreciation be brief, something in the way of an impressionistic postscript to a basically analytical study. In rendering this personal judgment, I should like to comment first upon Warren's evolving mastery of verse texture and then to conclude with a few words about Warren's "place" in modern American poetry.

SOME NOTES ON VERSE TEXTURE

In the June-July 1923 number of *The Fugitive* magazine, Robert Penn Warren, just turned eighteen, was one of five poets selected as "Qualified for the Nashville Prize"—a bonus that neither he nor fellow competitor Hart Crane finally won. Warren's entry, "Crusade," evinces many telltale signs of the recency of *The Waste Land*—a poem that "every Southern freshman, literarily inclined, knew by heart in 1922," according to Warren's own testimony.[2] Seeking "the Tomb of God," Warren's crusader finds only Eliotic doubt—"Can rock and dust presage a fabled heaven?"—and Eliotic imagery of death and sterility: "Skulls glaring white on red deserts at noon; . . . / Flies on bloated bodies rotting by the way." The one sign of personal talent in the poem is an appeal to eye and ear that sometimes emerges: "The long green wash of breakers swirling in."

In *Thirty-six Poems* the Eliot influence continues strong, particularly in the volume's two most ambitious poems, "Kentucky Mountain Farm" and "The Return: An Elegy." "Kentucky Mountain Farm" begins, like *The Waste Land*, with the cruel reawakening of springtime, that "season of the obscene moon whose pull / Disturbs the sod, the rabbit, the lank fox"; and the poem's sectioning in seven parts also suggests Eliot's influence. (The phrase "fractured atoms" in Part II was evidently lifted from "Gerontion.") Yet the style is pre-Eliot, with a late Victorian regularity of rhyme, meter, and stanza pattern. And the imagery is local and original, foreshadowing among other things the poet's lifelong passion for birds (a jay, a cardinal, and a hawk dominate three of the seven poem-segments) and his ideal of self-unification (the closing image of the leaf meeting its reflection represents parts of the self merging). In "The Return: An Elegy" the Eliotic manner is more noticeable, not only in the naturalistic rendering of death but in the style: the recurrence of key phrases, as in the structure of a musical composition; the Prufrockian conversation between parts of a divided self (*"the old fox is dead* / what have I said"); the intermixing of rhyming lines of irregular length to intensify the mood; and powerfully accumulating "if" clauses (like Eliot's "If there were only water") to render inexpressible grief and desire ("If I could pluck / ... For you my mother / ... Out of the dark the dark and swollen orchid of this sorrow"). That repetition of "the dark the dark" as noun and adjective risks obscurity, but is an effective mood-deepener.

Influence of poets besides Eliot is also apparent in the early poems; but Warren's borrowings, like Eliot's own, usually aim towards some original effect. The parallels with Marvell and Donne in "The Garden" and "Love's Parable," for example, are deliberate and extensive; yet their metaphysical style is sufficiently "made new," as Pound would have it, to speak to our own time about the problem of ruinous knowledge. And poems that have reminded readers of Thomas Hardy, like "Pacific Gazer" and "Calendar," muster some fine original effects among the Hardyesque accents; stanza 2 of "Calendar," for example, closes with a striking autumnal metaphor: "the frost will warp / The oak, and wind thumb / That cold-taut harp." The only oppressive influence I have found among Warren's poems is that of Hart Crane in "Problems of Knowledge," which employs the interrogative gambit and the density of imagery that often overloads Crane's syntax: "What years, what hours, has spider contemplation spun / Her film to snare the muscled fact?"

Such specific influences aside, Warren's status as a poet was assured almost from the beginning by his ear for word-music. Master of a remarkable variety of styles, he has always lavished care upon the sound of his lines as well as upon his rhetorical effects. "Late Subterfuge," for example, begins with a Pope-like or Johnsonian couplet—"The year dulls toward its eaves-dripping end. / We have kept honor yet, or lost a friend"—but it also includes lines that for internal rhyme and alliteration might date back to *Beowulf:* "The snake cold-coiled, secret in cane the weasel." In *Eleven Poems* as Warren's vision of the undiscovered self deepens the richness of his sound texture seems to deepen apace. "Original Sin: A Short Story" begins, for example, with a nightmare vision: with "locks like seaweed strung on the stinking stone, / The nightmare stumbles past. . . ." Here are seven "s" sounds, five "st" constructions, a "strung-stink-stone" progression all introduced by the "locks like" slant rhyme, not to mention the long vowel effects. In "Pursuit" Warren goes after the moods and rhythms of the sea, from its "sunlit hurlyburly" to its "fury / Of spume-tooth and dawnless sea-heave" in "the dire meridians, off Ireland." "End of Season" tells how "toward moon-set de Leon / Woke, while squat, Time clucked like the darkling ape"—and with those five "k" sounds, that last line matches the ape cluck for cluck, we might say. At the end of this poem *you* are offered advice: "deep and wide-eyed, dive / Down the glaucous glimmer where no voice can visit." Here, structured around the internal rhyme of "wide-eyed," are five "d" sounds and a three-part alliteration, "deep . . . dive . . . Down," followed by "glaucous glimmer" and "voice . . . visit." In "Crime" the poet again appeals both to eye and ear in telling how "the seasons stammer / Past pulse in the yellow throat of the field-lark," while in "Terror" he detonates a string of labial consonants: "Not picnics or pageants or the improbable / Powers of air. . . ." (The first stanza, in which this line appears, is an exercise in the grand style: a ten-line sentence built around three repetitions of the verb *suffice*.)

When fast pace is needed in "The World Comes Galloping" (part of the "Mexico" sequence), Warren bunches alliterative dactyls to catch the rocking rhythm of his crazed horseman: "banging the cobbles like castanets, / . . . Wall-eyed and wheezing, the lurching hammer-head, / The swaying youth. . . ." In "Billie Potts," the auditory magic leaps to the ear everywhere, in short phrases ("salt-lick and . . . lyric swale"), in richly textured couplets ("The lucent leaf is lifted, lank beard fingered, by no breeze, / Rapt in the fabulous complacency of fresco, vase, or frieze"), and in sustained Miltonic flights of euphony ("The bee knows, and the eel's cold ganglia burn . . ."). Under the spell of those liquid *l*'s and *n*'s and *s*'s, together with the incantatory repetition of long vowels in an *e-o* pattern, even the hard consonants take on a lyrical quality in this passage.

In *Brother to Dragons* the organ range of auditory effects is far too varied and prolific to catalogue here, but let us note a few: the sibilance of the minotaur's passing, for example ("when the hoof heaves— / Listen!—the foulness sucks like mire"), and the slow reptilian movement of the serpent Nidhogg, "whose cumbrous coils and cold dung chill / The roots of the world's tree." [3] Amid the blank verse and purple passages, some lighter effects are tucked away: a heroic couplet in response to a D.A.R. marker that falsifies the Lewis family's history ("But let that pass, for to the pious mind / Our history's nothing if it's not refined"), and an imitation of Robert Frost when the occasion warrants ("That seemed ungracious, not in the country manners, / The only manners left that aren't for show"—pp. 21, 25). The imitation Eliot obtrudes a bit in Warren's "Hollow Men" passage ("Wind, force without body, word without / Meaning, accident without essence"—p. 97), but the lengthy rhyming incantation in the style of Eliot's dramatic choruses seems perfectly appropriate as R.P.W. conjures up the book's night of infamy:

> Let now the night descend
> With all its graduated terrors,
> And in its yearning toward absoluteness now amend
> The impudent daylight's velleities, and errors,
> And let the dark's most absolute shame
> Amend the day's finicking shamelessnesses . . .
>
> . . . .
> For all life lifts and longs towards its own name.
>
> *(p. 121)*

In *Promises*, again, a short list of auditory effects may suffice to give the flavor of the whole: the lyric vowel texture of "The Flower" ("Bee drowsy and blowsy with white bloom," "scent and sun-honey of air," "Bemused with sea and slow / With June heat and perfume"); the assonance, consonance, and alliterative echoes in "Colder Fire" ("Pine-blackness mist-tangled, the peak black above: the glade gives / On . . . the hawk-hung delight / Of distance unspooled and bright space spilled"); the shifting moods of the sea as the poet addresses the moon in "Man in Moonlight" ("you smoothed the sweet Gulf asleep, like a babe at the breast" or "spangled spume-tangle on black rock, and seal barked at sea-roar"). A similar fusion of sound and sense transmits the spectacle of the tractor in "Hands Are Paid" (part of the "Boy's Will" sequence): "The tractor now, a-clank, a-shamble, / Grunts down the pike, the long way home." So much depends—Carlos Williams might say—on the trochaic substitution that simultaneously reinforces "Grunts" and matches the antique motor's irregular rhythm. Mention should also be made of some other comic effects in *Promises*—the "noses . . . imperfectly blown" in the poem about the Gillum family, or the dragon's spoor ("that field-mist is where his great turd steams") in "Dragon Country."

You, Emperors, and Others is perhaps the clearest example of Warren's synthesis of the old and new styles, respecting the formal discipline of the high Modern period to a surprising degree while exploiting the loosening effects sanctioned by "the New American Poetry." The loosening effects are evident in his individual lines, which sometimes resemble Blake's or Whitman's free verse laxity (in "Prognosis" and "The Letter about Money," for example); but his stanza patterns remain remarkably disciplined to a recurring rhyme pattern, even in these experimental exercises. "The Letter about Money," for example, consists of eight stanzas that at first look like free verse, but they disclose on closer inspection a recurrent *abbacdcdede* rhyme pattern. Again, space permits only the smallest sampling of this volume's auditory smorgasbord: Achilles withdrawing the spear from his victim in "Fatal Interview" ("and flesh-suction sighs sad, once"); the seeker of dawn in "The Letter about Money" ("then see . . . the snow peak go gory, / and the eagle will unlatch crag-clasp, / fall, and at breaking of wing-furl, bark glory"); and the cacophonous riot of harsh consonants—labials and glottal stops—describing the moment of death in "Between the Boxcars" ("when that blunt grossness, slam-banging, bang-slamming, blots black the last blue flash of sky"). The three sections of this last poem mark a progression from traditional rhyming quatrains, through Warren's distinctive "loose" style (irregular line lengths in a tightly disciplined rhyming pattern), and into genuine Whitmanesque free verse dependent on parallel syntax for its repetitions ("He has fled . . . ," "He has retired . . ."). The effect of the three styles is perhaps comparable to that of a cubist painting in trying to approach the central fact of death from three disparate angles.

In *Tale of Time* Warren largely shifts over to the metrics of "the New American Poetry." A few poems, like "The Mad Druggist" and parts of the "Delight" sequence, maintain a rhyme scheme; but most of the book resembles the Eliot-Pound-Williams free verse strain as opposed to the Yeats-Auden-Thomas discipline of the high Modern period. (Warren has become increasingly "American" and less "British" in this respect ever since *Thirty-six Poems*.) Here the intensity of experience seems principally to carry the poem, with the lines being broken up according to something like Pound's "musical phrase" or Williams's rhythm of breathing. Charles Olson's manifesto on Projective Verse, published in 1950, states three principles that we find increasingly evident in Warren's verse of these last two decades: (1) the primacy of content over form ("FORM IS NEVER MORE THAN AN EXTENSION OF CONTENT"); (2) a reliance on the rhythm of breathing ("And the line comes—I swear it—from the breath, from the breathing of the man who writes, at the moment he writes"); and (3) exploitation of the typewriter as a way of indicating this breathing rhythm ("due to its rigidity and its space precisions, it can, for a poet, indicate exactly the breath, the pauses, the suspensions even of syllables . . . which he intends. For the first time the poet has the stave and the bar a musician has had").[4]

A poem like "Insomnia" demonstrates these principles in that the content (a night visit to mother's grave) dictates the form (broken sentence syntax); the rhythm of breathing determines line lengths (under the emotional stress, the rhythm is actually that of panting); and the typewriter has been used to "score" the composition (the poem cannot be scanned except as seen on the page): "If to that place. Place of grass. / If to hour of whippoorwill, I. . . . / If now I, not a child, should come to / That place. . . ." Warren's special signature in this new style is his fondness for breaking his lines—a bit like a mad stonecutter, at times—so as to split up what normally would constitute units of grammatical syntax, separating preposition from object ("Like / A bursting blood blister"—"Elijah on Mount Carmel"), subject from verb ("Wind / Does not move"—"Stargazing"), adjective from noun ("Hoover was not a bad / Man"—"What Happened"), and so forth. The idea is presumably to accentuate, as breathing naturally does during speech, the initial words or phrases of the lines thus partitioned, so as to give unusual emphasis to the word "face," for example, in the following line from "Insomnia"; "What age has the soul, what / Face does it wear . . . ?"

Another feature of Warren's new style is a frequent recourse to elliptical grammar, as in "Chain Saw at Dawn in Vermont" (Part 2) where a single subject ("a man") is implicitly repeated with a long series of verbs in subsequent statements ("Is dying," "Wakes," "thinks," "wonders," "wonders why," "had not known," "So / Sweats"). On the other hand, Warren has not abandoned the careful craftsmanship acquired during his long sojourn with his Modern and Metaphysical masters. "Intuition," for example, uses colloquial diction and a radically self-mocking break in tone reminiscent of Donne: "suddenly / Life takes on a new dimension, and old pain / Is wisdom—Christ, believe that / And you'll believe anything. . . ." And "Saul at Gilboa" shows the old master of sound texture at work. Arranged in the periodic style appropriate to its epic subject, the first stanza moves through a relatively lyric texture (liquid *l*'s, long-vowelled spondees like "great stone" and "noon-blaze," and internal rhymes like "lions . . . iron" and "moonlight, bone-white") into an onomatopoeic noise storm suitable to the wind's rising:

> From landscape the color of lions.
> From land of great stone the color,
> At noon-blaze, of the droppings of lions,
> But harder than iron and,
> By moonlight, bone-white, and the crouched stone seizes,
> In its teeth, the night-wind, and the wind
> Yelps, the wind
> Yowls.

(The image of the great rock as a beast biting the wind till it yowls is a nice turn of metaphor.) Another little triumph of sound texture ends the poem as Samuel laments, "through / The enormous hollow of my head, History / Whistles like a wind." Samuel's breathstream cannot help but exhale like wind in saying this, what with the three *h* sounds encompassed by "through" on one side and "Whistles . . . wind" on the other.

In *Incarnations*, Warren continues to display the loosening effects of the "new" poetry. Two of these poems, "Myth on Mediterranean Beach" and "Her Hat," maintain the old-style rhyme scheme and recurring stanzaic pattern for ironic effect; and "Where They Come to Wait for the Body: A Ghost Story" actually sustains a *terza rima* pattern. But otherwise, the book is written in free form, with sentences being sectioned off into lines and stanzas according to the poet's "feel" for metrical emphasis. In "Riddle in the Garden" this free form style suits the theme nicely; the poem's run-on syntax, embracing the first nineteen lines in a single sentence, sustains Warren's osmosis theme ("for you / are part of the world") by connecting everything grammatically as well as thematically. And the poet's ear remains capacious as ever for sound texture. In "Paul Valéry Stood on the Cliff and Confronted the Furious Energies of Nature," Warren works up a minor windstorm of *h* and *w* and *wh* sounds in connection with those furious energies that Valéry confronted: "Where dust gritty as / Hot sand was hurled by / Sea-wind . . . , he / Walked, and white and far sail / Heeled now to windward. . . ." But when the energies of nature manifest themselves less furiously, as in the slow ripening of vegetable life, Warren's verse texture thickens luxuriantly: "Where the slow fig's purple sloth / Swells, I sit and meditate. . . ." (Or: "The plum, black yet bough-bound, bursts, and the gold ooze is, / Of bees, joy.")

In *Audubon*, Warren maintains his usual command of imagery ("And the large bird, / Long neck outthrust, wings crooked to scull air, moved / In a slow calligraphy . . ."), as well as his typical dialectical structure (Audubon, on seeing the crude cabin, thinks, "The human filth, the human hope"—which, as Louis Martz has observed, is a concise expression of the poem's theme). And the sound texture, when the occasion warrants, is as richly crafted as ever: "the bear, / Daft in the honey-light, yawns, / The bear's tongue . . . out-crisps to the curled tip, / It bleeds the black blood of the blueberry." The "new" style, however, predominates in the sense of Olson's dictum that form is never more than an extension of content. As in "Billie Potts," a combination of narration (focusing on the woman) and meditation (expressing the responses of Audubon and of Warren's persona) gives us the poem's content; but unlike "Billie Potts," *Audubon* relies solely upon the curve of experience—attended by a rising and subsiding emotional intensity—as its principle of formal ordering. The book's closing segment, "Tell Me A Story," typifies what I am speaking of:

> Long ago, in Kentucky, I, a boy, stood
> By a dirt road, in first dark, and heard
> The great geese hoot northward.
>
> I could not see them, there being no moon
> And the stars sparse. I heard them.
>
> I did not know what was happening in my heart.
>
> It was the season before the elderberry blooms,
> Therefore they were going north.
> The sound was passing northward.

By high Modern standards this poem risks banality. Aside from its one slant rhyme ("stars sparse"), it displays little technical virtuosity that might distinguish the passage from prose. What vindicates the piece as a poem is solely its emotional intensity—the "happening in my heart" that imparts quasi-mystic meaning to otherwise trivial details. The thrice-repeated assertion that the geese were going north is one such detail and that "I could not see them . . . I heard them," is another. If this stripped-down language is charged with meaning (as Pound declared every poem must be), the "charge" comes not through any linguistic pyrotechnics but through the inherent quality of the experience being transmitted, particularly as it recapitulates Audubon's quasi-mystical response to the birds in the previous segment, "Love and Knowledge." That previous segment also violates the Modern aesthetic by stating its theme baldly —"What is love? / One name for it is knowledge"—and elsewhere in *Audubon* Warren flouts the Modern "impersonality of art" doctrine with openly didactic exhortations and outcries ("Continue to walk in the world. Yes, love it!"—"We Are Only Ourselves").

Or Else presents a remarkable variety of forms and manners, featuring not only the musician's bar and stave but the painter's impressionistic eye. A few of these poems date back stylistically al-

most to the beginning of English poetry. "The Faring" resembles
Anglo-Saxon verse in its similes, periodic syntax, hyphenated com-
pounds, and balanced alliterations: "Once over water, to you
borne brightly, / . . . I, / Riding the spume-flash, by gull-cries
ringed, / Came." "Homage to Theodore Dreiser" (the "Psychological Profile" section) is a genuine *terza rima* performance, in the
fashion of Dante's *Divine Comedy;* and "Interjection # 8: Or,
Sometimes, Night" is an exercise in the grand style, its sixteen lines
comprising a single sentence in which the subject—"The unsleeping principle of delight"—is held away from its verb and comple-
ment ("Come into my mind") by thirteen intervening lines of
subordinate clauses and parallel structures. "There's a Grandfather's
Clock in the Hall" employs a Whitmanesque free verse, free-
association catalogue to render its sequence of dramatic vignettes:

And you are a child again watching the reflection of early
    morning sunlight on the ceiling above your bed,
Or perhaps you are fifteen feet under water and holding your breath as
    you struggle with a rock-snagged anchor, or holding
        your breath just long enough for one more long,
            slow thrust to make the orgasm really
                intolerable,
Or you are wondering why you do not really give a damn, as they
    trundle you off to the operating room,
Or your mother is standing up to get married and is very pretty and
    excited and is a virgin, and your heart overflows, and
        you watch her with tears in your eyes, or
She is the one in the hospital room and she is really dying.

They have taken out her false teeth, which are now in a
    tumbler on the bedside table, and you know that only
        the undertaker will ever put them back in. . . .

Here and in other poems Olson's "bar and stave" of the typewriter are an essential feature of Warren's prosody, for the composition of the lines and stanzas requires visual as well as auditory
perception of the poem. "Ballad of Mister Dutcher" and "I Am
Dreaming of a White Christmas" are as free-form as anything in the
Williams canon; and the book's closing poem, "A Problem in
Spatial Composition," renders the effect of a painting—or even a

motion picture—through a bit of pictographic typography that follows the hawk's descent to a tree branch:

> The hawk,
> Entering the composition at the upper left frame
> Of the window, glides,
> In the pellucid ease of thought and at
> His breathless angle,
> Down.
>   Breaks speed.
>   Hangs with a slight lift and hover.
>   Makes contact.
> The hawk perches on the topmost, indicative tip. . . .

In "Rattlesnake Country" the poet becomes an Impressionist painter noting the landscape's subtle mutations under the sky's changing light: "nothing / Happens. Except that, bit by bit, the mountains / Get heavier all afternoon." And in "Birth of Love" the nude bather calls up a fusion of the poet's metaphor and the painter's eye for light and shadow:

> The body,
> Profiled against the darkness of spruces, seems
> To draw to itself, and condense in its whiteness, what light
> In the sky yet lingers or, from
> The metallic and abstract severity of water, lifts. The body,
> With the towel now trailing loose from one hand, is
> A white stalk from which the face flowers gravely toward the high
>   sky.

Again, in the style of the "new" poetry, the language here is precise, stripped down, and dependent for its psychic "charge" upon the intensity of the experience being transmitted ("She moves, and in his heart he cries out . . .").

In and since his "Arcturus" poems, we find the old master displaying a lifetime's cumulative craft. In "A Way to Love God" the opening pictorial image, "where the incoming swell from the sunset Pacific / . . . leans and staggers to break," is mere prologue to an image of both pictorial and auditory delight: "the stars, silver, silver" over "the sea's virgin bosom unveiled / To give suck to the wavering serpent of the moon." This image, in turn, is juxtaposed immediately against the harsh cacophony of human history "in *plaza, piazza, place, platz,* and square" where "Boot heels, like history being born, on cobbles bang." In "Evening Hawk" a shift in rhythm from anapestic speed to spondaic retardation announces, with periodic dignity, the bird's arrival: ". . . riding / The last tumultuous avalanche of / Light above pines and the guttural gorge, / The hawk comes." And in "Answer to Prayer," the caliber of the consonance indicates how the character of the snow changes from before to after the prayer, the guttural "slip-tilt and crunch of re-freezing snow" being supplanted by the smoothly suspirant "soft veil and swish / Of flakes falling." In "Sister Water" the "k" sounds in "the cough and mastication of / The garbage truck in the next block" may suffice to make the line also cough slightly, whereas the long vowels and liquid consonants in "Dream of a Dream" enhance the dreamer's vision: "Moonlight stumbles with bright heel / In the stream, and the stones sing." Verse forms also range from free-form ("Old Nigger on One-Mule Cart," "Bicentennial") to tight-knit rhyming and stanzaic patterns, generally depending upon the lyric or narrative character of the poem's substance.

To conclude these notes on verse texture, we may say that like T. S. Eliot and Robert Lowell, Warren has developed throughout his poetic career in a continuing sequence of stylistic mutations, never resting in a style already mastered. Although we cannot do justice here to the full force of his technical virtuosity, it seems likely that even the critical discord described earlier in this chapter would resolve into harmony on the question of Warren's technical achievements, provided that each critic were permitted to muster up his own samples (and provided that each were sufficiently detached from the Paleface-Redskin acrimony). As our final problem of judgment, we turn to the question of Warren's "place" in the modern poetic hierarchy.

THE QUESTION OF "PLACE"

The definition of artistic status has ever been among the most troublesome vexations afflicting the literary establishment. Literary history is humiliatingly full of Twains and Whitmans and Melvilles who have languished unknown or misunderstood for a life-span while the Longfellows prospered in both popular and academic glory. T. S. Eliot admitted his own unease about this phenomenon in declaring that but for a quirk or two of luck, his old friend Conrad Aiken rather than Eliot himself might have been lionized as the leading poet of the age; and Pound stuttered in rage about Fitzgerald's *Rubáiyat* lying unread in the bookstores until Rossetti happened across a remaindered copy. In recent years political happenstance has had substantial impact upon American critical taste, elevating a book like *Catch-22* to spectacular fame while John Hawkes continues to be little known or read. Robert Lowell is a gifted and important poet, but who can say how much his artistic reputation benefited from his internationally celebrated run-in with Lyndon Johnson's White House? Even, or especially, within the literary establishment, the rejected dinner invitation brought acclaim to Lowell the artist-hero to a degree that might have astonished Lowell the poet-prisoner jailed during World War II for draft-resistance.

Admittedly, then, judgment of any poet's place and worth is a highly subjective and fallible business. Yet an estimate of Warren's "place" within the three generations of American poetry represented in his half-century career might be ventured. Concerning the "big five" of the high Modern period—Eliot, Pound, Williams, Stevens, and Hart Crane—one concession must be granted immediately: unlike Pound, Eliot, and Williams, Warren has not exerted appreciable influence on fellow poets (though he has gathered a large bouquet of their accolades). This granted, the only one of the "big five" with whom Warren is definitely out of the competitive running is T. S. Eliot, who as image-maker, structural architect, style-setter, critical theorist, and "spokesman for the age" still towers over all the others; even so, Warren at least resembles Eliot in his stylistic evolution and intellectual depth. And with respect to the other four poets, Warren's eleven volumes notably avoid the limitations that circumscribe their work.

At his best Warren approximates the lyric sensuousness of Wallace Stevens, for example, but without lapsing into the tedious redundancy that belabors Stevens's later work and without the deliberate narrowness that caused Stevens to exclude "gross realism" as a proper subject for poetry.[5] There is nothing in Warren's aesthetics that compares with Stevens's deliberate exclusion of reality from poetry. "The artist transforms us into epicures," Stevens says; "he is *un amoureux perpetuel* of the world that he contemplates . . . ; and finally . . . everything like a firm grasp of reality is eliminated from the aesthetic field. With these aphorisms in mind, how is it possible to condemn escapism? The poetic process is psychologically an escapist process." [6] Although this abstraction of poetry away from the sordidness of "gross realism" gave Stevens the "nobility" he found lacking in modern literature, this nobility came at the price of a limited moral, political, and religious imagination.[7] "Does it really matter," a colleague of mine once put it, "that Peter Quince ate the caviar?" Or that the emperor was able to lick up all the ice cream before it melted? And, not to ignore Stevens's later "meditative" verse, Warren's great interest in the problem of solipsism never led him into Stevens's closed circuit of contemplation, with reality and imagination chasing each other around in what Stevens admitted was a never-ending circle, "first clockwise, then anti-clockwise." [8] Even Stevens's style, his typical blank verse prosody, seems narrowly rendered compared to Warren's great technical range. While not denying Stevens's great power as an image-maker, then, I submit that a reader of Warren's whole poetic canon may be as richly rewarded as a reader of Stevens's.

As pathfinder, teacher, and benefactor to other artists, Ezra Pound has had few peers in literary history, but for inherent worth his *Personae* and *Cantos* are not unarguably superior to Warren's poetic achievement. Pound himself described the *Cantos* as a "botch"; for the second time, he felt he was "wrong from the start" for thinking of poetry as a "rag-bag" he could stuff any passing thoughts into.[9] For so indulging his eccentric and at times deranged intellect, Pound misused his lyric gift to an extent rarely, if ever, seen in serious poetry; and on the score of intellectual depth and discipline Warren may reasonably be advanced as *il miglior fabbro*. The same thing is true, in a different way, of Hart Crane, whose most successful poems—"Helen and Faustus," *Voyages*, parts of *The Bridge*—bespeak a gift of the first magnitude, but whose crash landings between flights of mysticism left both his life and his poetry a tragically overstrained patchwork of fragments.

To be sure, Crane's death at age thirty-two must mitigate our judgment, for at that age, Warren had not matched Crane's achievement. But it may be reasonably argued that in his three score years and ten, Warren has gone on to surpass Crane's achievement.

Of our "big five" Moderns, William Carlos Williams is the man who most resembles Warren in having turned out a prolific and consistently excellent output over a long lifetime. Here again, however, Warren may claim the greater mastery both in technical range—having written in a larger variety of styles—and in intellectual profundity. Williams, as a full-time doctor, never attempted to compete intellectually with the poet-professors of the Eliot-Pound-Warren ilk, and his touchiness on the question is something we never find in Warren. In "Aigeltinger," for example, Williams ridicules the gift he lacks: "They say I am not profound / But where is profundity, Aigeltinger . . . ? / Aigeltinger, you were profound." And in "The Visit," he bridles at being judged naive ("The / naive may be like a sunny day / . . . and is not to be despised"), and finally threatens to assault his critic-visitor: "Say I am less an artist / than a spadeworker but one / who has no aversion to taking / his spade to the head / of any who would derrogate / his performance in the craft." Not to "derrogate" Williams's performance or his charm, I again submit that a reader may be as well rewarded by the whole of Warren's verse canon as by the whole of Williams's. The fact that one poet has been much more widely read than the other should not prejudice this comparison.

Among the second generation of Moderns, contemporaries of Warren's who mostly followed in the steps of their Modern masters, Roethke, I think, may have the edge in lyric power and Lowell, in experimental daring. But for technical variety, depth and complexity of theme, and verbal gifts, Warren is of comparable status with those two and other notables of that generation: Shapiro, Nemerov, Scott, Tate, Eberhart, Wilbur, and others. And concerning the "third generation" of contemporary poets—those who have arisen since Olson's manifesto in 1950—Warren's place should be at least equal with any. Although Olson, Duncan, Creeley, Ginsberg, the later Lowell, and their contemporaries have largely succeeded in overthrowing the Modern period, "the New American Poetry" has yet to produce (or even, it may be, to attempt) a masterpiece, by common consensus even of its admirers.[10] Warren's own emergence as one of the "new" poets, in *Audubon* for example, may among other things help refute that impression.

Our final criterion in judging Warren's "place" among American poets is Henry James's premise that "an author's paramount charge is the cure of souls" (*Notes and Reviews*, New York: 1921, p. 19). In *Democracy and Poetry*, the two Jefferson Lectures published by the Harvard University Press in 1975, Warren uses the word "self" rather than "soul," but it is clear that the "cure of selves" is his ultimate concern, in the tradition of Arnold's and Wordsworth's and Shelley's defenses of poetry. Although devoted to poetry and art in general, *Democracy and Poetry* also defines Warren's personal purpose with the clarity and eloquence of a career's summation. The opening essay, "Democracy and the Diminished Self," updates the Fugitive-Agrarian revulsion against the erosion of individual worth and identity in a technocratic-commercial mass society; the other essay, "Poetry and Selfhood," defines the function of poetry as a counterforce to that erosion, primarily through its role in counteracting modern man's experience of alienation. Whereas science, technology, and urbanization have "cut [man] off from nature, . . . from society, from a sense of significance in his work, from, in the end, any sense of significance in his own existence," poetry sustains selfhood by reminding us "that abstract thought cannot grasp the meaning of existence and that feeling—passion—provides the knowledge that is the key of existence and action" (pp. 54, 48). When translated into effective form, such passion—here we may think of Warren's epiphanies—may evoke a reader's lost psychic unity: "what a glorious *klang* of being awakens to unify mind and body, to repair, if even for a moment, what Martin Buber has called 'the injured wholeness of man' " (p. 74). When rightly done, the art work likewise—we may think of "Billie Potts" and the osmosis of being—"binds our very physiological being to it in the context of the rhythms of the universe," with such compelling force that even scientists may "refer to artists as brother symbolists with merely a different kind of net for snaring 'reality' " (pp. 74, 51). And poetry restores the bond between self and community by its inherent act of communication. Not only does the reader relate to the fictive self in a work of literature, for "only insofar as the work establishes and expresses a self can it engage us"; but also the reader relates to the artist, who inevitably infuses his own identity into his handiwork (here we may think of Warren's "conversion" motif and his R.P.W. in *Brother to Dragons*): "The posited self of a lyric may be taken as purely fictional or as a shadowy persona of a literal self, the author. And this fact leads to the most subtle, complex, and profound relationship in literature. . . . It is not only the objective characters that serve as 'models' of selfhood; the work itself represents the author's adventures in selfhood" (pp. 70, 71). For Warren, as the interplay of his three ground themes has shown, those adventures in selfhood have produced a dialectical tension: "I suppose I see life, for all our yearning for and struggle toward primal or supernal unity, as a more or less oscillating process" (p. 93). But as poetry "helps one to grasp reality and to grasp one's own life," it renders its cure of souls by proving "that the self is a style of being, continually expanding in a vital process of definition, affirmation, revision, and growth" (pp. 92, 89).

In a lecture he delivered in 1966 and later published as a pamphlet entitled *A Plea in Mitigation: Modern Poetry and the End of an Era*, Warren formally acknowledged "the end of 'modernism,' that school of which the Founding Fathers were Eliot, Pound, and Yeats." He explained this demise by defining two ways of regarding poetry, as "prophecy" and as "art":

> When a new poetic period dawns, it always dawns with prophetic urgency: It brings with it the possibility of new experience. . . .
> But the time always comes when the prophetic force drains away. The poetry is repudiated—quite properly, for it no longer answers the life-need for defining identity, for establishing equilibrium in change. . . . At this point of the death of the poetry of an age . . . [the] body of poetry is torn apart and scattered but after this there may be a resurrection—a resurrection into "poetry as art."

Every piece of art, he said, originates as prophecy, as immediate living truth for its maker: "The individual writer . . . must be 'committed.' . . . As a writer—that is, in the moment of writing—he must think of poetry only as prophecy." [11]

It was in this role as prophet, I think, that Warren developed his major themes: the naturalistic dread and alienation in *Thirty-six Poems* (1935); the mounting identity crisis of *Eleven Poems on the Same Theme* (1942), "The Ballad of Billie Potts" (1944), and *Brother to Dragons* (1953), where a sanctimonious surface ego tries to stave off some fearsome inherent depravity; the enlargement of the osmosis of being theme in *Promises* (1957) and later books, providing some answer to both the naturalistic dread and the identity problem; and most recently the affirmations of "delight" coming on strongly. This prophetic impulse is what James Dickey had in mind when he classified Warren among those poets who can "give you the sense of poetry as a thing of final importance to life."

We may find one further implication in Dickey's statement, however. If, over the half-century span of Warren's verse, there is one quality that most unmistakably lifts him to the first rank of American poets, then that quality would have to be the remarkable power, clarity, and originality of his imagery, flowing copiously into every part of his poetic canon from the first part of his career to the last. By imagery we refer to that verbal construct which, beginning with simple pictorial power, may ascend to metaphorical, symbolic, and even mythic significance as it implies larger dimensions of meaning. We are speaking, that is, of the verbal figure that Aristotle called metaphor when, in *The Poetics* (Chapter 22), he declared, "But the greatest thing by far is to be a master of metaphor. It is the one thing that cannot be learned from others; and it is also a sign of genius. . . ." It is the agency by which, in Shelley's *A Defence of Poetry*, "poetry awakens and enlarges the mind itself," as the poet's "vitally metaphorical [language] . . . marks the before unapprehended relations of things." And it is the poet's ultimate gesture of communication, as Robert Frost—who said "Poetry is simply made of metaphor"—described it: "Mind must convince mind that it can uncurl and wave the same filaments of subtlety, soul convince soul that it can give off the same shimmers of eternity. At no point would anyone but a brute fool want to break off this correspondence." (I quote from "The Constant Symbol" and Frost's preface to *King Jasper* here.)

Defined thusly, the cumulative power of Warren's imagery in his eleven volumes is incalculable. Our whole discussion of the poetic vision of Robert Penn Warren has mostly consisted of studies in Warren's imagery, but in the amplitude of his work the poems and their imagery remain exegetically inexhaustible. To recall just a few instances of imagery ascending to metaphorical and even mythic significance, we may cite the protean metaphors of the undiscovered self, transmuting from old dog, old horse, and old people in *Eleven Poems* into minotaur, serpent, and Lilburn in *Brother to Dragons;* or, fixing upon the osmotic theme in "Billie Potts," we may recall how subtly the beastly face in the dark modulates from a pictorial image at the poem's outset ("Where no sun comes, the muskrat's astute face / Was lifted to the yammering jay; then dropped") to the mythic level—asserting a belief to live by—at the end: "the sad head lifting to the long return / . . . Carries its knowledge, navigator without star." Concerning the lapsarian theme, likewise, how forceful yet simple, and how deeply earned, is the concluding image in "Saul at Gilboa": "How beautiful are the young, walking! / If I could weep." The power of such imagery to illuminate experience, to interpret its meaning, or even to give us beliefs to live by would have to be one of Dickey's meanings in calling Warren's poetry a thing of final importance to life.

Few will argue against the contention that as prophet Warren has spoken movingly and meaningfully about some central issues of our time. But it is as art that his poetry must hope to survive—even though, as Warren observes, "any piece of art may again become prophecy" (he points to modern revivals of Donne and Blake as examples). How much of his poetry will ascend into the immortality of "poetry as art" remains to be seen. But his themes are likely to remain significant; and through a career that reaches back over a half century, encompassing schools of pre-Modern, Modern, and post-Modern aesthetics, he has displayed both growth and consistency in technical resources. With respect to the ageless elements of poetic technique—command of metaphor, control of tone and diction, powers of organization, mastery of sound effects, and the like—each phase of Warren's career has evinced a "morality of style" that is true to the classic standard.

As we think back to the highly polished, neo-metaphysical entries in *Thirty-six Poems;* the original dramatic and lyric power of *Eleven Poems* and "Billie Potts"; the large scale, multi-voiced verse-drama *Brother to Dragons;* the varied and sustained poem sequences in *Promises, You, Emperors* and *Tale of Time;* the surprising mastery of the "new" style in *Incarnations, Audubon,* and *Or Else*—as we view that whole corpus, Warren's "place" in American poetry seems insecure only because he is not widely enough read or understood. More than any other writer in American literature, it now appears, Warren has suffered neglect as a poet because of his greater fame as a novelist. But as Louis Martz has observed, Warren may eventually come to be known as a poet who also wrote novels. Whether or not that proves true, Warren clearly deserves to be more widely read as a poet. Both as "prophecy" and as "art" the poetic canon of Robert Penn Warren evinces such significance, versatility, and excellence as to rank him among the finest and most fertile talents of his age.

Notes

INTRODUCTION

[1] *Kenyon Review*, 1 (Winter, 1939): 82. I am indebted to Charles Bohner's *Robert Penn Warren* (New York: Twayne, 1964) for drawing my attention to this comment by Ransom; Allen Tate, "*The Fugitive*, 1922-1925: A Personal Recollection Twenty Years After," *Princeton University Library Chronicle*, 3 (April, 1942): 82.

[2] Morton D. Zabel, "Problems of Knowledge," *Poetry*, 48 (April, 1936): 37-41.

[3] *New York Times Book Review*, April 26, 1942, p. 4.

[4] *Virginia Quarterly Review*, 18 (Summer, 1942): 479-80.

[5] Dudley Fitts, "Of Tragic Stature," *Poetry*, 65 (November, 1944): 94-101.

[6] John Crowe Ransom, "The Inklings of 'Original Sin,'" *Saturday Review of Literature*, 27 (May 20, 1944): 10-11; *Nation*, 159 (November 25, 1944): 660, 662.

[7] *Sewanee Review*, 52 (Autumn, 1944): 575-78.

[8] Ruth Herschberger, "Poised between the Two Alarms," *Accent*, 4 (Summer, 1944): 240-46.

[9] *New York Times Book Review*, May 7, 1944, p. 4.

[10] William Van O'Connor, "Robert Penn Warren: 'Provincial' Poet," in *A Southern Vanguard*, ed. Allen Tate (New York: Prentice-Hall, 1947), p. 98.

[11] W. P. Southard, "The Religious Poetry of Robert Penn Warren," *Kenyon Review*, 7 (Autumn, 1945): 653-76.

[12] John L. Stewart, "The Achievement of Robert Penn Warren," *South Atlantic Quarterly*, 47 (October, 1948): 562-79.

[13] "The Present State of Poetry in the United States," *Kenyon Review*, 1 (Autumn, 1939): 397. Philip Rahv's essay, "Paleface and Redskin," appeared in the previous number (Summer, 1939) of this magazine, pp. 251-56.

[14] Randall Jarrell, "On the Underside of the Stone," *New York Times Book Review*, August 23, 1953, p. 6.

[15] Robert Lowell, "Prose Genius in Verse," *Kenyon Review*, 15 (Autumn, 1953): 619-25.

[16] Delmore Schwartz, "The Dragon of Guilt," *New Republic*, 129 (September 14, 1953): 17-18.

[17] *The New Yorker*, 29 (October 24, 1953): 157-58.

[18] Parker Tyler, "The Ambiguous Axe," *Poetry*, 83 (December, 1953): 167-71.

[19] John McCormick, "White Does and Dragons," *Western Review*, 18 (Winter, 1954): 163-67.

[20] Hugh Kenner, "Something Nasty in the Meat-House," *Hudson Review*, 6 (Winter, 1954): 605-10.

[21] Leslie Fiedler, "Seneca in the Meat-House," *Partisan Review*, 21 (March-April, 1954): 208-12.

[22] James Dickey, "In the Presence of Anthologies," *Sewanee Review*, 66 (Spring, 1958): 307-09.

[23] Kenneth Koch, "Fresh Air," in *The New American Poetry*, ed. Donald M. Allen (New York: Grove Press, 1960), p. 231.

[24] M. L. Rosenthal, "Out There in the Dark," *Nation*, 186 (January 18, 1958): 56–57.

[25] Morgan Blum, *"Promises* as Fulfillment," *Kenyon Review*, 21 (Winter, 1959): 97–120.

[26] Leonard Casper, "The Founding Fathers," *Western Review*, 22 (Autumn, 1957): 69–71.

[27] Floyd C. Watkins, "Billie Potts at the Fall of Time," *Mississippi Quarterly*, 11 (Winter, 1958): 19–28.

[28] Harriet Zinnes, "A New Word Needed," *Prairie Schooner*, 36 (Spring, 1962): 85–87.

[29] John Edward Hardy, "You, Robert Penn Warren," *Poetry*, 99 (October, 1961): 58–62.

[30] John Thompson, "A Catalogue of Poets," *Hudson Review*, 13 (Winter, 1960–61): 619–20.

[31] Dudley Fitts, "An Exercise in Metrical High Jinks," *New York Times Book Review*, October 23, 1960, p. 32.

[32] Louis D. Rubin, Jr., "The Eye of Time: Religious Themes in Robert Penn Warren's Poetry," *Diliman Review* (Philippines), 3 (July, 1955): 215–37.

[33] Louis L. Martz, "The Virtues of Collection," *Yale Review*, 50 (Spring, 1961): 445–46.

[34] Hyatt H. Waggoner, *American Poets: From the Puritans to the Present* (Boston: Houghton Mifflin, 1968), pp 543–59.

[35] Monroe K. Spears, "The Latest Poetry of Robert Penn Warren," *Sewanee Review*, 78 (Spring, 1970): 348–57.

[36] M. L. Rosenthal, "Robert Penn Warren's Poetry," *South Atlantic Quarterly*, 62 (Autumn, 1963): 499–507.

[37] *New Leader*, 50 (March 27, 1967): 25.

[38] Hayden Carruth, "In Spite of Artifice," *Hudson Review*, 19 (Winter, 1966–67): 693–94.

[39] John L. Stewart, *The Burden of Time: The Fugitives and Agrarians* (Princeton: Princeton University Press, 1965), pp. 523 and 540.

[40] Allen Shepherd, "Carrying Manty Home," *Four Quarters*, 21 (May, 1972): 101–10.

[41] *New York Times Book Review*, October 9, 1966, p. 4; *Saturday Review*, 69 (December 31, 1966): 24–25.

[42] *Southern Review*, n.s. 6 (Winter, 1970): 208–10.

[43] John Wain, "Robert Penn Warren: The Drama of the Past," *New Republic*, 115 (November 26, 1966): 16–18.

[44] George Core, "In the Heart's Ambiguity: Robert Penn Warren as Poet," *Mississippi Quarterly*, 22 (1969): 313–26.

[45] William Dickey, "A Place in the Country," *Hudson Review*, 20 (Summer, 1969): 357–59.

[46] *Partisan Review*, 37 (1970): 298–99.

[47] *Yale Reviews*, 59 (Summer, 1970): 564–69.

[48] *New York Times Book Review*, January 11, 1970, p. 5.

[49] *Partisan Review*, 38 (1971): 122–23.

[50] Allen Shepherd, "Warren's *Audubon:* 'Issues in Purer Form' and 'The Ground Rules of Fact,' " *Mississippi Quarterly*, 24 (1970): 47–56.

[51] Robert F. Clayton, *Library Journal*, 99 (October 15, 1974): 2607. Untitled review of *Or Else*.

[52] J. D. McClatchy, "Recent Poetry: Inventions and Obsessions," *Yale Review*, 64 (Spring, 1975): 429. This quotation may be found in the Modern Library edition of the novel, p. 126.

[53] Leonard Casper, *Robert Penn Warren: The Dark and Bloody Ground* (Seattle: University of Washington Press, 1960), pp. 56-87.

[54] Stewart, *Burden of Time*, pp. 515 and 530.

[55] John Lewis Longley, Jr., ed., *Robert Penn Warren: A Collection of Critical Essays* (New York: New York University Press, 1965), p. ix.

[56] George Palmer Garrett, "The Recent Poetry of Robert Penn Warren," in Longley, *Robert Penn Warren*, pp. 223, 230, 235.

CHAPTER 1

[1] Dixon Wecter, *Sam Clemens of Hannibal* (Boston: Houghton Mifflin, 1952), pp. 63-64. The comment occurs in a letter to Thomas Bailey Aldrich, 1893.

[2] Ernest Hemingway, *Across the River and into the Trees* (New York: Charles Scribner's Sons, 1970), p. 33.

[3] Vladimir Nabokov, *Speak, Memory* (New York: Grosset & Dunlap, 1951), p. 1.

[4] John Updike, *The Poorhouse Fair* (New York: Fawcett Crest, 1958), p. 80.

[5] "The Present State of Poetry in the United States," *Kenyon Review*, 1 (Autumn, 1939): 391.

[6] Mark Twain, *Autobiography* (New York: Harper and Brothers, 1924), 2: 7.

[7] For the source of Freud's letter, see note 9 of Chapter 3.

[8] C. G. Jung, *The Undiscovered Self* (New York: Mentor Books, 1959), pp. 107-8.

[9] J. G. Frazer, *The Golden Bough* (New York: Macmillan, 1935), 1: 236.

[10] William James, *The Varieties of Religious Experience* (New York: Mentor Books, 1958), p. 326; Jung, *Undiscovered Self*, p. 101.

[11] James, *Varieties*, p. 162.

[12] These are the closing sentences of Chapter 8 in *All the King's Men*.

[13] James, *Varieties*, p. 173.

[14] *All the King's Men* (New York: Modern Library, 1953), pp. 201 and 200.

[15] "Knowledge and the Image of Man," *Sewanee Review*, 63 (Winter, 1955): 182-92. Also in John Lewis Longley, ed., *Robert Penn Warren: A Collection of Critical Essays* (New York: New York University Press, 1965), pp. 237-46. I have quoted the latter version, p. 241.

[16] *Flood: A Romance of Our Time* (New York: Signet Books, 1965), pp. 366 and 353.

[17] James, *Varieties*, p. 321.

[18] *Ibid.*, pp. 195 and 186.

[19] *Selected Essays by Robert Penn Warren* (New York: Vintage Books, 1966), p. 197.

[20] *Ibid.*, pp. 205, 208.

[21] *Ibid.*, pp. 210-11.

[22] *Ibid.*, p. 222.

[23] *Ibid.*, pp. 225, 226-27.

[24] *Ibid.*, p. 222.

[25] James, *Varieties*, pp. 294, 302-03.

[26] *New Republic*, 54 (April 4, 1928):227. Review of John Hall Wheelock's col-

lection, *The Bright Dawn; Poetry,* 43 (March, 1934): 342-46. Review of John Peale Bishop's *Now with His Love.*

[27] *American Review,* 3 (May, 1934): 212-27. Review of several poets.

[28] *Poetry,* 49 (February, 1937): 279-82. Review of Robinson Jeffers' *Solstice and Other Poems.*

[29] *Accent,* 4 (Summer, 1944): 251-53.

[30] *New Republic,* 70 (February 24, 1932): 51-52.

[31] *American Review,* 2 (November, 1933): 27-45. (The two quoted excerpts appear on pp. 32 and 43.)

[32] *Virginia Quarterly Review,* 11 (January, 1935): 93-112. (Excerpts, pp. 93 and 97.)

[33] F. Cudworth Flint, "Five Poets," *Southern Review,* 1 (Winter, 1936): 672-74.

[34] *Kenyon Review,* 1 (Autumn, 1939): 384-98. (Excerpts, pp. 398 and 397.)

[35] Robert Penn Warren, *Selected Essays* (New York: Random House, 1958). Also issued in paperback (New York: Vintage Books, 1966), p. 25. Since I quote this edition so frequently, I shall hereafter cite references to it within my main text.

[36] *Modern Poetry, American and British,* ed. Kimon Friar and John Malcolm Brinnan (New York: Appleton, Century-Crofts, 1951), pp. 541-43; *New York Times Book Review,* 58 (August 23, 1953): 6, 25.

[37] "John Crowe Ransom: Some Random Remarks," *Shenandoah,* 14 (Spring, 1963): 19-21.

[38] "Notes on the Poetry of John Crowe Ransom at His Eightieth Birthday," *Kenyon Review,* 30 (Autumn, 1968): 319-49. (Excerpts, pp. 320, 343-44.)

[39] "Melville's Poems," *Southern Review,* n.s. 3 (Autumn, 1967): 799-855. Since I quote from this lengthy essay frequently, I am including page references within my main text. This first excerpt occurs on p. 801.

[40] *Who Speaks for the Negro?* (New York: Random House, 1965), p. 291.

[41] "Whittier," *Sewanee Review,* 79 (1971): 86-135. (Excerpts, pp. 108, 124, and 120.)

[42] Robert Penn Warren, *Homage to Theodore Dreiser* (New York: Random House, 1971), pp. 76, 151, 20, and 11.

CHAPTER 2

[1] Robert Penn Warren, *All the King's Men* (New York: Modern Library, 1953), p. 12.

[2] Nathanael West, *The Dream Life of Balso Snell* in *The Complete Works of Nathanael West* (New York: Farrar, Straus and Cuhady, 1957), p. 27.

[3] "Defensive processes are the psychical correlative of the flight reflex and perform the task of preventing the generation of pain from internal sources. . . . Humour can be regarded as the highest of these defense processes." Sigmund Freud, *Wit and Its Relation to the Unconscious;* also titled *Jokes and Their Relation to the Unconscious* in *The Complete Psychological Works of Sigmund Freud,* ed. James Strachey (London: Hogarth Press, 1957), 8: 233.

[4] The reference is again to the *Sewanee Review* essay, republished in John Lewis Longley, ed., *Robert Penn Warren: A Collection of Critical Essays* (New York: New York University Press, 1965), pp. 245-46.

[5] Warren used this phrase in a conversation with me at his home in Stratton, Vermont (September 1, 1964).

[6] Longley, *Robert Penn Warren,* p. 242.

[7] Ralph Waldo Emerson, *Selections from Ralph Waldo Emerson,* ed. Stephen E. Whicher (Boston: Houghton Mifflin, 1957), p. 55.

[8] See Emily Dickinson's poem, "I Heard a Fly Buzz When I Died."

[9] "A Conversation with Robert Penn Warren," *Four Quarters,* 21 (May, 1972): 8-9.

[10] John Edward Hardy's "poems about nothing" comment appeared in *Poetry,* 99 (October, 1961): 60. Dudley Fitts' dismissal of *You, Emperors, and Others* as "high jinks, . . . an artistic vacation" appeared in the *New York Times Book Review,* October 23, 1960, p. 32.

[11] John Updike, "The Art of Fiction," *Paris Review,* no. 45 (Spring, 1969): 94.

[12] Hawthorne's comment on Emerson appears in his Introduction to his *Mosses from an Old Manse.*

[13] Whicher, ed., *Selections from Ralph Waldo Emerson,* p. 269.

[14] *Selected Essays by Robert Penn Warren* (New York: Vintage Books, 1966), p. 237.

[15] William James, *The Varieties of Religious Experience* (New York: Mentor Books, 1958), p. 121.

[16] *Ibid.,* pp. 133 and 155.

[17] *Ibid.,* p. 155.

CHAPTER 3

[1] William James, *Pragmatism* (New York: Meridian, 1955), pp. 190-91.

[2] William James, *The Varieties of Religious Experience* (New York: Mentor Books, 1958), pp. 188-89, 326, 195, and 196.

[3] Howard Nemerov, "The Phoenix in the World," *Furioso* 3, no. 3, p. 36.

[4] C. G. Jung, *The Undiscovered Self* (New York: Mentor Books, 1959), pp. 107-08.

[5] *Ibid.,* p. 110.

[6] *Ibid.,* p. 93. See also note 20 to this chapter.

[7] James, *Varieties,* pp. 121, 124, and 186.

[8] *Ibid.,* p. 141.

[9] Sigmund Freud, *The Complete Psychological Works of Sigmund Freud,* James Strachey, ed. (London: The Hogarth Press, 1957), 14: 301.

[10] *All the King's Men* (New York: Modern Library, 1953), pp. 50 and 54. That Warren himself shares Willie Stark's attitude about dirt is corroborated in a note published by B. R. McElderry, Jr., in *Walt Whitman Review* 14 (December 1962): 91. McElderry inquired of Warren whether he was influenced by a comment by Walt Whitman about Matthew Arnold: "Arnold always gives you the notion that he hates to touch the dirt. . . . But everything comes out of the dirt— everything. . . ." Warren's reply was, "No, if I ever read Whitman's comment on Arnold (and a good comment it is, too), I had forgotten it."

[11] *Night Rider* (New York: Random House, 1939), p. 419.

[12] *Brother to Dragons* (New York: Random House, 1953), p. 118.

[13] John Updike, "The Art of Fiction," *Paris Review,* no. 45 (Spring, 1969): 101.

[14] James, *Varieties,* pp. 295 and 319.

[15] *Ibid.,* p. 304.

[16] Whitman's "inverted mysticism" is discussed by James E. Miller, Jr., in "*Song of Myself* as Inverted Mystical Experience," *PMLA,* 70 (September, 1955): 631-61.

[17] Garrett quotes this passage from Frederick McDowell ("Psychology and

Theme in *Brother to Dragons,*" *PMLA,* 70 (September, 1955): 565-86, as the start-ing point for his "The Function of the Pasiphae Myth in Brother to Dragons," *MLN,* 74 (April, 1959): 311-13. These two essays and Dennis M. Dooley's "The Persona R.P.W. in Warren's *Brother to Dragons*" rank among the best analyses of this poem. Dooley's essay—*Mississippi Quarterly,* 25 (1971): 19-30—shows R.P.W. undergoing a conversion from cynicism to acceptance in a fashion paralleling that of Thomas Jefferson. Garrett's essay conveys the insight that Warren's minotaur hidden in the labyrinth represents "the concealed *id* at the heart of the psyche." McDowell's discussion of the Oedipal motif between Lilburn and his mother, though very perceptive, misses a point, I believe, in calling Lilburn's brutal treat-ment of his loved ones "senseless." Lilburn's behavior is perverse, even perverted, certainly, but not senseless, since with each gradation of loyalty toward him—wife, brother, black Mammy, hound—he tests limits to prove how each love in turn will twist into betrayal of him, given sufficient pressure. There is logic and purpose here, not mere motiveless malignity.

[18] Warren, *Brother to Dragons,* pp. 32-33. Since I quote so widely from this book, I shall hereafter cite page references to it in parentheses within my main text.

[19] Jung, *Undiscovered Self,* p. 101.

[20] In his study of archetypes, Joseph Campbell, like Warren, follows Jung's lead in declaring the cleavage within the self to be modern man's most serious psycho-logical problem. In *The Hero with the Thousand Faces* (New York: Pantheon Books, 1953), p. 388, Campbell says, "The lines of communication between the conscious and unconscious zones of the psyche have all been cut, and we have been split in two."

CHAPTER 4

[1] Robert Penn Warren, "Knowledge and the Image of Man," *Sewanee Review,* 63 (Winter, 1955): 182.

[2] John Lewis Longley, ed., *Robert Penn Warren: A Collection of Essays* (New York: New York University Press, 1965), p. 241.

[3] Ralph Ellison, *Shadow and Act* (New York: Signet Books, 1964), p. 177.

[4] Warren, "Knowledge and the Image of Man," p. 182.

[5] *Flood: A Romance of Our Time* (New York: Signet Books, 1965), p. 353.

[6] *Who Speaks for the Negro?* (New York: Random House, 1965), pp. 266 and 265.

[7] Robert Penn Warren, *Or Else* (New York: Random House, 1974), p. 70.

[8] *Night Rider* (New York: Random House, 1948), p. 142.

[9] *At Heaven's Gate* (New York: Signet Books, 1949), p. 191.

[10] *All the King's Men* (New York: Modern Library, 1953), p. 172.

[11] *Ibid.,* p. 75.

[12] Warren, *Flood,* p. 336.

[13] Warren, *Brother to Dragons* (New York: Random House, 1953), p. 64.

[14] *Ibid.,* p. 62.

[15] *Ibid.,* p. 42.

[16] *Selected Essays by Robert Penn Warren* (New York: Vintage Books, 1966), p. 251.

[17] Warren, *All the King's Men,* p. 39.

[18] *Ibid.,* pp. 200 and 462.

[19] Warren, *Selected Essays,* pp. 229 and 211.

[20] *The Cave* (New York: Signet Books, 1959), pp. 144 and 361.

[21] *Brother to Dragons,* pp. 94, 95, 208, and 32.

[22] Warren, *The Cave,* pp. 227-29.

[23] Warren, *Brother to Dragons,* p. 215.

[24] Warren, *Selected Essays,* p. 229.

[25] September 1, 1964 in Stratton, Vermont.

[26] William Styron, *Set This House on Fire* (New York: Signet Books, 1959), pp. 246-48.

[27] S. T. Coleridge, "On Posey or Art" in *Miscellanies,* ed. T. Ashe (London, 1885), pp. 42-49. Cited in Richard Ellmann and Charles Feidelson, *The Modern Tradition* (New York: Oxford, 1964), p. 43.

[28] Preface to the 1800 edition of *Lyrical Ballads.*

[29] William James, *Pragmatism* (New York: Meridian, 1955), p. 189.

[30] Longley, *Robert Penn Warren,* pp. 241-42.

[31] William James, *The Varieties of Religious Experience* (New York: Mentor Books, 1958), pp. 54-55.

[32] John Updike, *The Centaur* (New York: Fawcett Crest, 1962), p. 220.

[33] James, *Pragmatism,* p. 187.

[34] Warren, *Selected Essays,* p. 253.

[35] Warren, *The Cave,* p. 291.

[36] James, *Varieties,* p. 297.

[37] "Robert Penn Warren," *The Vanderbilt Alumnus* (March-April 1970), p. 21.

[38] James, *Varieties,* p. 281.

[39] Warren, *Selected Essays,* p. 162.

[40] Nathaniel Hawthorne, *The American Notebooks,* ed. Randall Stewart (New Haven: Yale University Press, 1932), p. 98.

CHAPTER 5

[1] See John L. Stewart, *The Burden of Time: The Fugitives and Agrarians* (Princeton: Princeton University Press, 1965), pp. 459, 464, and 443. The comment by Peter Davison appears in *Atlantic Monthly* 218 (November, 1966): 163. All the other references in this paragraph are cited in my "Introduction: The Critical Reckoning."

[2] Roy Newquist, "Interview with Eleanor Clark and Robert Penn Warren," *Conversations* (Rand McNally and Company, 1962), p. 84.

[3] Warren, *Brother to Dragons* (New York: Random House, 1953), pp. 7 and 34. I am incorporating other references to this book within my main text.

[4] Charles Olson, "PROJECTIVE VERSE," in *The New American Poetry,* ed. Donald M. Allen (New York: Grove Press, 1960), pp. 387-89 and 393.

[5] Stevens's distaste for "gross realism" limited his admiration for Hemingway and Faulkner. In recommending them as lecturers in the Poetry Series at Princeton, Stevens wrote in a letter dated July 2, 1942: "But supposing that Hemingway shouldn't be available, what about Faulkner? For all his gross realism, Faulkner is a poet." Holly Stevens, ed., *The Letters of Wallace Stevens* (New York: Knopf, 1966), pp. 411-12.

[6] Wallace Stevens, "The Noble Rider and the Sound of Words," in *The Necessary Angel* (New York: Vintage, 1951), p. 30.

[7] *Ibid.,* pp. 12-13 and 23.

[8] Stevens, "Three Academic Pieces," in *The Necessary Angel*, p. 79.

[9] Noel Stock, in *The Life of Ezra Pound* (New York: Pantheon Books, 1970), pp. 457-58, reports a conversation between Pound and Daniel Cory dated early in October, 1966: "Cory brought up the subject of the cantos and the conflicting opinions they had aroused. Pound intervened firmly, describing the work as a 'botch.' And when Cory persisted, 'You mean it didn't come off?' the poet replied: 'Of course it didn't. . . . I picked out this and that thing that interested me, and then jumbled them into a bag. But that's not the way . . . to make . . . *a work of art*' " (Emphasis Pound's).

[10] Two of the most distinguished critics of "the New American Poetry," M. L. Rosenthal and Richard Kostelanetz, have commented upon this phenomenon.

[11] *A Plea in Mitigation: Modern Poetry and the End of an Era* was presented as a Eugenia Dorothy Blount Lamar Lecture at Wesleyan College in Macon, Georgia in February, 1966. The essay was printed by Southern Press, Inc. of Macon, Georgia the same year; the three quotations I have cited occur on pp. 1, 2-3, and 19.

Index of Warren's Works

Note: In this index titles of individual poems and essays are in Roman type; titles of books are in *italics*.

After Night Flight Son Reaches Bedside of Already Unconscious Father, 74
Aged Man Surveys Past Time, 2, 46, 49, 51
Ah, Anima! 119, 228
All the King's Men, 5, 17, 27–29, 31, 46, 52, 62, 90, 93, 102, 122, 123, 144–45, 155, 157–58, 192, 194, 195–96, 199, 202, 236, 241, 250, 252
American Portrait: Old Style, 115–16
And All That Came Thereafter, 93–94
Answer to Prayer, 111–12, 114, 267
Apology for Domitian, 129–30, 197
Arrogant Law, 169
At Heaven's Gate, 2, 28, 62, 122, 144, 157, 195, 199
Aubade for Hope, 5, 62
Audubon: A Vision, 16–17, 30, 36, 41, 104–05, 117, 122, 148, 192, 198, 205–06, 211, 224, 234, 235, 237, 242–43, 247–53, 263–64, 271, 275
Autumnal Equinox on Mediterranean Beach, 81–82

Ballad: Between the Boxcars, 80, 205, 260–61
Ballad of Billie Potts, The, 2, 3, 4, 5, 10, 13, 15, 18, 20, 27, 29, 31, 32, 34, 35, 36, 39, 42, 56, 77, 121, 122, 130, 137, 140, 144–46, 148–63, 164, 166, 179, 180, 183, 187, 194, 196, 198, 199, 200, 211–12, 216, 219, 229, 234, 247, 255, 258, 263–64, 271, 273, 274
Ballad of Mister Dutcher and the Last Lynching in Gupton, 195, 198, 265
Ballad of a Sweet Dream of Peace, 62, 130, 164–66, 199–200, 202–05, 219–20, 225
Band of Angels, 14, 90, 123, 194, 199
Bearded Oaks, 3, 52, 132, 134–35
Bear Track Plantation: Shortly after Shiloh, 128–29
Be Something Else, 103
Bicentennial, 117–19, 267

Birth of Love, 245–46, 266
Blackberry Winter (story), 52–53, 69, 70
Blow, West Wind, 85–86, 106
Boy's Will, Joyful Labor Without Pay, and Harvest Home (1918), 72–73, 202–03, 238, 260
Bramble Bush, The, 83, 221
Brightness of Distance, 213
Brotherhood in Pain, 110, 113, 227
Brother to Dragons, 1, 6–8, 13, 14, 19, 24, 27, 40, 64, 121, 122, 123, 130, 133, 137, 149, 157, 158, 163–64, 169–89, 192, 194, 196, 199, 200, 201, 215, 216, 218, 234, 250, 255, 259, 272, 273, 274, 275
Butterflies over the Map, 124

Calendar, 50, 257
Can I See Arcturus from Where I Stand? Poems 1975, 109–14, 213, 226–28, 246–47, 266–67
Cave, The, 199, 213, 215–16, 243
Chain Saw at Dawn in Vermont in Time of Drouth, 87, 106, 262
Child Next Door, The, 65–66
Clearly about You, 84, 166, 220
Cold Colloquy, 55, 131
Colder Fire, 218, 236, 238, 259
Colloquy with Cockroach, 83
Composition in Gold and Red-Gold, 86, 106, 222
Country Burying (1919), 68–69
Court-Martial, 67, 202
Cricket, on Kitchen Floor, Enters History, 84
Crime, 5, 132, 137, 142–43, 144–45, 172, 187, 196, 258
Croesus in Autumn, 50
Crusade, 256

Dark Night of the Soul, 70–71
Dark Woods, 67–68
Day Dr. Knox Did It, The, 93–94, 245

Dead Language, A: Circa 1885, 74
Debate: Question, Quarry, Dream,
   79
Delight, 240–41, 255, 261
Democracy and Poetry, 271–72
Dogwood, The, 68
Does the Wild Rose? 91–92, 222
Dragon Country: To Jacob Boehme,
   72, 83, 260
Dragon-Tree, 86–87, 239
Dream, 119, 228
Dream He Never Knew the End of,
   The, 224, 248–51
Dream of a Dream, 228–29, 267
Dream of a Dream the Small Boy
   Had, 223, 240
Driver, Driver, 104

Eidolon, 5, 55–56, 122, 251
Eleven Poems on the Same Theme,
   2, 18, 26, 31, 35, 43, 46, 107, 109, 113,
   121, 124, 130–49, 155, 157, 166, 170, 172,
   175, 178, 180, 187, 196, 215, 257–58,
   273, 274
Elijah on Mount Carmel, 123, 125–26,
   261
Enclave, The, 241–42
Enclaves, 96, 241–42
End of Season, 132, 140–42, 145, 258
Evening Hawk, 11_–_3, 227, 267
Event, The *(Tale of Time)*, 93
Event, The *(Incarnations)*, 102

Fall Comes in Back-Country Vermont,
   85, 93, 208, 222
Faring, The, 241, 265
Fatal Interview: Penthesilea and
   Achilles, 76–77, 260
Finisterre, 241
Flaubert in Egypt, 108, 234, 244
Flood: A Romance of Our Time, 30,
   158, 192, 194, 196, 199
Flower, The, 9, 66, 216–17, 236–37,
   246, 259
Fog, 210
Folly on Royal Street Before the Raw
   Face of God, 245
Foreign Shore, Old Woman, Slaughter
   of Octopus, 197
Forever O'Clock, 244
Founding Fathers, Nineteenth-Century
   Style, Southeast U.S.A., 201
Fox Fire: 1956, 74–75
Friends of the Family, or Bowling a
   Sticky Cricket, 219

Garden, The, 46, 50–51, 192–93, 257
Garden Waters, 59
Garland for You, 10, 73, 130, 164–70
Genealogy, 48
Go It, Granny—Go It, Hog! 165
Gold Glade, 67–68, 236, 238
Grasshopper Tries to Break Solipsism,
   210, 239
Gull's Cry, 65, 180, 218

Hands Are Paid, 73, 260
Harvard '61: Battle Fatigue, 124–25, 200
Hazel Leaf, The, 68
Heart of Autumn, 119, 227–28
Her Hat, 263
His Smile, 90–91
History, 200
Holly and Hickory, 77
Homage to Emerson, On Night Flight
   to New York, 90–92, 243
Homage to Theodore Dreiser (long
   essay), 36, 43–45
Homage to Theodore Dreiser (poem in
   Or Else), 108–09, 234, 244, 265

I Am Dreaming of a White Christmas,
   211, 225–26, 265
I Guess You Ought to Know Who
   You Are, 204
Incarnations: Poems 1966–1968, 15–16,
   96–104, 120, 205, 207–10, 223–24, 235,
   241–43, 255, 263, 275
Infant Boy at Midcentury, 201
In Italian They Call the Bird Civetta,
   78–79
In Moonlight, Somewhere, They Are
   Singing, 78
Insomnia, 89–90, 207, 239–40, 261–62
Interim, The, 88, 207
Interjection # 1: The Need for
   Re-evaluation, 211
Interjection # 2: Caveat, 42, 243–44
Interjection # 3: I Know a Place
   Where All Is Real, 244
Interjection # 4: Bad Year, Bad War:
   A New Year's Card, 1969, 108
Interjection # 5: Solipsism and
   Theology, 193
Interjection # 6: What You Sometimes
   Feel on Your Face at Night, 224–25
Interjection # 7: Remarks of Soul to
   Body, 245
Interjection # 8: Or, Sometimes, Night,
   244–45, 265
Internal Injuries, 96, 101–04, 208

In the Turpitude of Time: N.D., 75, 221
Intuition, 241, 262
Island of Summer, 96–101, 223–24
Ivy, The, 224

John Brown: The Making of a Martyr, 44, 90, 123, 194
Joy, 84, 238

Kentucky Mountain Farm, 51, 107, 193, 212, 256–57
Knockety-Knockety-Knock, 82
Knowledge and the Image of Man (essay), 19, 30, 39, 51, 63, 190, 191, 198, 234–35

Last Metaphor, The, 50, 63, 140
Late Subterfuge, 50, 59, 257
Leaf, The, 99–100, 208, 263
Legacy of the Civil War: Meditations on the Centennial, The, 90, 200
Letter about Money, Love, or Other Comfort, If Any, The, 167–69, 197–98, 260
Letter from a Coward to a Hero, 56–57
Letter of a Mother, 5, 51–52, 131
Letter to a Friend, 61–62
Little Boy and General Principle, 84
Little Boy and Lost Shoe, 86, 106
Little Boy on Voyage, 83
Loss, of Perhaps Love, in Our World of Contingency, 112–13
Love: Two Vignettes, 240
Love's Parable, 57–58, 63, 132, 134–35, 140, 255, 257
Lullaby: A Motion Like Sleep, 218–19, 236–37
Lullaby: Exercise in Human Charity and Self-Knowledge, 167, 220
Lullaby: Moonlight Lingers, 213–14
Lullaby: Smile in Sleep, 218

Mad Druggist, The, 88, 207, 261
Mad Young Aristocrat on Beach, 128
Man Coming of Age, 46, 53, 54, 122
Mango on the Mango Tree, The, 29, 159–60
Man in Moonlight, 68, 71–72, 259–60
Man in the Street, 127–28, 166
Masts at Dawn, 208, 224, 235
Meet Me in the Green Glen, 194
Mexico Is a Foreign Country: Five Studies in Naturalism (revised subtitle: Four Studies in Naturalism), 26, 29, 58–59, 124, 159, 192, 258
Midnight Outcry, 110
Mistral at Night, 223
Monologue at Midnight, 132, 134–36
Moonlight Observed from Ruined Fortress, 71
Moonrise, 97
Mortmain, 10, 74–76, 205, 206
Mother Makes the Biscuits, 83, 221
Multiplication Table, 91
Myth on Mediterranean Beach: Aphrodite as Logos, 15, 99, 209, 255, 263

Natural History *(Incarnations)*, 97, 98, 208–09
Natural History *(Or Else)*, 225
Nature of a Mirror, The, 106, 211
Necessity for Belief, The, 217
News of Unexpected Demise of Little Boy Blue, 82–83
News Photo, 108, 195
Night Is Personal, 209
Nightmare of Man, 83
Nightmare of Mouse, 83
Night Rider, 62, 123, 158, 194, 195, 199
Nocturne: Traveling Salesman in Hotel Bedroom, 80–81
Notes on a Life to Be Lived, 85–88, 106, 206
Nursery Rhymes, 82–83, 221

Obsession, 83–84
Old Nigger on One-Mule Cart Encountered Late at Night, 113–14, 246, 267
One Drunk Allegory, 92
Only Trouble, The, 102
Or Else: Poem/Poems 1968–1974, 17, 42, 44, 104–09, 193, 195, 197, 198, 205, 211, 214, 217, 224–26, 237, 243–46, 264–66, 275
Original Sin: A Short Story, 132, 137, 143–45, 148, 172, 175, 180, 196, 204, 258
Ornithology in a World of Flux, 77

Pacific Gazer, 47–48, 51, 241, 255, 257
Paradox, 112–13
Patriotic Tour and Postulate of Joy, 86, 239
Paul Valéry Stood on the Cliff and Confronted the Furious Energies of Nature, 210, 263
Penological Study, 101–02, 263

Picnic Remembered, 9, 53–55, 58, 64, 107, 113, 122, 132, 134–35, 236, 237
Place and Time, 93
Place Where Nothing Is, A, 98
Plea in Mitigation, A: Modern Poetry and the End of An Era, 272–73
Pondy Woods, 15, 217
Problem in Spatial Composition, A, 106–07, 265–66
Problems of Knowledge, 46, 257
Prognosis: A Short Story, the End of Which You Will Know Soon Enough, 205, 221, 260
Promises: Poems 1954–1956, 1, 6, 8–10, 14, 19, 20, 62, 64–73, 130, 148, 164, 180, 196–97, 201, 202–05, 206, 207, 208, 213–14, 216–20, 225, 231, 236–38, 246, 259–60, 273, 275
Pursuit, 39, 132, 137, 145–47, 196, 258

Question and Answer, 63, 132, 138

Ransom, 26
Rattlesnake Country, 107–08, 197, 244, 266
Reading Late at Night, Thermometer Falling, 105
Real Question Calling for Solution, A, 166, 220–21
Rebuke of the Rocks, 52
Red Mullet, The, 208–09
Resolution, 61, 236
Return, The, 55
Return, The: An Elegy, 5, 131, 206. 255, 256–57
Revelation, 5, 39, 131–32, 140, 206
Riddle in the Garden, 98, 209, 263
Rumor Unverified Stop Can You Confirm Stop, 219–20

Saul at Gilboa, 94–96, 262–63, 274
School Lesson Based on Word of Tragic Death of Entire Gillum Family, 69, 260
Scream, The, 102
Season Opens on Wild Boar in Chianti, 110, 114
Selected Essays, 37–40, 149, 241, 252
Selected Poems, 1923–1943, 1–5, 12, 26, 46–64, 124, 132, 200, 236, 237, 255
Selected Poems, 1923–1966, 13–15, 47, 70, 132, 150, 255
Selected Poems, 1923–1975, 18, 47, 84–96, 109, 115
Self That Stares, The, 169

Shoes in the Rain Jungle, 85, 92–93
Short Thoughts for Long Nights, 83–84
Sirocco, 64–65
Sister Water, 116–17, 267
Skiers, 242–43
Small Soldiers with Drum in Large Landscape, 29
Small White House, 85–86, 106
Snake, The, 73, 197
So Frost Astounds, 46
Some Quiet, Plain Poems, 77–79
So You Agree with What I Say? Well, What Did I Say? 126–27
Stargazing, 85, 103, 106, 261
Summer Storm (Circa 1916), and God's Grace, 69–70
Sunset Walk in Thaw-Time in Vermont, 214
Switzerland, 166, 236, 238

Tale of Time: New Poems, 1960–1966, 84–96, 103, 106, 123, 205–08, 222–23, 237, 239–41, 243, 246, 261–63, 275
Tale of Time (poem sequence), 88–90, 206–07, 239–40
Tell Me a Story, 264
Terror, 132, 137, 147–48, 258
There's a Grandfather's Clock in the Hall, 246, 265
Thirty-six Poems, 2, 12, 19, 26, 36, 46–64, 109, 131, 140, 241, 255, 256–57, 261, 273, 274
Three Poems in Time, 119, 227–28
Tiberius on Capri, 129, 197
Time as Hypnosis, 105, 211
To a Face in a Crowd, 47
To a Little Girl, One Year Old, in a Ruined Fortress, 64–66
Tonight the Woods Are Darkened, 68
To One Awake, 48
Toward Rationality, 2
Trying to Tell You Something, 227, 246–47
Two Pieces after Suetonius, 129–30, 197
Two Poems about Suddenly and a Rose, 222, 240
Two Studies in Idealism: Short Survey of American, and Human, History, 124–25, 128–29, 200

Variation: Ode to Fear, 26, 49, 51
Vision, A: Circa 1880, 75–76
Vision Under the October Mountain: A Love Poem, 87, 106, 222–23

Waiting, 117
Walk by Moonlight in Small Town, 70–71
Wart, The, 92
Watershed, 9, 60
Ways of Day, 87–88
Way to Love God, A, 110, 213, 226–27, 246, 266–67
Well House, The, 77–78
What Day Is, 96–98, 209, 223
What Happened, 88, 206–07, 262
What Was the Promise That Smiled from the Maples at Evening? 8, 67, 206, 213
What Were You Thinking, Dear Mother? 89, 207

Where They Come to Wait for the Body: A Ghost Story, 263
Who Speaks for the Negro? 43, 194
Wilderness: A Tale of the Civil War, 15, 194, 199
World Comes Galloping, The: A True Story, 58–59, 258
World Enough and Time: A Romantic Novel, 123, 194, 199
World Is a Parable, The, 103–04

You, Emperors, and Others: Poems, 1957–1960, 1, 6, 10–12, 15, 20, 27, 46, 73–84, 89, 126, 128, 130, 148, 164, 197–98, 205, 207, 210, 220–21, 236, 238–39, 260–61, 275
Youth Stares at Minoan Sunset, 114

General Index

Agrarian movement, 5, 90, 199, 271
Aiken, Conrad, 268
American Notebooks (Hawthorne), 253–54
"American Scholar, The" (Emerson), 92
Aristotle *(Poetics)*, 273
Arnold, Matthew, 232, 271, 281 n.10
Ash-Wednesday (Eliot), 51, 63, 139–40, 190, 240
atman (Hindu), 24, 232
Auden, W. H., 261

Baudelaire, Charles, 51
Being and Nothingness (Sartre), 207
Beowulf, 257, 265
Bergonzi, Bernard, 15
Bhagavad-Gita, 232
Bible, 25, 46, 74, 85, 94–96, 98, 125–26, 141, 157, 168, 170–71, 184, 208, 232, 243
"Billie in the Darbies" (Melville), 42

black humor, 49
Blake, William, 32, 51, 66, 83, 85, 86, 123, 161, 190, 202, 232, 239, 260, 274
Bloom, Harold, 18
Blum, Morgan, 9
Boehme, Jacob, 72
Bogan, Louise, 6, 255
Bohner, Charles, 17, 19, 277 n.1
Bradbury, John M., 18
Browning, Robert, 6
Buber, Martin, 271
Bunyan, John, 120

Campbell, Joseph, 282 n.20
Carruth, Hayden, 14
Casper, Leonard, 9, 18
Centaur, The (Updike), 235–36
Christianity, 24–25, 30, 40, 51, 53, 99, 123, 127, 157–58, 186, 192, 197, 204, 220, 232
Clarel (Melville), 41–42

Clark, Eleanor, 15, 283 n.2
Clayton, Robert F., 17
Coleridge, Samuel Taylor, 3, 20, 31–32, 35, 37, 39–40, 41, 42, 71, 97, 107, 160, 186, 191, 193, 198, 202, 212, 219, 221, 233
Conrad, Joseph, 37–40
Core, George, 15, 255
Cowan, Louise, 18
Crane, Hart, 1, 232, 256, 257, 268, 269–70
Cummings, E. E., 34–35

Dante, 25, 28, 160, 164, 203, 265
Davison, Peter, 255, 283 n.1
Defence of Poetry, A (Shelley), 191, 273
Dickey, James, 3, 8, 273–74
Dickey, William, 15
Dickinson, Emily, 49, 69, 98
"Divinity School Address" (Emerson), 24, 91–92
Donne, John, 57, 176–77, 186, 257, 262, 274
Dooley, Dennis M., 281–82 n.17
Dupee, F. W., 255

Eberhart, Richard, 18, 270
Ellis, Havelock, 235
Ellison, Ralph, 190
Eliot, T. S., 1, 2, 3, 6, 11, 21, 23, 28, 33, 34, 37, 39, 49, 50–51, 52, 63, 67, 77, 84, 90, 98, 99, 113, 138–40, 181, 182–83, 184, 186, 190, 192, 204, 240, 245, 246, 250, 256–57, 259, 261, 267, 268, 272
Emerson, Ralph Waldo, 13, 24, 52, 63, 66, 90–92, 100, 111, 232
"Experience" (Emerson), 100

"Fancy's Show Box" (Hawthorne), 25
Faulkner, William, 1, 9, 21, 22, 37–39, 52, 201, 210, 233, 250, 283 n.5
Fiedler, Leslie, 7, 255
Fitts, Dudley, 2, 11
Fitzgerald, F. Scott, 21, 235
Flint, F. Cudworth, 36
Four Quartets (Eliot), 33, 63, 77, 113, 184, 186, 204, 246
Fraser, G. S., 16
Frazer, Sir James, 26
Freud, Sigmund, 3, 5, 23, 26, 30, 49, 109, 130, 132–33, 147, 153, 157, 160, 173, 194, 198, 226, 280 n.3
Frost, Robert, 18, 21, 37–39, 66, 86, 203, 210, 259, 273

Fugitive (magazine), 5, 255, 277 n.1
Fugitive movement, 1, 2, 3, 18, 50, 90, 199, 271
Future of an Illusion, The (Freud), 133

Garrett, George P., 20, 172, 281–82 n.17
Garrigue, Jean, 14
"Gerontion" (Eliot), 49, 256
Ginsberg, Allen, 6, 270
"Grace" (Emerson), 24
Gregory, Horace, 3

Hardy, John Edward, 11
Hardy, Thomas, 257
Hawkes, John, 268
Hawthorne, Nathaniel, 25, 34, 90, 128, 253–54
"Hawthorne and His Mosses" (Melville), 25
Heller, Joseph *(Catch-22)*, 268
Hemingway, Ernest, 21, 22, 33, 37–39, 59, 64, 84, 98, 206, 235, 250, 283 n.5
Hero with the Thousand Faces, The (Campbell), 282 n.20
Herschberger, Ruth, 3, 5
"Hollow Men, The" (Eliot), 98, 139, 259
Hopkins, Gerard Manley, 21
Housman, A. E., 131
Huff, Mary Nance, 20

Imagist movement, 16, 40
Impressionism (painting), 86, 264–66

Jack, Peter Monro, 2
James, Henry, 15, 16, 205, 271
James, William, 26, 27–33, 43, 108–09, 120, 127–28, 132–34, 136, 139–40, 145, 148, 153, 157, 160–61, 226, 227, 233–35, 239, 245, 250
Jarrell, Randall, 6
Jefferson, Thomas, 7, 36, 41, 64, 171–89, 194, 196, 197, 200
Johnson, Dr. Samuel, 257
Joyce, James, 235
Jung, Carl Gustav, 26, 27, 29, 30, 113, 120, 130, 133–49, 152–53, 177, 186, 190, 194, 198

Keats, John, 34, 163, 240
Kenner, Hugh, 7, 255
Kierkegaard, Sören, 72
Koch, Kenneth, 8, 277 n.23
Kostelanetz, Richard, 284 n.10
Krutch, Joseph Wood, 58–59

Lanier, Sidney, 35
Lawrence, D. H., 59, 209
"Lifeguard" (Updike), 22
Longfellow, Henry Wadsworth, 268
Longley, John L., Jr., 19–20
"Love Song of J. Alfred Prufrock, The"
    (Eliot), 113, 257
Lowell, Robert, 6, 13, 18, 267, 268, 270

McClatchey, J. D., 17
McCormick, John, 7, 255
McCullers, Carson, 232
McDowell, Frederick P. W., 19, 172,
    281–82 n. 17
MacLeish, Archibald, 18, 34
Mailer, Norman ("Cannibals and
    Christians"), 129
Martien, Norman, 16
Martz, Louis, 12, 15, 16, 255, 263, 275
Marvell, Andrew, 2, 11, 37, 42, 50, 257
Melville, Herman, 9, 25, 31, 38–39, 40,
    41–43, 44, 171, 172, 210, 212, 253, 267
Miller, Henry, 209
Miller, James E., Jr., 162, 281 n.16
Milton, John, 50, 54, 62, 245, 258
Moby-Dick (Melville), 43, 210, 212
"Mr. Eliot's Sunday Morning Service"
    (Eliot), 99

Nabokov, Vladimir, 21, 22, 33, 163, 211,
    235
naturalism, 3, 22, 23, 58, 63, 84, 86,
    91, 98, 109, 130–31, 138–40, 153,
    184–89, 192, 204, 215, 217, 257
"Nature" (Emerson), 63, 91–92, 111
Nemerov, Howard, 135, 270
"New American Poetry," 6, 9, 12,
    260–67, 270, 277 n.23, 283 n.4, 284
    n.10
New Criticism, 13, 39–40, 245
"Nothing Gold Can Stay" (Frost), 21

O'Connor, William Van, 3, 5
"Ode on Intimations of Immortality"
    (Wordsworth), 54, 96, 222
"Ode to the West Wind" (Shelley), 82
Olson, Charles (Projective Verse), 261,
    263, 265, 270, 283 n.4
"Oven Bird, The" (Frost), 21

Paleface-Redskin controversy, 6–13, 267,
    277 n.13
Pater, Walter, 235, 236, 246
Plato, 112–14, 227
Poe, Edgar Allan, 25, 48, 163, 210, 241

Poorhouse Fair, The (Updike), 22
Pope, Alexander, 257
Porter, Katherine Anne, 20, 37–38
Pound, Ezra, 33, 149, 257, 261, 264, 268,
    269, 272, 284 n.9
"Pragmatism and Religion" (William
    James), 43, 127–28, 239
Pragmatism (The One and the Many:
    William James), 227, 233–34, 244
"Prayer in Spring, A" (Frost), 21
"Preface to the Lyrical Ballads"
    (Wordsworth), 233, 238, 253
"Preludes" (Eliot), 50–51, 139
Principles of Psychology (James), 153
Proust, Marcel, 79

Rabbit, Run! (Updike), 21
Rahv, Philip, 6, 277 n.13
Ransom, John Crowe, 1, 2, 3, 4, 5, 13,
    36, 40–41, 50
"Reluctance" (Frost), 21
"Resolution and Independence"
    (Wordsworth), 238
Rime of the Ancient Mariner, The
    (Coleridge), 3, 20, 31–33, 37, 39, 42,
    71, 107, 149, 160, 186, 202, 212, 219,
    241
Robinson, Edwin Arlington, 107
Roethke, Theodore, 21, 270
Romantic movement, 13, 21, 31–32, 52,
    71, 97–98, 178, 190, 202, 232, 246
Rosenthal, M. L., 9, 13–14, 284 n.10
Rousseau, Jean Jacques, 232
Rubin, Louis D., Jr., 12, 15, 255
Rushton, Peter, 2
Ruskin, John, 131

Salinger, J. D., 21
Santayana, George, 37
Sartre, Jean-Paul, 207
Schopenhauer, Arthur, 242
Schwartz, Delmore, 6, 255
Scott, Winfield Townley, 270
Sedgwick, William Ellery, 31
Shapiro, Karl, 270
Shelley, Percy Bysshe, 32, 82, 191, 271,
    273
Shepherd, Allen, 14, 16
"Sitting by a Bush in Broad Sunlight"
    (Frost), 203
Slater, Joseph, 15
"Sleepers, The" (Whitman), 167
Song of Myself (Whitman), 229–31
Southard, W. P., 4, 255
Spears, Monroe K., 13

Spinoza, Benedict, 63, 232
Stevens, Wallace, 18, 33, 85, 133, 163, 210, 226, 235, 241, 268–69, 283 n.5, 6, 7, 8
Stewart, John L., 5, 14, 19, 255, 283 n.1
"Stopping by Woods on a Snowy Evening" (Frost), 210
Stuart, Dabney, 18
Stuart, Jesse, 3
Studies in the History of the Renaissance (Pater), 235, 246
Styron, William, 232–33

Tate, Allen, 1, 13, 270
Thomas, Dylan, 21, 52, 121, 131, 162, 241, 261
Thompson, John, 11
Thoreau, Henry David, 24, 234
Thorp, Willard, 3
Tillich, Paul, 59
"Tintern Abbey" (Wordsworth), 163, 232
Tolstoy, Leo, 120
Transcendentalism, 24, 52, 90–92, 123–24, 232
Twain, Mark, 21, 22, 26, 52, 267
Tyler, Parker, 7

Undiscovered Self, The (Jung), 26–27, 121, 133–38, 140, 177
Updike, John, 21, 23, 80–81, 158, 235–36

Varieties of Religious Experience, The (James), 27–33, 109, 120, 132–33, 139–40, 160–61, 226, 235, 245, 250
Vendler, Helen, 16
Virgil, 164, 166, 203

Waggoner, Hyatt, 12
Wain, John, 15
Walden (Thoreau), 24
Waste Land, The (Eliot), 28, 52, 67, 113, 181, 250, 256–57
Watkins, Floyd C., 10
Welty, Eudora, 20, 37–38, 252
West, Nathanael, 49
West, Paul, 19
"When Lilacs Last in the Dooryard Bloom'd" (Whitman), 149
White Jacket (Melville), 41–42
Whitman, Walt, 6, 30, 38, 118, 149, 162, 167, 201, 225, 229–31, 234, 260, 265, 267, 281 n.10
Whittier, John Greenleaf, 40, 43, 44
Whittington, Curtis, Jr., 20
Wilbur, Richard, 270
Williams, William Carlos, 4, 260, 261, 265, 268, 270
Wit and Its Relation to the Unconscious (Freud), 280 n.10
Wolfe, Thomas, 21, 38
Wordsworth, William, 21, 32, 52, 54, 57, 64, 66, 67–68, 70, 71, 96, 111, 114, 115, 121, 131, 163, 190, 222, 232, 233, 234, 238, 248, 253, 271
World as Will and Idea, The (Schopenhauer), 242
"World Is Too Much With Us, The" (Wordsworth), 111

Yeats, William Butler, 20, 85, 253, 261, 272

Zabel, Morton, 1
Zeno, 113
Zinnes, Harriet, 10